The 5 Biggest Civil War Battles: Gettysburg, Chickamauga, Spotsylvania Court House, Chancellorsville, and The Wilderness

By Charles River Editors

Painting by Alfred Waud depicting a Confederate advance at Chickamauga

About Charles River Editors

Charles River Editors was founded by Harvard and MIT alumni to provide superior editing and original writing services, with the expertise to create digital content for publishers across a vast range of subject matter. In addition to providing original digital content for third party publishers, Charles River Editors republishes civilization's greatest literary works, bringing them to a new generation via ebooks.

Sign up here to receive updates about free books as we publish them, and visit Our Kindle Author Page to browse today's free promotions and our most recently published Kindle titles.

Introduction

The Battle of Chancellorsville (May 2-6, 1863)

"My God! It is horrible—horrible; and to think of it, 130,000 magnificent soldiers so cut the pieces by less than 60,000 half-starved ragamuffins!" – Horace Greeley, Editor of the *New York Tribune*

Of all the Civil War battles fought, and of all the victories achieved by Robert E. Lee at the command of the Confederate Army of Northern Virginia, the Battle of Chancellorsville is considered the most tactically complex and ultimately the most brilliant Confederate victory of the war.

In early May 1863, the Army of the Potomac was at the height of its power as it bore down on Robert E. Lee's Army of Northern Virginia near Fredericksburg, where the Confederates had defeated them the previous December. The Union behemoth had spent most of the winter season being reorganized and drilled by "Fighting Joe" Hooker, an aggressive commander who had fought hard at places like Antietam. With an army nearing 130,000 men, Hooker's Army of the Potomac was twice the size of the Army of Northern Virginia.

With that advantage, Hooker proposed a daring and aggressive two pronged attack that aimed to keep Lee's army occupied in front of Fredericksburg while marching around its left. Meanwhile a cavalry raid well in the rear was intended to cut Lee's lines of supplies and possibly retreat. Hooker's plan initially worked perfectly, with the division of his army surprising Lee. At the end of May 1, Lee was outnumbered 2-1 and now had to worry about threats on two fronts.

Incredibly, Lee once again decided to divide his forces in the face of the enemy, sending Stonewall Jackson to turn the Union army's right flank while the rest of the army maintained positions near Fredericksburg. The Battle of Chancellorsville is one of the most famous of the Civil War, and the most famous part of the battle was Stonewall Jackson's daring march across the Army of the Potomac's flank, surprising the XI Corps with an attack on May 2, 1863. Having ignored warnings of Jackson's march, the XI Corps was quickly routed. The surprise was a costly success, however, as Jackson was mortally wounded after being mistakenly fired upon by his own men.

Having seized the initiative, half of Lee's army launched desperate attacks on Hooker's forces near the Wilderness over the next 2 days, while simultaneously defending against Union attacks around Fredericksburg that pushed the other half of his army back several miles on May 3. Ultimately, Hooker, who may have suffered a concussion during the battle, decided to pull both parts of his army back across the Rappahannock River on May 4, requiring a careful extrication over the next few days as Lee's army tried to destroy them while they were still on the southern bank of the river.

Lee's heavily outnumbered army had just won the most stunning victory of the war, but it cost them Stonewall Jackson. Moreover, the reorganization of the armies and the battle itself played an influential role in the way the Pennsylvania Campaign and the Battle of Gettysburg unfolded later that summer.

The 5 Biggest Civil War Battles comprehensively covers the campaign and the events that led up to the battle, the fighting itself, and the aftermath of the battle. Accounts of the battle by important participants are also included, along with maps of the battle and pictures of important people, places, and events. You will learn about the Battle of Chancellorsville like you never have before, in no time at all.

Barlow Knoll, on the northernmost section of the battlefield

The Battle of Gettysburg (July 1-3, 1863)

The names of history's most famous battles still ring in our ears today, their influence immediately understood by all. Marathon lent its name to the world's most famous race, but it also preserved Western civilization during the First Persian War. Saratoga, won by one of the colonists' most renowned war heroes before he became his nation's most vile traitor. Hastings ensured the Normans' success in England and changed the course of British history. Waterloo, which marked the reshaping of the European continent and Napoleon's doom, has now become part of the English lexicon. In Charles River Editors' Greatest Battles in History series, readers can get caught up to speed on history's greatest battles in the time it takes to finish a commute, while learning interesting facts long forgotten or never known.

Without question, the most famous battle of the American Civil War took place outside of the small town of Gettysburg, Pennsylvania, which happened to be a transportation hub, serving as the center of a wheel with several roads leading out to other Pennsylvanian towns. From July 1-3, Robert E. Lee's Confederate Army of Northern Virginia tried everything in its power to decisively defeat George Meade's Union Army of the Potomac, unleashing ferocious assaults that inflicted nearly 50,000 casualties in all.

Day 1 of the battle would have been one of the 25 biggest battles of the Civil War itself, and it ended with a tactical Confederate victory. But over the next two days, Lee would try and fail to dislodge the Union army with attacks on both of its flanks during the second day and Pickett's Charge on the third and final day. Meade's stout defense held, barely, repulsing each attempted assault, handing the Union a desperately needed victory that ended up being one of the Civil War's turning points.

After the South had lost the war, the importance of Gettysburg as one of the "high tide" marks of the Confederacy became apparent to everyone, making the battle all the more important in the years after it had been fought. While former Confederate generals cast about for scapegoats, with various officers pointing fingers at Robert E. Lee, James Longstreet, and James Stuart, historians and avid Civil War fans became obsessed with studying and analyzing all the command decisions and army movements during the entire campaign. Despite the saturation of coverage, Americans refuse to grow tired of visiting the battlefield and reliving the biggest battle fought in North America.

The 5 Biggest Civil War Battles comprehensively covers the entire Pennsylvania campaign, analyzes the decisions made by the battle's most important leaders, and explains the aftermath of the Union victory and the legacies that were made and tarnished by the battle. Along with bibliographies, maps of the battle, and pictures of important people and places, you will learn about the Battle of Gettysburg like you never have before, in no time at all.

The Battle of Chickamauga (September 19-20, 1863)

"I know Mr. Davis thinks he can do a great many things other men would hesitate to attempt. For instance, he tried to do what God failed to do. He tried to make a soldier of Braxton Bragg."
– General Joseph E. Johnston

Americans have long been fascinated by the Civil War and its biggest battles, particularly Gettysburg, Antietam, and Shiloh, all of which involved Robert E. Lee or Ulysses S. Grant. But the second biggest battle of the entire war mostly gets overlooked among casual readers, despite the fact it represented the last great chance for the Confederates to salvage the Western theater.

In mid-September, the Union Army of the Cumberland under General William Rosecrans had taken Chattanooga, but rather than be pushed out of the action, Army of Tennessee commander Braxton Bragg decided to stop with his 60,000 men and prepare a counterattack south of Chattanooga at a creek named Chickamauga. To bolster his fire-power, Confederate President Jefferson Davis sent 12,000 additional troops under the command of Lieutenant General James Longstreet, whose corps had just recently fought at Gettysburg in July.

On the morning of September 19, 1863, Bragg's men assaulted the Union line, which was established in a wooded area thick with underbrush along the river. That day and the morning of the next, Bragg continue to pummel Union forces, with the battle devolving from an organized succession of coordinated assaults into what one Union soldier described as "a mad, irregular battle, very much resembling guerrilla warfare on a vast scale in which one army was bushwhacking the other, and wherein all the science and the art of war went for nothing."

Late that second morning, Rosecrans was misinformed that a gap was forming in his front line, so he responded by moving several units forward to shore it up. What Rosecrans didn't realize, however, was that in doing so he accidentally created a quarter-mile gap in the Union center, directly in the path of Longstreet's men. Described by one of Rosecrans' own men as "an angry flood," Longstreet's attack was successful in driving one-third of the Union Army off the field, with Rosecrans himself running all the way to Chattanooga, where he was later found weeping and seeking solace from a staff priest.

As the Confederate assault continued, George H. Thomas led the Union left wing against heavy Confederate attack even after nearly half of the Union army abandoned their defenses and retreated from the battlefield, racing toward Chattanooga. Thomas rallied the remaining parts of the army and formed a defensive stand on Horseshoe Ridge, with more units spontaneously rallying to the new defensive line. Thomas and his men managed to hold until nightfall, when they made an orderly retreat to Chattanooga while the Confederates occupied the surrounding heights, ultimately besieging the city. Dubbed "The Rock of Chickamauga", Thomas's heroics ensured that Rosecrans' army was able to successfully retreat back to Chattanooga.

In the aftermath of the Battle of Chickamauga, several Confederate generals blamed the number of men lost during what would be the bloodiest battle of the Western Theater on Bragg's incompetence, also criticizing him for refusing to pursue the escaping Union army. General Longstreet later stated to Jefferson Davis, "Nothing but the hand of God can help as long as we have our present commander."

The 5 Biggest Civil War Battles comprehensively covers the campaign and the events that led up to the battle, the fighting itself, and the aftermath of the battle. Accounts of the battle by important participants are also included, along with maps of the battle and pictures of important people, places, and events. You will learn about the Battle of Chickamauga like you never have before, in no time at all.

The Battle of the Wilderness (May 5-7, 1864)

"Numbers meant little—in fact, they were frequently an encumbrance on the narrow trails. Visibility was limited, making it extremely difficult for officers to exercise effective control. Attackers could only thrash noisily and blindly forward through the underbrush, perfect targets for the concealed defenders." – Col. Vincent J. Esposito

With Robert E. Lee's Army of Northern Virginia continuing to frustrate the Union Army of the Potomac's attempts to take Richmond in 1862 and 1863, President Lincoln shook things up by turning command of all the armies of the United States to Ulysses S. Grant in March 1864. , Lee had won stunning victories at battles like Chancellorsville and Second Bull Run by going on the offensive and taking the strategic initiative, but Grant and Lincoln had no intention of letting him do so anymore. Attaching himself to the Army of the Potomac, Grant ordered Army of the Potomac commander George Meade, "Lee's army is your objective point. Wherever Lee goes, there you will go also."

From May 5-7, the two most famous generals of the Civil War squared off for the first time. The 100,000 strong Army of the Potomac was double the size of Lee's hardened but battered Army of Northern Virginia. It was a similar position to the one George McClellan had in 1862 and Joe Hooker had in 1863, and Grant's first attack, at the Battle of the Wilderness, followed a similar pattern. Nevertheless, Lee proved more than capable on the defensive.

The Battle of the Wilderness was fought so close to where the Battle of Chancellorsville took place a year earlier that soldiers encountered skeletons that had been buried in shallow graves in 1863. Moreover, the woods were so thick that neither side could actually see who they were shooting at, and whole brigades at times got lost in the forest. Both armies sustained heavy casualties while Grant kept attempting to move the fighting to a setting more to his advantage, but the heavy forest made coordinated movements almost impossible.

On May 5 and May 6, both armies attempted desperate attacks and counterattacks to strike a knockout blow, but they were ultimately unable to dislodge each other. Given the terrain and the nature of the fighting, it was one of the most horrendous battles of the war, with some wounded men literally burning to death in fires ignited by the battle that sparked the nearby underbrush and spread rapidly. The defending Confederates technically won a tactical victory by holding their ground, but they did so at a staggering cost, inflicting 17,000 casualties on the Army of the Potomac and suffering 11,000 of their own.

On May 7, Grant disengaged his army from the battle. His objective had been frustrated by Lee's skillful defense, the same position as Hooker at Chancellorsville, McClellan on the Virginian Peninsula, and Burnside after Fredericksburg. His men got the familiar dreadful feeling that they would retreat back toward Washington, as they had too many times before. This time, however, Grant made the fateful decision to keep moving south, inspiring his men by telling them that he was prepared to "fight it out on this line if it takes all Summer." The Battle of the Wilderness would only be the beginning of the Overland Campaign, not the end of it.

The 5 Biggest Civil War Battles comprehensively covers the campaign and the events that led up to the battle, the fighting itself, and the aftermath of the battle. Accounts of the battle by important participants are also included, along with maps of the battle and pictures of important people, places, and events. You will learn about the Wilderness like you never have before, in no time at all.

The Battle of Spotsylvania Court House (May 8-21, 1864)

"The appalling sight presented was harrowing in the extreme. Our own killed were scattered over a large space near the "angle," while in front of the captured breastworks the enemy's dead, vastly more numerous than our own, were piled upon each other in some places four layers deep, exhibiting every ghastly phase of mutilation. Below the mass of fast-decaying corpses, the convulsive twitching of limbs and the writhing of bodies showed that there were wounded men still alive and struggling to extricate themselves from the horrid entombment. Every relief possible was afforded, but in too many cases it came too late. The place was well named the "Bloody Angle." – Horace Porter, *Campaigning with Grant*

At the Battle of the Wilderness (May 5-7, 1864), Ulysses S. Grant and Robert E. Lee had fought to a standstill in their first encounter, failing to dislodge each other despite incurring nearly 30,000 casualties between the Union Army of the Potomac and the Confederate Army of Northern Virginia. Despite the fierce fighting, Grant continued to push his battered but resilient army south, hoping to beat Lee's army to the crossroads at Spotsylvania Court House, but Lee's army beat Grant's to Spotsylvania and began digging in, setting the scene for on and off fighting from May 8-21 that ultimately inflicted more casualties than the Battle of the Wilderness. In fact, with over 32,000 casualties among the two sides, it was the deadliest battle of the Overland Campaign.

Although the Battle of Spotsylvania technically lasted nearly 2 weeks, it is best remembered for the fighting that took place on May 12 at a salient in the Confederate line manned by Richard

S. Ewell's corps. Known as the Mule Shoe, a Union assault on the salient produced 24 hours of the most savage fighting conducted during the war, forever christening that point in the line as the Bloody Angle. Although Winfield Scott Hancock's II Corps established a temporary breakthrough, the Confederates were ultimately able to repulse the Union soldiers in bloody hand-to-hand fighting.

After their inability to break Lee's line on May 12, Grant continued to probe Lee's line for weaknesses, attempting to gain a perceptible advantage. However, by 1864 Civil War soldiers had become adept at digging in and building the kind of trenches that would dominate the fighting of World War I 50 years later. By winning the race to Spotsylvania, the Confederates had enough time to dig in and prepare for the kind of defensive fighting that made assaults futile. On May 20, Grant began the process of disengaging from his lines and marching the Army of the Potomac further south, forcing Lee into another race toward the North Anna River. The two armies had suffered a combined 50,000 casualties in about 15 days of fighting, but the Overland Campaign was still only half finished.

The 5 Biggest Civil War Battles comprehensively covers the events that led up to the battle, the fighting itself, and the aftermath of the battle. Accounts of the battle by important participants are also included, along with maps of the battle and pictures of important people, places, and events. You will learn about the Battle of Spotsylvania Court House like you never have before, in no time at all.

The 5 Biggest Civil War Battles: Gettysburg, Chickamauga, Spotsylvania Court House, Chancellorsville, and The Wilderness

About Charles River Editors

Introduction

The Battle of Chancellorsville

   Chapter 1: Preparing for the Chancellorsville Campaign

   Chapter 2: Getting the Jump on Lee

   Chapter 3: May 1

   Chapter 4: May 2

   Chapter 5: May 3

   Chapter 6: Hooker Withdraws

   Chapter 7: The Aftermath of Chancellorsville

   Bibliography

The Battle of Gettysburg

   Chapter 1: The Battle of Brandy Station

   Chapter 2: Lee Invades Pennsylvania

     Meade Takes Command

   Chapter 3: July 1, 1863

   Chapter 4: July 2, 1863

     Longstreet's Assault

     Ewell's Attack

   Chapter 5: July 3, 1863

     Lee's Plan

     East Cavalry Field

     Pickett's Charge

     Farnsworth's Charge

   Chapter 6: Controversy over Lee's Retreat

   Chapter 7: Who's to Blame?

     Lee?

     Longstreet?

     Stuart?

     The Army of the Potomac?

   Meade Bibliography

   Hancock Bibliography

- Chamberlain Bibliography
- Lee Bibliography
- Longstreet Bibliography
- Stuart Bibliography
- The Battle of Chickamauga
  - Chapter 1: The Summer of 1863
  - Chapter 2: Davis's Cross Roads
  - Chapter 3: Concentrating the Army of the Cumberland
  - Chapter 4: September 19
  - Chapter 5: The Morning of September 20
  - Chapter 6: The Union Blunder
  - Chapter 7: The Rock of Chickamauga
  - Chapter 8: The Aftermath of Chickamauga
  - Bibliography
- The Battle of the Wilderness
  - Chapter 1: Grant Comes East
  - Chapter 2: Entering the Wilderness
  - Chapter 3: May 5
  - Chapter 4: May 6
  - Chapter 5: The Campaign Continues
  - Bibliography
- The Battle of Spotsylvania Court House
  - Chapter 1: Racing to Spotsylvania
  - Chapter 2: May 8
  - Chapter 3: Digging In
  - Chapter 4: May 10
  - Chapter 5: May 11
  - Chapter 6: The Bloody Angle
  - Chapter 7: Lee Lives to Fight Another Day
  - Bibliography

The Battle of Chancellorsville

Chapter 1: Preparing for the Chancellorsville Campaign

"My plans are perfect. May God have mercy on General Lee for I will have none." – Joseph Hooker

After the Union debacle at the Battle of Fredericksburg, the fighting in the Eastern theater of the Civil War during 1862 was done, and the decisive Confederate victory buoyed the Confederacy's hopes. Confederate commander Robert E. Lee was described by the *Charleston Mercury* as "jubilant, almost off-balance, and seemingly desirous of embracing everyone who calls on him." The results of Antietam and the Maryland Campaign from 3 months earlier were apparently old news or forgotten by the *Mercury*, which boasted, "General Lee knows his business and the army has yet known no such word as fail."

Naturally, Fredericksburg represented one of the low points of the Civil War for the North, with the Army of the Potomac having suffered an almost unheard of 8:1 ratio in losses compared to Lee's army. Lincoln reacted to the news by writing, "If there is a worse place than hell, I am in it." It showed too, as noted by Pennsylvania Governor Andrew Curtin, who told Lincoln after touring the battlefield, "It was not a battle, it was a butchery". Curtin noted the president was "heart-broken at the recital, and soon reached a state of nervous excitement bordering on insanity." Radical Republicans frustrated at the prosecution of the war took it out on the generals and the Lincoln Administration; Michigan Senator Zachariah Chandler claimed, "The President is a weak man, too weak for the occasion, and those fool or traitor generals are wasting time and yet more precious blood in indecisive battles and delays." Perhaps the *Cincinnati Commercial* summed up the battle best in reporting, "It can hardly be in human nature for men to show more valor or generals to manifest less judgment, than were perceptible on our side that day."

Although there was jubilant talk in the South of the North giving up the fight imminently after Fredericksburg, it was clearly premature. Lee had concluded an incredibly successful year for the Confederates in the East, but the South was still struggling. The Confederate forces in the West had failed to win a major battle, suffering defeat at places like Shiloh in Tennessee and across the Mississippi River. As the war continued into 1863, the southern economy continued to deteriorate. Southern armies were suffering serious deficiencies of nearly all supplies as the Union blockade continued to be effective as stopping most international commerce with the Confederacy. Moreover, the prospect of Great Britain or France recognizing the Confederacy had been all but eliminated by the Emancipation Proclamation.

Given the unlikelihood of forcing the North's capitulation, the Confederacy's main hope for victory was to win some decisive victory or hope that Abraham Lincoln would lose his reelection bid in 1864, and that the new president would want to negotiate peace with the Confederacy. Understandably, this colored Confederate war strategy, and unquestionably Lee's, in 1863, which goes a long way toward explaining what happened at Chancellorsville and Gettysburg.

As for those battles, Burnside would not be with the Army of the Potomac during them. In January, a month removed from Fredericksburg, Lincoln fired the man who believed he was not up to the job of commanding the Army of the Potomac but took it anyway to prevent Joe Hooker from becoming the commanding general. As fate would have it, Burnside was replaced by Joe Hooker.

Darius N. Couch, who was in command of the II Corps during the Chancellorsville campaign, described some of the measures Hooker took to whip his demoralized army back into a strong fighting force:

"For some days there had been a rumor that Hooker had been fixed upon for the place, and on the 26th of January it was confirmed. This appointment, undoubtedly, gave very general satisfaction to the army, except perhaps to a few, mostly superior officers, who had grown up with it, and had had abundant opportunities to study Hooker's military character; these believed that Mr. Lincoln had committed a grave error in his selection. The army, from its former reverses, had become quite disheartened and almost sulky; but the quick, vigorous measures now adopted and carried out with a firm hand had a magical effect in toning up where there had been demoralization and inspiring confidence where there had been mistrust. Few changes were made in the heads of the general staff departments, but for his chief-of-staff Hooker applied for Brigadier-General Charles P. Stone, who, through some untoward influence at Washington, was not given to him. This was a mistake of the war dignitaries, although the officer finally appointed to the office, Major-General Daniel Butterfield, proved himself very efficient. Burnside's system of dividing the army into three grand divisions was set aside, and the novelty was introduced of giving to each army corps a distinct badge, an idea which was very popular with officers and men."

Couch

One noteworthy change Hooker also made in his command structure that Couch did not mention is that he organized all of his cavalry into one corps under George Stoneman, instead of continuing to attach separate brigades of cavalry to the individual corps in the army. This had led to uncoordinated uses of the cavalry, diluting the Union cavalry's ability to conduct reconnaissance and also weakening their impact in battle. Hooker was following Lee's lead in placing the cavalry under one command, but he committed what's considered one of the greatest blunders of the Chancellorsville campaign by thereafter sending the entire cavalry on a raid behind enemy lines instead of using them in their traditional roles of screening the army and conducting reconnaissance.

Joe Hooker

As Hooker was adding to his army and reorganizing it, Lee was actually detaching some of his army due to a shortage of supplies. In late March 1863, Lee reported, 'The men are cheerful, and I receive but few complaints, still I do not consider it enough to maintain them in health and vigor, and I fear they will be unable to endure the hardships of the approaching campaign. Symptoms of scurvy are appearing among them, and, to supply the place of vegetables, each regiment is directed to send a daily detail to gather sassafras buds, wild onions, garlic, lamb's quarter, and poke sprouts; but for so large an army the supply obtained is very small."

In addition to that hardship, Lee had detached about 15,000 from Longstreet's corps to defend against potential Union assaults made on the Peninsula, as McClellan had done the year before.

When supplies became an issue, Lee ordered Longstreet's men to start gathering supplies around the countryside in Virginia and North Carolina, with the hope that the supplies could be gathered in time before the rest of the army had to face a major attack. As it would turn out, two of Longstreet's divisions, John Bell Hood's and George Pickett's, would be over 100 miles away and way too far away to march back in time to join a battle.

Lee

Hooker was ready to place his reorganized juggernaut in motion by mid-April, and with that in mind he devised a simple strategy that called on Stoneman's cavalry to conduct a raid deep behind enemy lines, destroying the Confederate supply lines and cutting Lee's communications with Richmond. Hooker figured this would compel Lee to abandon his line along the

Rappahannock River and Fredericksburg and withdraw closer to Richmond, at which time the Army of the Potomac would start giving chase. As it turned out, heavy rains forced a delay in the cavalry raid, but as the battle of Chancellorsville itself would suggest, Lee would not have abandoned his current defensive line anyway.

Having witnessed a host of setbacks in 1862 and Burnside's "Mud March" fiasco at the beginning of 1863, President Lincoln was understandably upset, complaining, "I greatly fear it is another failure already." But after Hooker's first plan was scrapped, he came up with an even more ambitious second plan while discussing it with the leaders in Washington in late April. Once again the cavalry would be sent on a raid far to the south of Lee's lines, but this time Hooker planned to demonstrate along Fredericksburg with much of his army in an attempt to keep Lee's attention while also stealthily marching three of his corps across the Rappahannock several miles to the west, positioning them to strike Lee's left and rear. With supply lines and communication lines cut in his rear, Hooker figured Lee would be forced to fall back, and with this plan a large chunk of Hooker's army would already be across the Rappahannock ready to pursue.

Hooker's plan

As Hooker's army prepared to march, he rightly labeled the Army of the Potomac "the finest army on the planet", and historians have largely credited him for his plan. Porter Alexander agreed, writing in his memoirs, "On the whole I think this plan was decidedly the best strategy conceived in any of the campaigns ever set foot against us. And the execution of it was, also, excellently managed, up to the morning of May 1st.

On the other hand, Hooker was taking a major risk by dividing his army, with one part of it across the river and the other part of it on the other side in no position to come to its support. Longstreet noted the predicament this strategy could cause in his memoirs, and he even went so far as to suggest his belief that Lee should've invited the movement and stood ready to fight a defensive battle:

> "General Hooker had split his army in two, and was virtually in the condition which President Lincoln afterwards so graphically described in his letter addressed to him June 5 following,--viz.:
>
> 'I would not take any risk of being entangled upon the river, like an ox jumped half over a fence and liable to be torn by dogs front and rear, without a fair chance to gore one way or to kick the other.'
>
> My impression was, and is, that General Lee, standing under his trenches, would have been stronger against Hooker than he was in December against Burnside, and that he would have grown stronger every hour of delay, while Hooker would have grown weaker in morale and in confidence of his plan and the confidence of his troops. He had interior lines for defence, while his adversary was divided by two crossings of the river, which made Lee's sixty thousand for defence about equal to the one hundred and thirteen thousand under General Hooker. By the time that the divisions of Pickett and Hood could have joined General Lee, General Hooker would have found that he must march to attack or make a retreat without battle. It seems probable that under the original plan the battle would have given fruits worthy of a general engagement. The Confederates would then have had opportunity, and have been in condition to so follow Hooker as to have compelled his retirement to Washington, and that advantage might have drawn Grant from Vicksburg; whereas General Lee was actually so crippled by his victory that he was a full month restoring his army to condition to take the field. In defensive warfare he was perfect. When the hunt was up, his combativeness was overruling."

Chapter 2: Getting the Jump on Lee

Hooker had designed a grand strategy, and during the first few days he put it in motion, it went nearly flawlessly. On April 27, the column of nearly 40,000 Union soldiers led by Henry Slocum, the XII Corps commander, began marching west to cross the Rappahannock and Rapidan rivers miles upstream and went completely undetected by Lee. In conjunction with that movement, Hooker began demonstrating near Fredericksburg with a large part of his army, as if he was about to force a crossing like Burnside had done in December. Couch explained the dispositions:

> In order to confound Lee, orders were issued to assemble the Sixth, Third, and First corps under Sedgwick at Franklin's Crossing and Pollock's Mill, some three miles below Fredericksburg, on the left, before daylight of the morning of the 29th, and throw two bridges across and hold them. This was done under a severe fire of sharp-shooters. The Second Corps, two divisions, marched on the 28th for Banks's Ford, four miles to

the right; the other division, Gibbon's, occupying Falmouth, near the river-bank, was directed to remain in its tents, as they were in full view of the enemy, who would readily observe their withdrawal.

Slocum

With these distractions, the plan called for the three corps (V, XI and XII) being guided by Slocum to arrive near Chancellorsville around April 30, which consisted of one mansion at a crossroads between the Orange Turnpike and Orange Plank Road. This was essential because the "Wilderness" was directly to the west of Chancellorsville, and it was so tangled that coordinated troop activity in that sector would be all but impossible, as Grant and Lee would find out a year later in May 1864. While they were concentrating there, Stoneman's cavalry set out on April 30 to harry Lee's lines in the south, Couch's II Corps was able to cross on April 30 miles west of Fredericksburg, and the III Corps under Dan Sickles was able to cross the Rappahannock the night of April 30. By the morning of May 1, Hooker had nearly 70,000 men around Chancellorsville, more than Lee's entire army, and Hooker still had John Sedgwick's VI Corps and John Reynolds's I Corps trying to cross in Lee's front a few miles south of Fredericksburg.

As the Army of the Potomac conducted these movements from April 27-30, Lee's army stayed in its defensive line near Fredericksburg, largely unaware of Hooker's intentions. Hooker's movements had worked perfectly, and he had Lee in just the position he had hoped for when concocting the plan. On April 30, Hooker issued General Orders No. 47, prematurely congratulating his army:

> "It is with heartfelt satisfaction the commanding general announces to the army that the operations of the last three days have determined that our enemy must either ingloriously fly, or come out from behind his defenses and give us battle on our own ground, where certain destruction awaits him.
>
> The operations of the Fifth, Eleventh, and Twelfth Corps have been a succession of splendid achievements."

Chapter 3: May 1

After the war, one of the most famous quotes of the battle allegedly came from Hooker, as reported in a history of the campaign published early in the 20th century. According to author and Civil War veteran John Bigelow Jr., there was a famous exchange between Hooker and division commander Abner Doubleday, in which Doubleday asked Hooker on the march toward Gettysburg, "What was wrong with you at Chancellorsville? Some say you were injured by a shell, and others that you were drunk; now tell us what it was." Hooker allegedly replied, "Doubleday, I was not hurt by a shell, and I was not drunk. For once I lost confidence in Hooker, and that is all there is to it."

Modern historians have strongly disputed that any such exchange took place, and it would certainly be out of character for Hooker, whose arrogance strongly turned off many of his comrades. But in an effort to explain why Hooker conducted such an ambitious campaign only to halt an offensive on May 1 when he had Lee where he wanted, it has often been said that Hooker lost his nerve.

While that has long been an accepted version of what happened, Hooker's General Orders on April 30 indicate that Hooker's plan was to march into a position that would force Lee to retreat or come out of his defenses to attack Hooker. In other words, Hooker's words suggest that he intended to fight a defensive battle all along if Lee would actually give battle, a possibility Hooker largely discounted.

It's also understandable why Hooker figured Lee wouldn't stand his ground and fight. To do so, Lee would have to shift at least part of his army a few miles to the west to face the Union soldiers gathering there, moving his men out of the vicinity of Fredericksburg even while two whole corps of the Army of the Potomac was in their front there. Essentially, Lee would have to split his forces and face the enemy in two fronts, while being heavily outnumbered in both.

Lee had not correctly anticipated what Hooker was doing with the column that set off on April 27 to head to Chancellorsville, but as he explained in his report after the campaign, the fact that Sedgwick and Reynolds were only demonstrating with their corps south of Fredericksburg during those days suggested to him that they were not intended to be the main thrust against his army:

> "No demonstration was made opposite any other part of our lines at Fredericksburg, and the strength of the force that had crossed and its apparent indisposition to attack indicated that the principal effort of the enemy would be made in some other quarter. This impression was confirmed by intelligence received from General Stuart that a large body of infantry and artillery was passing up the river. During the forenoon of the 29th, that officer reported that the enemy had crossed in force near Kelly's Ford on the preceding evening. Later in the day he announced that a heavy column was moving from Kelly's toward Germanna Ford, on the Rapidan, and another toward Ely's Ford, on that river. The routes they were pursuing after crossing the Rapidan converge near Chancellorsville, whence several roads lead to the rear of our position at

Fredericksburg."

Lee had sent one of the two divisions of Longstreet's corps that had stayed with his army under Richard Anderson toward Chancellorsville on April 29, but that division and the few Confederate forces posted along the Rappahannock crossings in that area would clearly be no match for the several corps Hooker had near Chancellorsville on May 1. Lee had to choose whether he would withdraw as Hooker expected or whether he would stay and fight.

As Longstreet alluded to in his memoirs, Lee was aggressive when he sensed an opportunity, and on May 1 he gambled that Sedgwick and Reynolds were merely a diversionary force that would not cause him trouble if he shifted the vast majority of his army to face the rest of Hooker's men near Chancellorsville. Thus, nearly 80% of Lee's army began marching west toward Chancellorsville in the early morning, leaving about 10,000 Confederates in Marye's Heights outside of Fredericksburg to defend against the 40,000 Union soldiers in their front. The rest of Lee's army, consisting of under 50,000 men, marched to the Zoan and Tabernacle churches along the Orange Turnpike and Orange Plank Road about two miles east of Chancellorsville. With that, the Confederates were outnumbered by 30,000 on their right and about 20,000 on their left.

While the Confederates started digging in along the Turnpike and the Plank Road, Hooker directed two divisions from George Meade's V Corps to head east down the River Road toward Banks's Ford, where they would guard a crossing for the rest of the army, the other division from the V Corps to head east on the Turnpike, and the XII Corps to march down the Plank Road, which meant these divisions would march straight into Confederate positions. Hooker kept Oliver Howard's XI Corps, Couch's II Corps, and Sickles's III Corps in reserve.

Hooker had a sizable numbers advantage, but he was sending three different columns down three different roads, making a coordinated attack practically impossible. As a result, the three roads would see piecemeal actions, beginning with Sykes's division of Meade's Corps hitting Lafayette McLaws's division on the Turnpike. The two sides pushed each other back and forth, while Richard Anderson's division found itself fighting elements of the XII Corps and XI Corps along the Plank Road. While the Union fought along those two roads, Meade's other divisions marched unopposed on the River Road toward Banks's Ford.

When McLaws's division had pushed Sykes's division back along the Turnpike, they got within a mile of Chancellorsville and were able to see the environment Hooker was positioned in. Lee explained in his report:

"At 11 a.m. the troops moved forward upon the Plank and old Turnpike roads, Anderson, with the brigades of Wright and Posey, leading on the former; McLaws, with his three brigades, preceded by Mahone's, on the latter. Generals Wilcox and Perry, of Anderson's division, co-operated with McLaws. Jackson's troops followed Anderson on the Plank road. Colonel Alexander's battalion of artillery accompanied the advance. The enemy was soon encountered on both roads, and heavy skirmishing with infantry and artillery ensued, our troops pressing steadily forward. A strong attack upon General McLaws was repulsed with spirit by Semmes' brigade, and General Wright, by direction of General Anderson, diverging to the left of the Plank road, marched by way of the unfinished railroad from Fredericksburg to Gordonsville, and turned the enemy's right. His whole line thereupon retreated rapidly, vigorously pursued by our troops until they arrived within about 1 mile of Chancellorsville. Here the enemy had assumed a position of great natural strength, surrounded on all sides by a dense forest filled with a tangled undergrowth, in the midst of which breastworks of logs had been constructed, with trees felled in front, so as to form an almost impenetrable abatis. His artillery swept the few narrow roads by which his position could be approached from the front, and commanded the adjacent woods."

Jackson

While Lee's report makes clear that Hooker was in a strong defensive position, it was also in a position that would make troop movements much more difficult. On the other hand, the ground that the Union divisions were fighting over was high ground with enough openings to place and use artillery. However, instead of pushing his reserves forward, during the middle of the fighting Hooker ordered his advanced divisions to fall back to Chancellorsville, shocking the subordinates who were commanding men in the middle of the fray. As Couch explained:

"Meade was finally pushed out on the left over the Banks's Ford and turnpike roads, Slocum and Howard on the right along the Plank road, the left to be near Banks's Ford by 2 P. M., the right at the junction of its line of movement with the turnpike at 12 M. No opposition was met, excepting that the division marching over the turnpike came upon the enemy two or three miles out, when the sound of their guns was heard at Chancellorsville, and General Hooker ordered me to take Hancock's division and proceed to the support of those engaged. After marching a mile and a half or so I came upon Sykes, who commanded, engaged at the time in drawing back his advance to the position he then occupied. Shortly after Hancock's troops had got into a line in front, an order was received from the commanding general 'to withdraw both divisions to Chancellorsville.' Turning to the officers around me, Hancock, Sykes, Warren, and others, I told them what the order was, upon which they all agreed with me that the ground should not be abandoned, because of the open country in front and the commanding position. An aide, Major J. B. Burt, dispatched to General Hooker to this effect, came back in half an hour with positive orders to return. Nothing was to be done but carry out the command, though Warren suggested that I should disobey, and then he rode back to see the general. In the meantime Slocum, on the Plank road to my right, had been ordered in, and the enemy's advance was between that road and my right flank. Sykes was first to move back, then followed by Hancock's regiments over the same road. When all but two of the latter had withdrawn, a third order came to me, brought by one of the general's staff: 'Hold on until 5 o'clock.' It was then perhaps 2 P. M. Disgusted at the general's vacillation and vexed at receiving an order of such tenor, I replied with warmth unbecoming in a subordinate: 'Tell General Hooker he is too late, the enemy are already on my right and rear. I am in full retreat.'"

Hooker was thus ceding the high ground around the roads and opting to dig in near the Wilderness instead, leaving some of the corps commanders beside themselves. George Meade complained, "My God, if we can't hold the top of the hill, we certainly can't hold the bottom of it!" Couch also considered it the moment the battle was lost, writing, "Proceeding to the Chancellor House, I narrated my operations in front to Hooker, which were seemingly satisfactory, as he said: 'It is all right, Couch, I have got Lee just where I want him; he must fight me on my own ground.' The retrograde movement had prepared me for something of the kind, but to hear from his own lips that the advantages gained by the successful marches of his lieutenants were to culminate in fighting a defensive battle in that nest of thickets was too much, and I retired from his presence with the belief that my commanding general was a whipped man. The army was directed to intrench itself."

On the night of May 1, Lee still had to decide whether to pull his army back or attack Hooker. He was still hoping to destroy the entire portion of Hooker's army at Chancellorsville before Sedgwick and Reynolds began pushing back his sparse defensive line near Fredericksburg. Jackson agreed with him, and as the two met that night to discuss their options. Jackson biographer Robert Lewis Dabney described their meeting:

> "When Friday night arrived, Generals Lee and Jackson met, at a spot where the road to the Catharine Iron Furnace turned southwestward from the plank-road, which was barely a mile in front of Hooker's works. Here, upon the brow of a gentle hill, grew a cluster of pine-trees, while the gound was carpeted with the clean, dry sedge and fallen leaves. They selected this spot, with their respective Staffs, to bivouac, while the army lay upon their weapons, a few yards before them, and prepared to sleep upon the ground, like their men. General Stuart had now joined them, and reported the results of his reconnoissances upon the south and west of Hooker's position. He had ascertained that the Federal commander had left a whole corps, under General Reynolds, at Ely's Ford, to guard his communications there, and that he had massed ninety thousand men around Chancellorsville, under his own eye, fortifying them upon the east, south and, southwest, as has been described. But upon the west and northwest his encampments were open, and their movements were watched by Stuart's pickets, who were secreted in the wilderness there. He had also ascertained, that almost all their cavalry had broken through the line of the Rapid Ann in one body, and had invaded the south, followed and watched by the brigade of W. H. Lee, evidently bent upon a grand raid against the Confederate communications. Generals Lee and Jackson now withdrew, and held an anxious consultation. That Hooker must be attacked, and that speedily, was clear to the judgments of both."

"The Last Meeting" between Lee and Jackson

As Lee realized, however, "It was evident that a direct attack upon the enemy would be attended with great difficulty and loss, in view of the strength of his position and his superiority of numbers." Thanks to reports from Stuart's cavalry that Hooker's left was well-defended (thanks to Meade's march on River Road) and his right was "in the air" with an open flank, Lee decided "to endeavor to turn his right flank and gain his rear, leaving a force in front to hold him in check and conceal the movement." In other words, having already split his army in two in the face of a larger army, Lee now planned to split his army into three by having some of his command march around Hooker's right, defying all military convention. Dabney explained:

"General Lee had promptly concluded, that while, on the one hand, immediate attack was proper, some more favorable place for assault must be sought, by moving farther toward Hooker's right. The attempt to rout ninety thousand well armed troops, entrenched at their leisure, by a front attack, with thirty-five thousand, would be too prodigal of patriot blood, and would offer too great a risk of repulse. He had accordingly already commanded his troops to commence a movement toward their left, and communicated his views to General Jackson, who warmly concurred in their wisdom. A report was about this time received from General Fitz Hugh Lee, of Stuart's command, describing the position of the Federal army, and the roads which he held with his cavalry leading to its rear. General Jackson now proposed to throw his command entirely into Hooker's rear, availing himself of the absence of the Federal cavalry, and the presence of the Confederate horse, and to assail him from the West, in concert with Anderson and McLaws. Stuart was there with his active horsemen to cover this movement; and he believed that it could be made with comparatively little risk, and, when accomplished, would enable him to crush the surprised enemy. He well knew that he was apparently proposing a 'grand detachment'; a measure pronounced by military science so reprehensible, in the presence of an active adversary."

With that decision, the stage was set for two of the most dramatic days of the Civil War.

Chapter 4: May 2

Having decided on the night of May 1 to try to turn Hooker's right flank, the Confederates went about getting a guide who could lead Jackson's command on the march. Charles C. Wellford, the man who owned the nearby Catherine Furnace, gave Jackson's mapmaker information about a road near Catherine Furnace that would take them to Brock Road and allow Jackson to march northwest toward Wilderness Tavern, placing them squarely in the flank and rear of Howard's XI Corps. The backwoods route was intended to hide the march from Union pickets, and the lack of Union cavalry to screen the Army of the Potomac made the stealthy march that much likelier to succeed.

As Jackson began marching his command that morning along a 12 mile route, Lee started digging in with Anderson's division and McLaws's division in Hooker's front along the Turnpike and the Plank Road. With Jackson's 28,000 men marching around Hooker's right, Lee now had less than 15,000 soldiers holding the line in front of Hooker's 70,000. Meanwhile, Hooker was also still digging in, and to bolster his numbers he ordered Reynolds to leave the Fredericksburg front and march to Chancellorsville to join the right flank. It was a circuitous march that had no hope of reaching Chancellorsville on May 2.

One of the great myths of Stonewall Jackson's legendary flank attack on May 2 is that it came as a complete surprise to the Army of the Potomac when the Confederates came bursting out of the woods on their flank. In fact, despite Stuart's cavalry screening the march in order to hide it to the best of their ability, there were several different times during the day that Union forces spotted the Confederate column and alerted their superiors. As Darius Couch explained:

"On the morning of May 2d our line had become strong enough to resist a front attack unless made in great force; the enemy had also been hard at work on his front, particularly that section of it between the Plank road and turnpike. Sedgwick, the previous night, had been ordered to send the First Corps (Reynolds's) to Chancellorsville. At 7 A. M. a sharp cannonade was opened on our left, followed by infantry demonstrations of no particular earnestness. Two hours later the enemy were observed moving a mile or so to the south and front of the center, and later the same column was reported to the commander of the Eleventh Corps by General Devens, whose division was on the extreme right flank. At 9:30 A. M. a circular directed to Generals Slocum and Howard called attention to this movement and to the weakness of their flanks."

News of Jackson's flank march reached Hooker within hours of its start, and Hooker guessed that it was either a retreat or a flanking march, so at 9:30 he warned XI Corps commander Oliver Howard, "We have good reason to suppose the enemy is moving to our right. Please advance your pickets for purposes of observation as far as may be safe in order to obtain timely information of their approach." Howard claimed later that morning that his corps was "taking measures to resist an attack from the west."

While Hooker was inviting Lee to attack around Chancellorsville, he ordered Sedgwick's VI Corps to "attack the enemy in his front [if] an opportunity presents itself with a reasonable expectation of success". Despite having a 4-1 advantage in manpower, Sedgwick decided to be cautious, possibly remembering what had happened when Union soldiers tried to storm Marye's Heights during the Battle of Fredericksburg the previous December. As a result, Sedgwick decided not to attack the Confederate line, manned by Jubal Early's greatly stretched division. Sedgwick has been heavily criticized by historians ever since, but he rationalized his decision in his post-campaign report:

"The following day, Saturday, May 2, Reynolds' corps was withdrawn from my command, and ordered to proceed to headquarters of the army, at or near Chancellorsville, one division, General Wheaton's, of the Sixth Corps, being sent by General Newton to cover his crossing and take up his bridge. I was also ordered to take up all the bridges at Franklin's crossing and below before daylight. This order was received at 5.25 a.m., after daylight, and could not, of course, be executed without attracting the observation of the enemy, and leaving him free to proceed against the forces under General Hooker."

Sedgwick

Lee had divided his army once on May 1 and again on May 2 by betting on Sedgwick's inaction in front of Early, and Sedgwick played right into it. Meanwhile, as Hooker was giving Sedgwick discretionary orders to possibly advance, he decided to try to intercept Jackson's column by moving Sickles's III corps "cautiously toward the road followed by the enemy, and harass the movement as much as possible". This order took the III Corps south past the high ground at Hazel Grove and interposed it between Richard Anderson's division and Jackson's column. By the time the men of the III Corps reached their destination, however, a rearguard conducted by the 23rd Georgia Infantry kept Sickles from harassing Jackson's advance. The 23rd Georgia would lose a majority of its men defending Jackson's rear, and eventually two brigades from A.P. Hill's famous "Light Division" had to reinforce them to cover Jackson.

Around 3:00, Jackson and cavalry officer Fitzhugh Lee were able to scout the Union's lines from high ground near the Plank Road. Despite Howard having told Hooker that he was preparing for the possibility of an attack on his flank, Jackson found Howard's men idling around, completely unprepared for what was about to hit them. In addition to being unprepared, the XI Corps was composed of a bunch of raw recruits who had never seen battle, and those who had seen action performed poorly at Second Manassas. The very reason they were on the far right was because Hooker didn't intend to use them for major combat operations.

As Jackson's men reached the crossroads near Wilderness Tavern, the opening in the area allowed him to form battle lines that straddled the Orange Turnpike in the rear of the XI Corps. They would then be marching through thick underbrush that not only completely obscured them but also scratched them up and tore their clothes. Despite the inevitable noises made by 21,000 men moving forward through a forest, and the scurrying of various animals out of the forest, Howard's corps still remained unprepared, and many of them were mostly concerned with cooking their dinner.

Sometime between 5-6 p.m., Jackson's men came hurdling out of the forest and fell upon Howard's hapless corps, many of whom had stacked unloaded rifles while sitting around campfires. Almost immediately, Jackson's attack rolled up Devens's division, and though Schurz's division tried to form an emergency defensive line in Jackson's front, they were quickly swept aside after finding themselves flanked on both sides. Dabney described the initial moments of the attack:

> "With a wild hurrah, the line of Rodes burst upon them from the woods, and the first volley decided their utter rout. The second line, commanded by Colston, unable to restrain their impetuosity, rushed forward at the shout, pressed upon the first, filling up their gaps, and firing over their heads, so that thenceforward the two were almost merged into one, and advanced together, a dense and impetuous mass. For three miles the Federalists were now swept back by a resistless charge. Even the works which confronted the west afforded them no protection; no sooner were they manned by the enemy, than the Confederates dashed upon them with the bayonet, and the defenders were either captured or again put to flight. The battle was but a continued onward march, with no other pause than that required for the rectification of the line, disordered by the density of the woods."

As Dabney's account suggests, the nature of the flank attack ensured that the Confederate officers began losing control of their commands almost immediately as they began rushing forward, but the XI Corps was even more out of control. Howard tried to valiantly rally his routed corps as they began fleeing in a panicked rout eastward, but he was no George H. Thomas and this was no Chickamauga. Most of his soldiers simply ran right past him until they reached Fairview, an open field near Hooker's headquarters at the Chancellor house. The vanguard of Jackson's attack, Robert Rodes's division, chased them the entire way until being brought to heel by the artillery posted there shortly after 7:00. Hooker tried to rally an emergency defensive line by pulling one of Sickles's III Corps divisions, who due to unusual sound acoustics had not heard any of the fighting despite the fact it was going on just 2.5 miles away from them, but it was the fading daylight that would ultimately blunt the Confederate attack.

The greatest resistance Jackson faced in his attack was the temptations that invited his men to stop their pursuit, including food, personal artifacts, guns, and other supplies. Jackson continued to order his subordinates, "Press forward", and he tried to urge the soldiers to keep up what had now become a disorganized pursuit. The XI Corps had lost ¼ of its strength, 2,500 men (nearly half of whom had been captured), in an hour, while its general officers suffered a substantial number of casualties trying to rally their men. By the time the flank attack had petered out,

Jackson's men were within sight of Hooker's headquarters at Chancellorsville, and Sickles's III Corps was now positioned between Jackson and the rest of Lee's force.

Lee had not been idle during Jackson's flank attack either, as explained by his nephew, cavalry officer Fitzhugh Lee, after the war: "During the flank march of his great lieutenant, Lee reminded the troops in his front of his position by frequent taps on different points of their lines, and when the sound of cannon gave notice of Jackson's attack, Lee ordered that Hooker's left be strongly pressed to prevent his sending re-enforcements to the point assailed."

Jackson's flank march permanently tarnished Oliver Howard's career and reputation, and he was well aware of it. In his post-campaign report, he took pains to try to explain what happened on the night of May 2:

"At about 6 p.m. I was at my headquarters, at Dowdall's Tavern, when the attack commenced. I sent my chief of staff to the front when firing was heard. General Schurz, who was with me, left at once to take command of his line. It was not three minutes before I followed. When I reached General Schurz's command, I saw that the enemy had enveloped my right, and that the First Division was giving way. I first tried to change the front of the deployed regiments. I next directed the artillery where to go; then formed a line by deploying some of the reserve regiments near the church. By this time the whole front on the north of the Plank road had given way. Colonel Buschbeck's brigade was faced about, and, lying on the other side of the rifle-pit embankment, held on with praiseworthy firmness. A part of General Schimmelfennig's and a part of General Krzyzanowski's brigades moved gradually back to the north of the Plank road and kept up their fire. At the center and near the Plank road there was a blind panic and great confusion. By the assistance of my staff and some other officers, one of whom was Colonel Dickinson, of General Hooker's staff, the rout was considerably checked, and all the artillery, except eight pieces, withdrawn. Some of the artillery was well served, and told effectively on the advancing enemy. Captain Dilger kept up a continuous fire until we reached General Betty's position.

Now as to the causes of this disaster to my corps:

1. Though constantly threatened and apprised of the moving of the enemy, yet the woods was so dense that he was able to mass a large force, whose exact whereabouts neither patrols, reconnaissances, nor scouts ascertained. He succeeded in forming a column opposite to and outflanking my right.

2. By the panic produced by the enemy's reverse fire, regiments and artillery were thrown suddenly upon those in position.

3. The absence of General Barlow's brigade, which I had previously located in reserve

and en echelon with Colonel von Gilsa's, so as to cover his right flank. This was the only general reserve I had. My corps was very soon reorganized near Chancellorsville, and relieved General Meade's corps, on the left of the general line. Here it remained until Wednesday morning, when it resumed its position, as ordered, at the old camp."

Although the flank attack began to lose its steam as the sun went down, Jackson remained active all along his front, and in the process of conducting his own personal reconnaissance during the night, he positioned himself between the lines. Along with some of his staff, Jackson rode so closely to the Union line that some of the horses in his party were shot during a Union musket volley:

"He had now advanced a hundred yards beyond his line of battle, evidently supposing that, in accordance with his constant orders, a line of skirmishers had been sent to the front, immediately upon the recent cessation of the advance. He probably intended to proceed to the place where he supposed this line crossed the turnpike, to ascertain from them what they could learn concerning the enemy. He was attended only by a half dozen mounted orderlies, his signal officer, Captain Wilbourne, with one of his men, and his aide, Lieutenant Morrison, who had just returned to him. General A. P. Hill, with his staff also proceeded immediately after him, to the front of the line, accompanied by Captain Boswell of the Engineers, whom General Jackson had just detached to assist him. After the General and his escort had proceeded down the road a hundred yards, they were surprised by a volley of musketry from the right, which spread toward their front, until the bullets began to whistle among them, and struck several horses."

After that close call, Jackson, Hill, and the staffers started riding back toward their own lines, only to be confused for Union soldiers by their own men, soldiers of the 18th North Carolina:

"General Jackson was now aware of their proximity, and perceived that there was no picket or skirmisher between him and his enemies. He therefore, turned to ride hurriedly back to his own troops; and, to avoid the fire, which was, thus far, limited to the south side of the road, he turned into the woods upon the north side. It so happened that General Hill, with his escort, had been directed by the same motive almost to the same spot.

As the party approached within twenty paces of the Confederate troops, these, evidently mistaking them for cavalry, stooped, and delivered a deadly fire. So sudden and stunning was this volley, and so near at hand, that every horse which was not shot down, recoiled from it in panic, and turned to rush back, bearing their riders toward the approaching enemy. Several fell dead upon the spot, among them the amiable and courageous Boswell; and more were wounded. Among the latter was General Jackson. His right hand was penetrated by a ball, his left forearm lacerated by another, and the same limb broken a little below the shoulder by a third, which not only crushed the bone, but severed the main artery. His horse also dashed, panic-stricken, toward the enemy, carrying him beneath the boughs of a tree which inflicted severe blows, lacerated his face, and almost dragged him from the saddle. His bridle hand was now powerless, but seizing the reins with the right hand, notwithstanding its wound, he arrested his career, and brought the animal back toward his own lines.

General Jackson drew up his horse, and sat for an instant gazing toward his own men, as if in astonishment at their cruel mistake, and in doubt whether he should again venture to approach them."

After personally dressing Jackson's wounds, Hill briefly took command of the Second Corps, until he was himself wounded in the legs, leaving him unable to walk or ride a horse. Hill relinquished command to Rodes, who realized he was over his head and directed JEB Stuart himself to take temporary command of the Second Infantry Corps, a decision Lee seconded when news reached him.

A.P. Hill

Jackson had been nearly hit by Union gunfire, and after he was injured, a litter started trying to carry him to the rear while coming under Union artillery fire, causing even more troubles:

"The party was now met by a litter, which someone had sent from the rear; and the General was placed upon it, and borne along by two soldiers, and Lieutenants Smith and Morrison. As they were placing him upon it, the enemy fired a volley of canister-shot up the road, which passed over their heads. But they had proceeded only a few steps before the discharge was repeated, with a more accurate aim. One of the soldiers bearing the litter was struck down, severely wounded; and had not Major Leigh, who was walking beside it, broken his fall, the General would have been precipitated to the ground. He was placed again upon the earth; and the causeway was now swept by a hurricane of projectiles of every species, before which it seemed that no living thing could survive. The bearers of the litter, and all the attendants, excepting Major Leigh and the General's two aides, left him, and fled into the woods on either hand, to escape the fatal tempest; while the sufferer lay along the road, with his feet toward the foe, exposed to all its fury.

It was now that his three faithful attendants displayed a heroic fidelity, which deserves to go down with the immortal name of Jackson to future ages. Disdaining to save their lives by deserting their chief, they lay down beside him in the causeway, and sought to protect him as far as possible with their bodies. On one side was Major Leigh, and on the other Lieutenant Smith. Again and again was the earth around them torn with volleys of canister, while shells and minie balls flew hissing over them, and the stroke of the iron hail raised sparkling flashes from the flinty gravel of the roadway. General Jackson struggled violently to rise, as though to endeavor to leave the road; but Smith threw his arm over him, and with friendly force held him to the earth, saying: "Sir, you must lie still; it will cost you your life if you rise." He speedily acquiesced, and lay quiet; but none of the four hoped to escape alive. Yet, almost by miracle, they were unharmed; and, after a few moments, the Federalists, having cleared the road of all except this little party, ceased to fire along it, and directed their aim to another quarter."

After being painfully carried back behind the Confederate lines, Jackson had his left arm amputated. When Lee heard of Jackson's injuries, he sent his religious leader Chaplain Lacy to Stonewall with the message, "Give him my affectionate regards, and tell him to make haste and get well, and come back to me as soon as he can. He has lost his left arm, but I have lost my right arm."

In a chaotic turn of events, the Confederacy's famous cavalry chief, JEB Stuart, was now in charge of the bulk of Lee's infantry. Making matters even more difficult for a general who had been leading cavalry the entire war, he had to reorganize the corps, which had gotten intermingled and disorganized in the attack. Stuart reported after the battle:

"It was already dark when I sought General Jackson, and proposed, as there appeared nothing else for me to do, to take some cavalry and infantry over and hold the Ely's Ford road. He approved the proposition, and I had already gained the heights overlooking the ford, where was a large number of camp-fires, when Captain [R. H. T.] Adams, of General A. P. Hill's staff, reached me post-haste, and informed me of the sad calamities which for the time deprived the troops of the leadership of both Jackson and Hill, and the urgent demand for me to come and take command as quickly as possible. I rode with rapidity back 5 miles, determined to press the pursuit already so gloriously begun. General Jackson had gone to the rear, but General A. P. Hill was still on the ground, and formally turned over the command to me. I sent also a staff officer to General Jackson to inform him that I would cheerfully carry out any instructions he would give, and proceeded immediately to the front, which I reached at 10 p.m.

   I found, upon reaching it, A. P. Hill's division in front, under Heth, with Lane's, McGowan's, Archer's, and Heth's brigades on the right of the road, within half a mile of Chancellorsville, near the apex of the ridge, and Pender's and Thomas' on the left. I found that the enemy had made an attack on our right flank, but were repulsed. The fact, however, that the attack was made, and at night, made the apprehensive of a repetition of it, and necessitated throwing back the right wing, so as to meet it. I was also informed that there was much confusion on the right, owing to the fact that some troops mistook friends for the enemy and fired upon them. Knowing that an advance under such circumstances would be extremely hazardous, much against my inclination, I felt bound to wait for daylight. General Jackson had also sent me word to use my own discretion. The commanding general was with the right wing of the army, with which I had no communication except by a very circuitous and uncertain route. I nevertheless sent a dispatch to inform him of the state of affairs, and rode around the lines restoring order, imposing silence, and making arrangements for the attack early next day. I sent Col. E. P. Alexander, senior officer of artillery, to select and occupy with artillery positions along the line bearing upon the enemy's position, with which duty he was engaged all night."

Stuart

As if the day hadn't gone poorly enough, Hooker ordered Sickles to make an attack later in the night, only for his men to be mistaken by the XII Corps artillery near Fairview as Confederates. The lone Union assault of the day would be halted by friendly fire.

Around the same time that night, Hooker fired off an order to Sedgwick, still around Fredericksburg, and ordered him to attack with all dispatch. Hooker had now correctly assumed that the Confederates in Sedgwick's front were a skeleton force, and the order to attack was sound, but unfortunately the manner in which he directed Sedgwick to attack required a 14 mile countermarch. Sedgwick reported:

"That night at 11 o'clock I received an order, dated 10.10 p.m., directing me to cross the Rappahannock at Fredericksburg immediately upon receipt of the order, and move in the direction of Chancellorsville until I connected with the major-general commanding; to attack and destroy any force on the road, and be in the vicinity of the general at daylight.

I had been informed repeatedly by Major-General Butterfield, chief of staff, that the force in front of me was very small, and the whole tenor of his many dispatches would have created the impression that the enemy had abandoned my front and retired from the city and its defenses had there not been more tangible evidence than the dispatches in question that the chief of staff was misinformed."

Due to Sedgwick's inaction earlier on May 2 and the nature of the orders that night, Sedgwick's men spent the entire day idle in front of an enemy ¼ their size.

Chapter 5: May 3

The morning of May 3

The Battle of Chancellorsville is best remembered for Stonewall Jackson's legendary flank attack on the night of May 2, but the battle would be decided on May 3. Despite the debacle suffered by the XI Corps, the Army of the Potomac still outnumbered Lee's army in the vicinity, and Jackson's corps (now commanded by Stuart) was still separated from the rest. Lee was determined to ensure Jackson's corps linked up with the rest of the army by attacking Sickles, whose III Corps stood between them along Hazel Grove.

In one of the most fateful decisions of the war, Lee's objective was actually obtained by Hooker's own orders. Early that morning, as the Confederates were preparing an attack despite being outnumbered by nearly 40,000 men, Hooker pulled the III Corps back from Hazel Grove to the Plank Road, covering his flanks and forming a horseshoe defensive line so that Sickles's corps would not be a salient in the line capable of being hit by both wings of the Confederate army around Chancellorsville. With that ground being ceded, Porter Alexander, who had been tasked by Stuart with conducting reconnaissance for placing artillery, was allowed to simply establish about 30 guns on the high ground at Hazel Grove. Alexander explained the consequences of Hooker's poor decision in his memoirs, "Altogether, I do not think there was a more brilliant thing done in the war than Stuart's extricating that command from the extremely critical position in which he found it."

As Hooker abandoned the high ground at Hazel Grove in favor of Fairview, Stuart's artillery began bombarding the Union positions from the high ground, not only forcing General Hooker's troops from Fairview but essentially decimating the Union lines while destroying Hooker's headquarters at Chancellor House. Of this turn of events, Stuart wrote, "As the sun lifted the mist that shrouded the field, it was discovered that the ridge on the extreme right was a fine position for concentrating artillery. I immediately ordered thirty pieces to that point, and, under the happy effects of the battalion system, it was done quickly. The effect of this fire upon the enemy's batteries was superb."

With Stuart's artillery now posted, the Confederates attacked all along the line at dawn, with Stuart's men advancing along the Plank Road from the west while Anderson and McLaws attacked up the Turnpike and Plank Road on the other side of Hooker's army. Stuart launched a savage attack with three divisions all advancing forward together, two of which were in support just a few hundred yards behind. Although many of them had exhausted themselves routing the XI Corps the night before, they were up to the challenge, as Stuart reported:

"At early dawn, Trimble's division composed the second line and Rodes' division the third. The latter had his rations on the spot, and, as his men were entirely without food, was extremely anxious to issue. I was disposed to wait a short time for this purpose; but when, as preliminary to an attack, I ordered the right of the first line to swing around and come perpendicular to the road, the order was misunderstood for an order to attack, and that part of the line became engaged. I ordered the whole line to advance and the second and third lines to follow. As the sun lifted the mist that shrouded the field, it was discovered that the ridge on the extreme right was a fine position for concentrating artillery. I immediately ordered thirty pieces to that point, and, under the happy effects of the battalion system, it was done quickly. The effect of this fire upon the enemy's batteries was superb.

In the meantime the enemy was pressing our left with infantry, and all the re-enforcements I could obtain were sent there. Colquitt's brigade, of Trimble's division, ordered first to the right, was directed to the left to support Pender. Iverson's brigade, of the second line, was also engaged there, and the three lines were more or less merged into one line of battle, and reported hard pressed. Urgent requests were sent for re-enforcements, and notices that the troops were out of ammunition, &c. I ordered that the ground must be held at all hazards; if necessary, with the bayonet. About this time also our right connected with Anderson's left, relieving all anxiety on that subject. I was now anxious to mass infantry on the left, to push the enemy there, and sent every available regiment to that point.

About 8 a.m. the works of the enemy directly in front of our right were stormed, but the enemy's forces retiring from the line facing Anderson, which our batteries enfiladed, caused our troops to abandon these works, the enemy coming in their rear. It was stormed a second time, when I discovered the enemy making a flank movement to the left of the road, for the purpose of dislodging our forces, and hastened to change the front of a portion of our line to meet this attack, but the shortness of the time and the deafening roar of artillery prevented the execution of this movement, and our line again retired. The third time it was taken, I made disposition of a portion of Ramseur's brigade to protect the left flank. Artillery was pushed forward to the crest, sharpshooters were posted in a house in advance, and in a few moments Chancellorsville was ours (10 a.m.). The enemy retired toward Ely's Ford, the road to United States Ford branching one-half mile west of Chancellorsville.

In this hotly contested battle the enemy had strong works on each side of the road, those on the commanding ridge being heavily defended by artillery. The night also had given him time to mass his troops to meet this attack, but the desperate valor of Jackson's corps overcame every obstacle and drove the enemy to his new line of defense, which his engineers had constructed in his rear, ready for occupation, at the intersection of the Ely's Ford and United States Ford roads."

While the Union and Confederate armies fought all along the lines, the Confederate artillery at Hazel Grove became an absolute menace, providing artillerists the opportunity to strike the heart of Hooker's positions. In his seminal history *Lee's Lieutenants*, biographer Douglas Southall Freeman described one artillery exchange during the day: "At Hazel Grove, in short, the finest artillerists of the Army of Northern Virginia were having their greatest day. They had improved guns, better ammunition and superior organization. With the fire of battle shining through his spectacles, William Pegram rejoiced. 'A glorious day, Colonel,' he said to Porter Alexander, 'a glorious day!'"

If Hooker had not regretted his decision to evacuate Hazel Grove earlier in the morning, he probably did around 9:00 a.m., when an artillery shell hit a pillar of the Chancellor house while he was standing near it. Hooker later noted that the shattered pillar struck him "violently... in an erect position from my head to my feet." It's long been speculated that Hooker suffered a concussion, but initially he refused to relinquish command to Couch or any of his staffers. Hooker's injury has long been cited as yet another reason why his generalship became more cautious after May 1.

Even before Hooker was injured, Darius Couch, Hooker's second-in-command, was bewildered not only by the lack of communications coming from Hooker but also the overly cautious timidity that Hooker was displaying:

"Upon the south porch of that mansion General Hooker stood leaning against one of its pillars, observing the fighting, looking anxious and much careworn. After the fighting had commenced I doubt if any orders were given by him to the commanders on the field, unless, perhaps, 'to retire when out of ammunition.' None were received by me, nor were there any inquiries as to how the battle was going along my front. On the right flank, where the fighting was desperate, the engaged troops were governed by the corps and division leaders. If the ear of the commanding general was, as he afterward stated, strained to catch the sound of Sedgwick's guns, it could not have heard them in the continuous uproar that filled the air around him; but as Sedgwick, who was known as a fighting officer, had not appeared at the time set - daylight - nor for some hours after, it was conclusive evidence that he had met with strong opposition, showing that all of Lee's army was not at Chancellorsville, so that the moment was favorable for Hooker to try his opponent's strength with every available man. Moreover, the left wing might at that very time be in jeopardy, therefore he was bound by every patriotic motive to strike hard for its relief. If he had remembered Mr. Lincoln's injunction ('Gentlemen, in your next fight put in all of your men'), the face of the day would have been changed and the field won for the Union arms."

In addition to injuring and likely concussing Hooker, who would spend the next hour in a daze before temporarily relinquishing command, the Confederate artillery ultimately made Fairview untenable for the Union line, the closest open high ground near Hazel Grove and the point at which Lee and Stuart were able to link their forces back together around 10:00 a.m. Stuart had made himself conspicuous during the fighting, as Couch explained:

"In the meanwhile Stuart was pressing the attack. At one time his left was so strongly resisted that his three lines were merged into one. To a notice sent him that the men were out of ammunition, he replied that they must hold their ground with the bayonet. About this time Stuart's right connected with Anderson's left, uniting thus the detached portions of General Lee's army. He then massed infantry on his left and stormed the Federal works. Twice he was repulsed, but the third time Stuart placed himself on horseback at the head of the troops, ordered the charge, carried the intrenchments, and held them, singing with ringing voice, 'Old Joe Hooker, won't you come out of the wilderness?' An eye-witness says he could not get rid of the impression that Harry of Navarre led the charge, except that Stuart's plume was black, for everywhere the men followed his feather. Anderson at the same time moved rapidly upon Chancellorsville, while McLaws made a strong demonstration in his front. At 10 A. M. the position at Chancellorsville was won, and Hooker had withdrawn to another line nearer the Rappahannock. Preparations were at once made by Lee to attack again, when further operations were arrested by intelligence received from Fredericksburg."

Lee's aide-de-camp, Charles Marshall, described the climactic scene:

"Lee's presence was the signal for one of those uncontrollable bursts of enthusiasm which none can appreciate who has not witnessed them. The fierce soldiers, with their faces blackened with the smoke of battle, the wounded crawling with feeble limbs from the fury of the devouring flames, all seemed possessed with a common impulse. One long unbroken cheer, in which the feeble cry of those who lay helpless on the earth blended with the strong voices of those who still fought, rose high above the roar of battle and hailed the presence of a victorious chief. He sat in the full realization of all that soldiers dream of—triumph; and as I looked at him in the complete fruition of the success which his genius, courage, and confidence in his army had won, I thought that it must have been from some such scene that men in ancient days ascended to the dignity of gods."

Despite this important success, whatever relief Lee felt upon linking back up with Stuart was almost immediately tempered by news that his right was collapsing against Sedgwick near Fredericksburg. Early had ordered to hold the line unless his men were attacked by "overwhelming numbers," in which case he was to withdraw his men to the south toward Richmond. But if Sedgwick seemed to be withdrawing from in front of him, Early was supposed to shift his men west and join the rest of Lee's army near Chancellorsville.

As it turned out, Early would begin to inadvertently retreat from his defensive line before Sedgwick even attacked on May 3, thanks to miscommunication. Early explained what happened in his memoirs:

"During the morning I rode to Lee's Hill for the purpose of observing the enemy's movements from that point, and I observed a considerable portion of his infantry in motion up the opposite river bank. While I was, in company with Generals Barksdale and Pendleton, observing the enemy's manoeuvre and trying to ascertain what it meant, at about 11 o'clock A. M., Colonel R. H. Chilton, of General Lee's staff, came to me with a verbal order to move up immediately towards Chancellorsville with my whole force, except a brigade of infantry and Pendleton's reserve artillery, and to leave at

Fredericksburg the brigade of infantry and a part of the reserve artillery to be selected by General Pendleton, with instructions to the commander of this force to watch the enemy's movements, and keep him in check if possible, but if he advanced with too heavy a force to retire on the road to Spottsylvania Court-House-General Pendleton being required to send the greater part of his reserve artillery to the rear at once.

   This order took me very much by surprise, and I remarked to Colonel Chilton that I could not retire my troops without their being seen by the enemy, whose position on Stafford Heights not only overlooked ours, but who had one or two balloons which he was constantly sending up from the heights to make observations, and stated that he would inevitably move over and take possession of Fredericksburg and the surrounding Heights. The Colonel said he presumed General Lee understood all this, but that it was much more important for him to have troops where he was, than at Fredericksburg, and if he defeated the enemy there he could easily retake Fredericksburg; he called my attention to the fact, which was apparent to us all, that there was a very heavy force of infantry massed on the slopes near Falmouth which had moved up from below, and stated that he had no doubt the greater portion of the force on the other side was in motion to reinforce Hooker. He repeated his orders with great distinctness in the presence of General Pendleton, and in reply to questions from us, said that there could be no mistake in his orders.

   This was very astounding to us, as we were satisfied that we were then keeping away from the army, opposed to General Lee, a much larger body of troops than my force could engage or neutralize if united to the army near Chancellorsville. It is true that there was the force massed near Falmouth and the indications were that it was moving above, but still there was a much larger force of infantry stationed below, which evinced no disposition to move. While we were conversing, information was brought me that the enemy had abandoned his lower crossing, and that our skirmishers had advanced tothe Pratt house, but he still, however, maintained his position at the mouth of Deep Creek with a division of infantry and a number of guns on our side of the river.

   The orders as delivered to me left me no discretion, and believing that General Lee understood his own necessities better than I possibly could, I did not feel justified in acting on my own judgment, and I therefore determined to move as directed. It subsequently turned out that Colonel Chilton had misunderstood General Lee's orders, which were that I should make the movement indicated if the enemy did not have a sufficient force in my front to detain the whole of mine, and it was to be left to me to judge of that, the orders, in fact, being similar to those given me at first. It also turned out that the troops seen massed near Falmouth were the 1st corps under Reynolds, moving up to reinforce Hooker, and that the 6th corps, Sedgwick's own, remained behind. "

Early

Early was alerted to the mistake in time to form his whole defensive line again by the early morning of May 3, but he was still vastly outnumbered. Early split his forces south of Fredericksburg and west of them, contesting the south while hoping Union fears about Marye's Heights would allow him to hold that position with fewer men. As a result, Marye's Heights, which had been turned into an unassailable fortress by Longstreet's corps in December 1862, was now manned by just two brigades, led by William Barksdale and Harry Hays.

When the fighting started near Marye's Heights that morning, it probably felt like déjà vu to the Union soldiers who knew full well that nearly 8,000 men had fallen in front of the dreaded stone wall at the base of Marye's Heights. And sure enough, the initial two assaults were repulsed by the two hard-pressed Confederate brigades holding it. How much longer they might have held the position against further assaults is unclear, because a flag of truce for the purposes of collecting the dead and wounded allowed Union soldiers to literally walk up to the rifle pit and see how undermanned the Confederates truly were. With that critical information, a third Union charge at the point of bayonets drove the remnants of the two Confederate brigades out of their rifle pits on Marye's Heights in minutes. For the first time in the campaign, one of Lee's lines had been broken by the Union.

Confederate casualties behind the stone wall at Marye's Heights

With his position now becoming untenable, Early began to fight while retreating to the south; having been attacked by overwhelming numbers, he was following Lee's orders and pulling his men away from Chancellorsville. Had Lee been at the scene, he almost certainly would have ensured that Early retreated west toward the rest of the army, but instead Early's retreat south would open up Sedgwick's path to Lee's rear at Chancellorsville.

Though Early was retreating away from the rest of the army, his men successfully delayed Sedgwick for hours around Fredericksburg on May 3, helped in large measure by the brigade of Cadmus Wilcox, who explained the nature of the Early's retreat from Fredericksburg:

> "Seeing a group of officers near Stansbury's house, I rode to them, and met Generals Barksdale and Hays. The former informed me that the enemy were in considerable force in and below Fredericksburg (this was the first intimation I had of the fact), and expressed some anxiety as to his right flank, and said that he should have reenforcements. I now determined not to move my command up the road until I knew definitely the intention of the enemy, and ordered them in the ravine opposite Dr.

Taylor's, where they would be near and yet out of sight. I now rode to the vicinity of the Marye house, to see and confer with General Barksdale. While near the house, I saw great numbers of the enemy in Fredericksburg, and a battery in the street running near the cemetery was firing occasional shots at a battery of ours to the left of the Plank road. I returned to my command without seeing General Barksdale, and, on my return, saw several regiments of the enemy's infantry moving out of the upper edge of the town. I had been with my command but a few minutes when one of General Barksdale's staff reported to me that the general was hard pressed, and wanted me to send him a regiment. I instantly ordered the Tenth Alabama to move in the direction of the Marye house, and rode rapidly in that direction myself, and when in the open field and high ground between Stansbury's and the Plank road, saw Hays' brigade moving over in the direction of the Plank road. This I supposed to be for the support of General Barksdale, but upon inquiry from one of Hays' regiments learned that the enemy had taken Marye's Hill end a portion of two of Barksdale's regiments, and that Hays' brigade was falling back to the Telegraph road. Soon a courier from General Barksdale confirmed this report, and with a suggestion from General Barksdale that I also had better fall back to the Telegraph road. On the left of the Plank road the ground in rear of Marye's Hill is higher, and overlooks and commands well that hill. Believing that my own and Hays' brigade could form in line, extending from near Stansbury's house along the crests of the hills toward the Plank road, and contest the field at least for a time successfully, with the enemy, I asked General Hays not to cross the Plank road, but to remain with me. This he declined doing, having been ordered to fall back to the Telegraph road, and was soon out of sight."

Wilcox

As a result of Lee's orders, and much to Wilcox's confusion and chagrin, instead of reforming a defensive line west of Fredericksburg, Hays and Barksdale retreated south and fell back with the rest of Early's division. Thankfully for the Confederates, Wilcox opted to continue fighting a delayed retreat west, buying time for Lee to hurry men east from Chancellorsville to try to stop Sedgwick's advance. Wilcox reported his initial stand:

"Finding myself alone on the left of the Plank road, with the enemy in full view on the crests of the first range of hills in rear of Fredericksburg, and with three times my own force clearly seen and in line, I felt it a duty to delay the enemy as much as possible in his advance, and to endeavor to check him all that I could should he move forward on the Plank road. With this view, I formed my brigade promptly in line along the crests of the hills running near Stansbury's house, at right angles to the Plank road. Two rifled pieces of Lewis' battery were placed in position to the rear of the left of my line, and two slightly in front of my right, which rested some 500 or 600 yards in front of Guest's house. Skirmishers were thrown forward, covering my entire front. As soon as the four pieces of artillery were in position, they opened fire upon the enemy's lines, some 800 or 900 yards to the front. This held the enemy in check for some time. At length they deployed skirmishers to the front and began to advance. This was slow, and, delayed by frequent halts, they seemed reluctant to advance. The enemy now brought a six-gun battery to the front on the left of the Plank road, not far from Marye's house, and opened with a fire of shells upon my line. The enemy's skirmishers now advanced and engaged ours, not nearer, however, than 350 or 400 yards, their solid lines remaining some distance behind the skirmishers. The enemy's battery having fired for some time, both the skirmishers and lines in rear advanced. They had also moved by a flank across the Plank road, and it was reported to me that they were moving up on the far side of the road, and were on a line with my right flank. The artillery was now directed to withdraw; then the skirmishers rejoined their regiments, and all moved to the rear on the River road, half a mile in rear of Dr. Taylor's, where they were halted for a few minutes."

Sedgwick continued pushing west down the Turnpike while Wilcox waited for reinforcements, and around 5:00 p.m., the two lines found themselves just 5 miles away from Lee's rear around Salem Church. Finally, Wilcox was joined by 4 brigades, pulled from McLaws and Anderson, bringing the Confederate forces up to 10,000 men. Wilcox described the climactic finale of the fighting in the east in his post-war report:

The enemy's artillery ceased to fire near 5 p.m. Their skirmishers then advanced; a spirited fire ensued between the skirmishers for some fifteen or twenty minutes. Ours then retired, firing as they fell back. The enemy's skirmishers pursued, followed by their solid lines of infantry and still a third line in rear. On either side of the road, as they advanced from the toll-gate, were open fields, and the ground slightly ascending. These fields continued to within about 250 yards of the church, and then woods, thick, but of small growth. When the front line of the enemy reached this wood, they made a slight halt; then, giving three cheers, they came with a rush, driving our skirmishers rapidly before them. Our men held their fire till their men came within less than 80 yards, and then delivered a close and terrible fire upon them, killing and wounding many and causing many of them to waver and give way. The enemy still press on, surround the school-house, and capture the entire company of the Ninth Alabama stationed in it, and, pressing hard upon the regiment in rear of the school-house, throw it in confusion and disorder, and force it to yield ground. The Ninth Alabama, in rear of this regiment, spring forward as one man, and, with the rapidity of lightning, restore the continuity of our line, breaking the lines of the enemy by its deadly fire and forcing him to give way, and, following him so that he could not rally, retake the school-house, free the captured company, and in turn take their captors. The entire line of the enemy on the right of the road is repulsed, and our men follow in rapid pursuit. The regiment that had given way to the first onset of the enemy now returned to the attack and joined in the pursuit. The enemy did not assail with the same spirit on the left of the road, and were more easily repulsed, and now are followed on either side of the road, which is crowded with a confused mass of the discomfited enemy. With a good battery to play upon this retreating mass, the carnage would have been terrific. There was no rallying or reforming of this line. Another line came up the Plank road at a double-quick, and, filing to the right and left, formed line in front of my brigade. This line was scarcely formed before they were broken by the fire of my men, and fled to the rear.

The pursuit continued as far as the toll-gate. Semmes' brigade and my own were the only troops that followed the retreating enemy. In rear of the gate were heavy reserves of the enemy. Our men were now halted and reformed, it being quite dark, and retired, not pursued by the enemy, leaving pickets far to the front in the open field. The vigor of the enemy's attack at the church was doubtless due to the fact that they believed there was only one brigade to resist them, and that they anticipated an easy affair of it, while the number of dead and wounded left on the field attests the obstinacy of the resistance of our men--200 of the former and more than 150 of the latter, and largely over 200 prisoners not wounded and 1 Federal flag captured.

Thus ended this spirited conflict at Salem Church; a bloody repulse to the enemy, rendering entirely useless to him his little success of the morning at Fredericksburg. The rear of our army at Chancellorsville was now secure and free from danger, and the Sixth Army Corps of the enemy and a part of the Second were now content to remain on the defensive.

Although Wilcox exuberantly described the result as a "bloody repulse", the truth is that Sedgwick was running out of daylight to continue his advance. As a result, Lee's rear was saved. Hooker would later complain that Sedgwick had not advanced as promptly as he should've, no doubt annoyed by what he considered Sedgwick's second straight day of failure: "My object in ordering General Sedgwick forward ...was to relieve me from the position in which I found myself at Chancellorsville...In my judgment General Sedgwick did not obey the spirit of my order, and made no sufficient effort to obey it...When he did move it was not with sufficient confidence or ability on his part to manoeuvre his troops."

Chancellorsville is not the most famous battle of the war, and it's best remembered for the events of May 2, but the action on May 3 may have been the most tactically complex of the war. Lee's army had made assaults on two parts of the Union line at Chancellorsville to ensure that his army linked back up, while still managing to maintain a defensive line and halt Sedgwick's advance on the right, thus conducting a successful offensive on his left and a successful defense on his right. The casualty count attests to the fact that the fighting was just as fierce as it was complex. Over 21,000 men were killed, wounded, or captured on May 3, 1863, making it the second bloodiest day in American history, barely behind the Battle of Antietam.

Chapter 6: Hooker Withdraws

"As to the charge that the battle was lost because [Hooker] was intoxicated, I have always stated that he probably abstained from the use of ardent spirits when it would have been far better for him to have continued in his usual habit in that respect. The shock from being violently thrown to the ground, together with the physical exhaustion resulting from loss of sleep and the anxiety of mind incident to the last six days of the campaign, would tell on any man." – Darius Couch

Lee had managed to win every gamble he took from May 1-3, and he had masterfully defended his right while simultaneously striking at Hooker on his left, but the armies woke up on the morning of May 4 with the Army of the Potomac still heavily outnumbering the Army of Northern Virginia near Chancellorsville and near Salem Church just west of Fredericksburg. Hooker's flanks and Sedgwick's flanks rested on the Rapidan and Rappahannock rivers respectively, which meant they were secure, but with their forces divided and Lee's army between them, Hooker was worried that the advantage of interior lines gave Lee a chance to destroy one of the two separated armies.

Throughout May 4, Hooker dug in, and the lack of offensive activity convinced Lee that he could detach more of Anderson's division to confront Sedgwick to the right. Lee was also able to recall Early's division, which now marched back north and reoccupied Marye's Heights on Sedgwick's left flank, linking up with the men from McLaws's division and Anderson's division opposite Sedgwick. Lee hoped to attack Sedgwick, now slightly outnumbering him, but delays in Anderson's march and hesitation by McLaws resulted in the attack not starting until 6:00 p.m. Sedgwick had spent all day drawing up defensive lines to protect his retreat back across the Rappahannock, so he was able to repulse the half-hearted offensive that night.

After the Confederate attack stopped and night fell, Sedgwick began extricating his command at Banks's Ford, recrossing the Rappahannock during the night of May 4-5. Hooker had taken a defensive stance and had idled all day near Chancellorsville, yet he now used Sedgwick's withdrawal as the pretext for a withdrawal of his own. Before doing so, however, he called a council of war on the night of May 4 and discussed the matter with his principal subordinates. Couch recounted that night's council of war:

"At 12 o'clock on the night of the 4th - 5th General Hooker assembled his corps commanders in council. Meade, Sickles, Howard, Reynolds, and myself were present; General Slocum, on account of the long distance from his post, did not arrive until after the meeting was broken up. Hooker stated that his instructions compelled him to cover Washington, not to jeopardize the army, etc. It was seen by the most casual observer that he had made up his mind to retreat. We were left by ourselves to consult, upon which Sickles made an elaborate argument, sustaining the views of the commanding general. Meade was in favor of fighting, stating that he doubted if we could get off our guns. Howard was in favor of fighting, qualifying his views by the remark that our present situation was due to the bad conduct of his corps, or words to that effect. Reynolds, who was lying on the ground very much fatigued, was in favor of an advance. I had similar views to those of Meade as to getting off the guns, but said I 'would favor an advance if I could designate the point of attack.' Upon collecting the suffrages, Meade, Reynolds, and Howard voted squarely for an advance, Sickles and myself squarely no; upon which Hooker informed the council that he should take upon himself the responsibility of retiring the army to the other side of the river. As I stepped out of the tent Reynolds, just behind me, broke out, 'What was the use of calling us together at this time of night when he intended to retreat anyhow?'

Thus, during the next day, Hooker began the process of pulling his command back across the river, a delicate process that started with removing the artillery and clearing the roads so that the infantry would not get bottled up. In the early morning hours of May 6, the rest of the corps began crossing the river, with Meade's V Corps protecting the retreat on the south bank. Even still, Couch, who was in command on the south bank of the Rapidan because Hooker was already across, claimed he was tempted to try to fight:

"Near midnight I got a note from Meade informing me that General Hooker was on the other side of the river, which had risen over the bridges, and that communication was cut off from him. I immediately rode over to Hooker's headquarters and found that I was in command of the army, if it had any commander. General Hunt, of the artillery, had brought the information as to the condition of the bridges, and from the reports there seemed to be danger of losing them entirely. After a short conference with Meade I told him that the recrossing would be suspended, and that 'we would stay where we were and fight it out,' returning to my tent with the intention of enjoying what I had not had since the night of the 30th ultimo - a good sleep; but at 2 A. M., communication having been reestablished, I received a sharp message from Hooker, to order the recrossing of the army as he had directed, and everything was safely transferred to the north bank of the Rappahannock."

As a result, the Army of the Potomac was safely back on the other side of the river by May 6, greatly surprising Lee, who was still making plans to attack Hooker in hopes of destroying his command against the Rapidan. Incredibly, upon withdrawing back across the river and retreating, Hooker issued General Orders No. 49, which actually congratulated his army on their recent achievements:

"The major-general commanding tenders to this army his congratulations on its achievements of the last seven days. If it has not accomplished all that was expected, the reasons are well known to the army. It is sufficient to say they were of a character not to be foreseen or prevented by human sagacity or resource.

In withdrawing from the south bank of the Rappahannock before delivering a general battle to our adversaries, the army has given renewed evidence of its confidence in itself and its fidelity to the principles it represents. In fighting at a disadvantage, we would have been recreant to our trust, to ourselves, our cause, and our country.

Profoundly loyal, and conscious of its strength, the Army of the Potomac will give or decline battle whenever its interest or honor may demand. It will also be the guardian of its own history and its own fame.

By our celerity and secrecy of movement, our advance and passage of the rivers were undisputed, and on our withdrawal not a rebel ventured to follow.

The events of the last week may swell with pride the heart of every officer and soldier of this army. We have added new luster to its former renown. We have made long marches, crossed rivers, surprised the enemy in his intrenchments, and whenever we have fought have inflicted heavier blows than we have received.

We have taken from the enemy 5,000 prisoners; captured and brought off seven pieces of artillery, fifteen colors; placed hors de combat 18,000 of his chosen troops; destroyed his depots filled with vast amounts of stores; deranged his communications; captured prisoners within the fortifications of his capital, and filled his country with fear and consternation.

We have no other regret than that caused by the loss of our brave companions, and in this we are consoled by the conviction that they have fallen in the holiest cause ever submitted to the arbitrament of battle."

Whether Hooker truly believed the contents of his orders or not, the rest of his officers and the rank-and-file were well aware of what their retreat meant.

The following day, on May 7, Stoneman's cavalry reentered Union lines east of Richmond on the Peninsula. Hooker's poor use of Stoneman's cavalry had deprived him of necessary reconnaissance on May 2 and made it that much easier for Stuart's cavalry to determine the XI Corps had its right flank in the air. For his part, Stoneman had accomplished nothing of importance, failing to destroy any of the supply lines or communication lines Hooker anticipated he would.

Chapter 7: The Aftermath of Chancellorsville

The Chancellorsville campaign officially came to an end with Hooker's withdrawal on May 6, but the most important casualty of the campaign would not come until 4 days later.

After being wounded and carried behind the lines on the night of May 2, Stonewall Jackson had his arm amputated, after which he was transported to Thomas C. Chandler's plantation well behind the battle lines to convalesce. He seemed to be recovering, and his wife and newborn daughter joined him at the plantation, but his doctors were unaware Jackson was exhibiting common symptoms that indicated oncoming pneumonia. Jackson lay dying in the Chandler plantation outbuilding on Sunday, May 10, 1863 with his wife Anna at his side. He comforted his wife, telling her, "It is the Lord's Day…my wish is fulfilled. I always wanted to die on Sunday." Near the end, a delirious Jackson seemed to have his mind on war, blurting out, "Tell A. P. Hill to prepare for actions! Pass the infantry to the front! Tell Major Hawks…" His final words were "Let us cross over the river, and rest under the shade of the trees."

The loss of Jackson was a crushing one for the Confederacy and Lee's army. In his post-campaign report, Lee wrote of his fallen subordinate, "The movement by which the enemy's position was turned and the fortune of the day decided was conducted by the lamented Lieutenant-General Jackson, who, as has already been stated, was severely wounded near the close of the engagement on Saturday evening. I do not propose here to speak of the character of this illustrious man, since removed from the scene of his eminent usefulness by the hand of an inscrutable but all-wise Providence. I nevertheless desire to pay the tribute of my admiration to the matchless energy and skill that marked this last act of his life, forming, as it did, a worthy conclusion of that long series of splendid achievements which won for him the lasting love and gratitude of his country."

The Battle of Chancellorsville is widely remembered as Lee's greatest victory. Historian Robert Krick, who wrote a history of the campaign and titled his book *Lee's Greatest Victory*, notes, "Lee's Chancellorsville consisted of a pastiche of unbelievably risky gambits that led to a great triumph. Hooker's campaign, after the brilliant opening movements, degenerated into a tale of opportunities missed and troops underutilized." And from a tactical standpoint, there's no question that Chancellorsville was Lee's masterpiece. Every gamble paid off, every decision he made ended up being the right one, and he was assisted by skilled subordinates like Stuart and Jackson. He seamlessly switched between taking the offensive and skillfully defending on two separate fronts over the course of several days, and he ultimately forced an army more than twice the size of his to withdraw and abort the campaign.

However, as Longstreet noted in his memoirs, the context of the Chancellorsville campaign cannot be forgotten. Lee had gained a complete strategic and tactical victory, but it was more a result of Hooker becoming cautious. The casualties among the two sides were 17,000 Union soldiers killed, captured or wounded, with about 13,000 Confederates killed, captured, or wounded. In other words, Lee lost nearly 25% of his army, and though he inflicted 4,000 more casualties on Hooker's army, the Army of the Potomac lost about 15% of its manpower. The Confederates were undermanned and lacked the resources of the Union throughout the war, and while Lee had blunted the latest offensive by the Army of the Potomac, the campaign all but ended with the two armies in the same positions they had been in 10 days earlier. No matter how many times Lee won a battle like Chancellorsville, the Confederacy would still lose the war. As Longstreet would put it in his memoirs, "The battle as pitched and as an independent affair was brilliant, and if the war was for glory could be called successful, but, besides putting the cause upon the hazard of a die, it was crippling in resources and of future progress, while the wait of a few days would have given time for concentration and opportunities against Hooker more effective than we experienced with Burnside at Fredericksburg. This was one of the occasions where success was not a just criterion."

Naturally, an analysis of Chancellorsville far different today given the hindsight of knowing the Civil War's final result than it was in May 1863. At the time, Chancellorsville was one of the most stunning battles of the Civil War, and Lincoln was shook to the core, exclaiming after the battle, "My God! My God! What will the country say?" At the same time, the South's joy at hearing of the victory was completely dampened by the loss of Jackson, and Longstreet recalled that when he rejoined the army, "I found [Lee] in sadness, notwithstanding that he was contemplating his great achievement and brilliant victory of Chancellorsville, for he had met with great loss as well as great gains. The battle had cost heavily of his army, but his grief was over the severe wounding of his great lieutenant, General Thomas Jonathan Jackson, the head of the Second Corps of the Army of Northern Virginia; cut off, too, at a moment so much needed to finish his work in the battle so handsomely begun."

Ultimately, Chancellorsville's most decisive impact and legacy can be found in the many ways it shaped Lee's subsequent Pennsylvania Campaign. At the beginning of 1863, Lee felt the Confederate cause needed the kind of decisive victory and master stroke that could win the war with one grand battle. It's why Lee constantly felt compelled to attack an army twice his army's size multiple times at Chancellorsville, and his failure to knockout Hooker made him that much more anxious to win a crushing victory at Gettysburg.

Lee's impatience with the status quo after Chancellorsville also induced him to invade Pennsylvania in the first place. Knowing that victories on Virginia soil meant little to an enemy that could simply retreat, regroup, and then return with more men and more advanced equipment, Lee would next set his sights on a Northern invasion, aiming to turn Northern opinion against the war and against President Lincoln. With his men already half-starved from dwindling provisions, Lee intended to confiscate food, horses, and equipment as they pushed north, and he also hoped to influence Northern politicians into giving up their support of the war by penetrating into Harrisburg or even Philadelphia. Given the right circumstances, Lee's army might even be able to capture either Baltimore or Philadelphia and use the city as leverage in peace negotiations.

Before Lee even made that invasion, the results at Chancellorsville led to major reorganizations of both armies that directly influenced how Gettysburg was fought. Not surprisingly, there were some serious shakeups in Chancellorsville's aftermath as Union generals pointed the fingers at each other. Hooker had a list of scapegoats, including XI Corps commander Oliver O. Howard, cavalry leader George Stoneman, and VI Corps commander John Sedgwick. Of course, just as many blamed Hooker, pointing out that a sizable amount of the Army of the Potomac had barely fought at all during the Chancellorsville campaign. The strongest critic was II Corps commander Darius N. Couch, who vowed never to serve under Hooker again and subsequently transferred out of the Army of the Potomac back to Pennsylvania to lead the state militia. He would be succeeded by Winfield Scott Hancock as the new commander of the II Corps, and Hancock would be the most conspicuous Union hero during the last two days of Gettysburg, including during Pickett's Charge.

Hancock

George Meade would later privately claim in a letter to his wife, "Hooker never lost his head, nor did he ever allow himself to be influenced by me or my advice. The objection I have to Hooker is that he did not and would not listen to those around him; that he acted deliberately on his own judgment, and in doing so, committed, as I think, fatal errors. If he had lost his head, and I had been placed in command, you may rest assured a very different result would have been arrived at, whether better or worse for us cannot be told now."

On May 10, 1863, as Stonewall Jackson lay dying, Meade wrote to his wife, "There is a great deal of talking in the camp, and I see the press is beginning to attack Hooker. I think these last operations have shaken the confidence of the army in Hooker's judgment, particularly among the superior officers. I have been much gratified at the frequent expression of opinion that I ought to be placed in command. Three of my seniors (Couch, Slocum and Sedgwick) have sent me word that they were willing to serve under me. Couch, I hear, told the President he would not serve any longer under Hooker, and recommended my assignment to the command. I mention all this confidentially. I do not attach any importance to it, and do not believe there is the slightest probability of my being placed in command."

Meade would get his private wish. Lincoln would relieve Hooker of command just a few days before the Battle of Gettysburg and name Meade the new commander of the Army of the Potomac. Meade would hold his ground during the battle and become the first Union general to inflict a decisive defeat upon Lee and his Army of Northern Virginia.

In the wake of Stonewall Jackson's death, Lee reorganized his army, creating three Corps out of the previous two, with A.P. Hill and Richard S. Ewell "replacing" Jackson. Hill had been a successful division commander, but he was constantly battling bouts of sickness that left him disabled, which would occur at Gettysburg. Ewell had distinguished himself during the Peninsula Campaign, but he suffered a serious injury during Second Manassas that historians often credit as making him more cautious in command upon his return. Ewell is often blamed for the Confederate loss at Gettysburg because of his inaction on Day 1 of the battle. Late in the afternoon of the battle's first day, Lee sent discretionary orders to Ewell that Cemetery Hill be taken "if practicable", but ultimately Ewell chose not to attempt the assault. Lee's order has been criticized because it left too much discretion to Ewell, leaving historians to speculate on how the more aggressive Stonewall Jackson would have acted on this order if he had lived to command this wing of Lee's army, and how differently the second day of battle would have proceeded with Confederate possession of Culp's Hill or Cemetery Hill. Discretionary orders were customary for General Lee because Jackson and Longstreet, his other principal subordinate, usually reacted to them aggressively and used their initiative to act quickly and forcefully. Ewell's decision not to attack, whether justified or not, may have ultimately cost the Confederates the battle. Edwin Coddington, widely considered the historian who wrote the greatest history of the battle, concluded, "Responsibility for the failure of the Confederates to make an all-out assault on Cemetery Hill on July 1 must rest with Lee. If Ewell had been a Jackson he might have been able to regroup his forces quickly enough to attack within an hour after the Yankees had started to retreat through the town. The likelihood of success decreased rapidly after that time unless Lee were willing to risk everything."

General Ewell

The second day of the fighting at Gettysburg may have also been dramatically shaped by the experiences at Chancellorsville. On Day 2 of the battle, Union III Corps commander Dan Sickles disobeyed Meade's orders and took it upon himself to advance his entire corps one half mile forward to a peach orchard, poising himself to take control of higher ground. Some historians assert that Sickles had held a grudge against Meade for taking command from his friend Joseph Hooker and intentionally disregarded orders, but it has also been speculated by some historians that Sickles moved forward to occupy high ground in his front due to the devastation unleashed against the III Corps at Chancellorsville once Confederates took high ground and operated their artillery on Hazel Grove. Sickles's decision at Gettysburg created a gap in the Union line that shaped hours of fighting and resulted in Sickles having the III Corps nearly annihilated in the process.

Given the unorthodox and controversial generalship at the battle, the mortal wounding of Stonewall Jackson at the pinnacle of his brilliant career, and the decisive impact it had on the men that fought it and the battle that came after it, it's no wonder that Chancellorsville continues to fascinate Americans nearly 150 years after it was fought.

Bibliography

Alexander, Edward P. Fighting for the Confederacy: The Personal Recollections of General Edward Porter Alexander. Edited by Gary W. Gallagher.

Catton, Bruce. Glory Road. Garden City, NY: Doubleday and Company, 1952.

Cullen, Joseph P. "Battle of Chancellorsville." In Battle Chronicles of the Civil War: 1863, edited by James M. McPherson. Connecticut: Grey Castle Press, 1989.

Freeman, Douglas S. Lee's Lieutenants: A Study in Command. 3 vols. New York: Scribner, 1946.

Furgurson, Ernest B. Chancellorsville 1863: The Souls of the Brave. New York: Knopf, 1992.

Gallagher, Gary W. The Battle of Chancellorsville. National Park Service Civil War series. Conshohocken, PA: U.S. National Park Service and Eastern National, 1995.

Hebert, Walter H. Fighting Joe Hooker. Lincoln: University of Nebraska Press, 1999.

Krick, Robert K. Chancellorsville—Lee's Greatest Victory. New York: American Heritage Publishing Co., 1990.

Sears, Stephen W. Chancellorsville. Boston: Houghton Mifflin, 1996.

The Battle of Gettysburg

Chapter 1: The Battle of Brandy Station

In the spring of 1863, General Lee discovered that McClellan had known of his plans and was able to force a battle at Antietam before all of General Lee's forces had arrived. General Lee now believed that he could successfully invade the North again, and that his defeat before was due in great measure to a stroke of bad luck. In addition, General Lee hoped to supply his army on the unscathed fields and towns of the North, while giving war ravaged northern Virginia a rest. After Chancellorsville, Longstreet and Lee met to discuss options for the Confederate Army's summer campaign. Longstreet advocated detachment of all or part of his corps to be sent to Tennessee, citing Union Maj. General Ulysses S. Grant's advance on Vicksburg, the critical Confederate stronghold on the Mississippi River. Longstreet argued that a reinforced army under Bragg could defeat Rosecrans and drive toward the Ohio River, compelling Grant to release his hold on Vicksburg. Lee, however, was opposed to a division of his army and instead advocated a large-scale offensive (and raid) into Pennsylvania. In addition, General Lee hoped to supply his army on the unscathed fields and towns of the North, while giving war ravaged northern Virginia a rest.

Knowing that victories on Virginia soil meant little to an enemy that could simply retreat, regroup, and then return with more men and more advanced equipment, Lee set his sights on a Northern invasion, aiming to turn Northern opinion against the war and against President Lincoln. With his men already half-starved from dwindling provisions, Lee intended to confiscate food, horses, and equipment as they pushed north--and hopefully influence Northern politicians into giving up their support of the war by penetrating into Harrisburg or even Philadelphia. Given the right circumstances, Lee's army might even be able to capture either Baltimore or Philadelphia and use the city as leverage in peace negotiations.

In the wake of Jackson's death, Lee reorganized his army, creating three Corps out of the previous two, with A.P. Hill and Richard S. Ewell "replacing" Stonewall. Hill had been a successful division commander, but he was constantly battling bouts of sickness that left him disabled, which would occur at Gettysburg. Ewell had distinguished himself during the Peninsula Campaign, suffering a serious injury that historians often credit as making him more cautious in command upon his return.

In early June, the Army of Northern Virginia occupied Culpeper, Virginia. After their victories at Fredericksburg and Chancellorsville against armies twice their size, Confederate troops felt invincible and anxious to carry the war north into Pennsylvania. Assuming his role as Lee's "Eyes of the Army" for the Pennsylvania Campaign, Stuart bivouacked his men near the Rappahannock River, screening the Confederate Army against surprise Union attacks. Taken with his recent successes, Stuart requested a full field review of his units by General Lee, and on

June 8, paraded his nearly 9,000 mounted troops and four batteries of horse artillery for review, also charging in simulated battle at Inlet Station about two miles southwest of Brandy Station. While Lee himself was unavailable to attend the review, some of the cavalrymen and newspaper reporters at the scene complained that all Stuart was doing was "feeding his ego and exhausting the horses." He began to be referred to as a "headline-hunting show-off."

Despite the critics, Stuart basked in the glory. Renowned Civil War historian Stephen Sears described the scene, "The grand review of June 5 was surely the proudest day of Jeb Stuart's thirty years. As he led a cavalcade of resplendent staff officers to the reviewing stand, trumpeters heralded his coming and women and girls strewed his path with flowers. Before all of the spectators the assembled cavalry brigade stretched a mile and a half. After Stuart and his entourage galloped past the line in review, the troopers in their turn saluted the reviewing stand in columns of squadrons. In performing a second "march past," the squadrons started off at a trot, then spurred to a gallop. Drawing sabers and breaking into the Rebel yell, the troopers rush toward the horse artillery drawn up in battery. The gunners responded defiantly, firing blank charges. Amidst this tumult of cannon fire and thundering hooves, a number of ladies swooned in their escorts' arms."[1]

However much Stuart enjoyed "horsing around", there was serious work to be done. The following day, Lee ordered Stuart to cross the Rappahannock and raid Union forward positions, shielding the Confederate Army from observation or interference as it moved north. Already anticipating this imminent offensive move, Stuart had ordered his troops back into formation around Brandy Station. Here, Stuart would endure the first of two low points in his military career: the Battle of Brandy Station, the largest predominantly cavalry engagement of the Civil War.

Union Maj. General Joseph Hooker interpreted Stuart's presence around Culpeper as a precursor to a raid on his army's supply lines. In response, he ordered his cavalry commander, Maj. General Alfred Pleasonton, to take a combined force of 8,000 cavalry and 3,000 infantry on a raid to "disperse and destroy" the 9,500 Confederates. Crossing the Rappahannock River in two columns on June 9,1863 at Beverly's Ford and Kelly's Ford, the first infantry unit caught Stuart completely off-guard, and the second surprised him yet again. Suddenly the Confederates were being battered both front and rear by mounted Union troops.

In addition to being the largest cavalry battle of the war, the chaos and confusion that ensued across the battlefield also made Brandy Station unique in that most of the fighting was done while mounted and using sabers. One account of the battle noted, "Of the bodies that littered the field that day, the vast majority were found to have perished by the sword."

---

[1] Sears, Stephen W. *Gettysburg*. Page 64.

After 10 hours of charges and countercharges that swept back and forth across Fleetwood Hill (where Stuart had headquartered the night before) involving drawn sabers and revolvers, Pleasonton decided to withdraw his exhausted men across the Rappahannock River. Stuart immediately claimed a Confederate victory because his men had managed to hold the field and inflicted more casualties on the enemy while forcing Pleasonton to withdraw before locating Lee's infantry. But Stuart was trying to save face, and nobody else, including Lee, took his view of the battle. The fact was, the Southern cavalry under Stuart had not detected the movement of two large columns of Union cavalry and had fallen prey to not one but *two* surprise attacks. Two days later the Richmond *Enquirer* reported, "If Gen. Stuart is to be the eyes and ears of the army we advise him to see more, and be seen less. Gen. Stuart has suffered no little in public estimation by the late enterprises of the enemy."[2]

Lee was now painfully aware of the increased competency of the Union cavalry, as well as the decline of the seemingly once-invincible Southern mounted armed forces under Stuart. Moreover, Stuart was now smarting from the negative publicity and the hit his reputation had taken at Brandy Station. The prideful, vainglorious cavalry leader hoped to bring glory to himself.

Chapter 2: Lee Invades Pennsylvania

During the first weeks of summer of 1863, as Stuart screened the army and completed several well-executed offenses against Union cavalry, many historians think it likely that he had already planned to remove the negative effect of Brandy Station by duplicating one of his now famous circumnavigating rides around the enemy army. But as Lee began his march north through the Shenandoah Valley in western Virginia, it is highly unlikely that is what he wanted or expected.

Before setting out on June 22, the methodical Lee gave Stuart specific instructions as to the role he was to play in the Pennsylvania offensive: as the "Eyes of the Army" he was to guard the mountain passes with part of his force while the Army of Northern Virginia was still south of the Potomac River, and then cross the river with the remainder of his army and screen the right flank of Confederate general Richard Stoddert Ewell's Second Corps as it moved down the Shenandoah Valley, maintaining contact with Ewell's army as it advanced towards Harrisburg.
But instead of taking the most direct route north near the Blue Ridge Mountains, Stuart chose a much more ambitious course of action.

Stuart decided to march his three best brigades (under Generals Hampton and Fitzhugh Lee, and Col. John R. Chambliss) between the Union army and Washington, north through Rockville to Westminster, and then into Pennsylvania--a route that would allow them to capture supplies along the way and wreak havoc as they skirted Washington. In the aftermath, the *Washington*

---

[2]   Wert, Jeffry D. *Cavalryman of the Lost Cause: A Biography of J.E.B. Stuart*. Page 251.

Star would write: "The cavalry chief [Stuart] interpreted his marching orders in a way that best suited his nature, and detached his 9000 troopers from their task of screening the main army and keeping tabs on the Federals. When Lee was in Pennsylvania anxiously looking for him, Stuart crossed the Potomac above Washington and captured a fine prize of Federal supply wagons . . . ."[3]

But to complicate matters even more, as Stuart set out on June 25 on what was probably a glory-seeking mission, he was unaware that his intended path was blocked by columns of Union infantry that would invariably force him to veer farther east than he or Lee had anticipated. Ultimately, his decision would prevent him from linking up with Ewell as ordered and deprive Lee of his primary cavalry force as he advanced deeper and deeper into unfamiliar enemy territory. According to Halsey Wigfall (son of Confederate States Senator Louis Wigfall) who was in Stuart's infantry, "Stuart and his cavalry left [Lee's] army on June 24 and did not contact [his] army again until the afternoon of July 2, the second day of the [Gettysburg] battle."[4]

According to Stuart's own account, on June 29 his men clashed briefly with two companies of Union cavalry in Westminster, Maryland, overwhelming and chasing them "a long distance on the Baltimore road," causing a "great panic" in the city of Baltimore. On June 30, the head of Stuart's column then encountered Union Brig. General Judson Kilpatrick's cavalry as it passed through Hanover--reportedly capturing a wagon train and scattering the Union army--after which Kilpatrick's men were able to regroup and drive Stuart and his men out of town. Then after a twenty-mile trek in the dark, Stuart's exhausted men reached Dover, Pennsylvania, on the morning of July 1 (which they briefly occupied).

Late on the second day of the battle, Stuart finally arrived, bringing with him the caravan of captured Union supply wagons, and he was immediately reprimanded by Lee. One account describes Lee as "visibly angry" raising his hand "as if to strike the tardy cavalry commander."[5] While that does not sound like Lee's style, Stuart has been heavily criticized ever since, and it has been speculated Lee took him to task harshly enough that Stuart offered his resignation. Lee didn't accept it, but he would later note in his after battle report that the cavalry had not updated him as to the Army of the Potomac's movements.

Given great discretion in his cavalry operations before the battle, Stuart's cavalry was too far removed from the Army of Northern Virginia to warn Lee of the Army of the Potomac's movements. As it would turn out, Lee's army inadvertently stumbled into Union cavalry and then the Union army at Gettysburg on the morning of July 1, 1863, walking blindly into what

---

[3]   Stepp, John W. & Hill, William I. (editors), *Mirror of War, the Washington Star reports the Civil War*. Page 199.
[4]   Eaton, Clement. *Jefferson Davis*. Page 178.
[5]   Philips, David. *Crucial Land Battles*. Page 75.

became the largest battle of the war.

Meade Takes Command

Though he had privately confided to his wife that he desired command of the Army of the Potomac, Meade never publicly expressed his wishes to those in charge, thus avoiding the political squabbling among generals. On June 28, however, he got his wish.

Before sunrise on that morning, a messenger entered Major General George Meade's field headquarters, shook the sleeping general and said, "I'm afraid I've come to give you some trouble, General."[6] Jumping to his feet, Meade's first thought was that he was being arrested-- probably for arguing with Hooker on the battlefield. Informed that he had replaced Maj. General Joseph Hooker as commander of the Army of the Potomac (Lincoln had passed over his friend, the more qualified John F. Reynolds), Meade at first protested, stating that he didn't want the job. Informed that his promotion was not a "request," Meade hitched up his sagging long underwear, ran his fingers through his thinning hair and said, "Well, I've been tried and condemned without a hearing, and I suppose I shall have to go to the execution."[7] Historians have also speculated that it may well have been Mead's foreign birth that got him selected over Reynolds. As such, he was excluded from running for the U. S. Presidency and therefore posed no future threat to Lincoln, as Reynolds may have if successful. Of course, that doesn't square with reports that Reynolds turned the offer down.

In addition to being informed by Hooker that he was in command, Meade received a telegram from general-in-chief Henry Halleck:

"General:
You will receive with this the order of the President placing you in command of the Army of the Potomac. Considering the circumstances, no one ever received a more important command; and I cannot doubt that you will fully justify the confidence which the Government has reposed in you.
You will not be hampered by any minute instructions from these headquarters. Your army is free to act as you may deem proper under the circumstances as they arise. You will, however, keep in view the important fact that the Army of the Potomac is the covering army of Washington, as well as the army of operation against the invading forces of the rebels. You will therefore manoeuvre and fight in such a manner as to cover the Capital and also Baltimore, as far as circumstances will admit. Should General Lee move upon either of these places, it is expected that you will either anticipate him or arrive with him, so as to give him battle.
All forces within the sphere of your operations will be held subject to your orders.

---

[6] Stevens, Joseph E. *1863: The Rebirth of a Nation*. Page 230.
[7] Stevens, Joseph E. *1863: The Rebirth of a Nation*. Page 231.

Harper's Ferry and its garrison are under your direct orders.

You are authorized to remove from command and send from your army any officer or other person you may deem proper; and to appoint to command as you may deem expedient.

In fine, General, you are intrusted with all the power and authority which the President, the Secretary of War, or the General-in-Chief can confer on you, and you may rely on our full support.

You will keep me fully informed of all your movements and the positions of your own troops and those of the enemy, so far as known.

I shall always be ready to advise and assist you to the utmost of my ability.

Very respectfully,

Your obedient servant,

H. W. Halleck, General-in-Chief."

Meade then issued General Orders No. 67:

By direction of the President of the United States, I hereby assume command of the Army of the Potomac.

As a soldier, in obeying this order—an order totally unexpected and unsolicited—I have no promises or pledges to make.

The country looks to this army to relieve it from the devastation and disgrace of a foreign invasion. Whatever fatigues and sacrifices we may be called upon to undergo, let us have in view, constantly, the magnitude of the interests involved, and let each man determine to do his duty, leaving to an all-controlling Providence the decision of the contest.

It is with great diffidence that I relieve in the command of this army an eminent and accomplished soldier, whose name must ever appear conspicuous in the history of its achievements; but I rely upon the hearty support of my companions in arms to assist me in the discharge of the duties of the important trust which has been confided to me.

George G. Meade, Major General, commanding.

When word of Meade's promotion spread around camp, it certainly surprised many men. After all, Meade lacked charisma, did not exude confidence, and did not arouse enthusiasm among his men by his presence. In fact, considering the many times he'd been wounded (or nearly wounded), many considered him a danger to his men and to himself. Even his trusty horse "Old Baldy" had been wounded under him at Second Bull Run and again at Antietam. Ultimately, the best thing his men could say about him was that at least he had never made any ruinous mistakes.

Assuming command of the Army of the Potomac on June 28 at Prospect Hall in Frederick,

Maryland, (with his second son, George, now part of his staff), Meade had his work cut out for him, though few apparently considered his position. Having to first locate his forces, he then had to review Hooker's strategy, study the most recent intelligence reports, and then determine the appropriate course of action, all the while keeping an eye fixed on Lee. Ultimately disregarding Hooker's plans to strike into the Cumberland Valley, Meade opted to march on Harrisburg, Pennsylvania to move toward the Susquehanna River, keeping his troops between Lee's army and Washinton.

Upon taking command, Meade began drawing up defensive positions around northern Maryland about a dozen miles south of Gettysburg. His proposed line would be referred to as the Pipe Creek Circular, but it would never be implemented due to actions outside of Meade's control.

It is believed that one of the first notices Lee got about the Army of the Potomac's movements actually came from a spy named "Harrison", a man who apparently worked undercover for Longstreet but of whom little is known. Harrison reported that General George G. Meade was now in command of the Union Army and was at that very moment marching north to meet Lee's army. According to Longstreet, he and Lee were supposedly on the same page at the beginning of the campaign. "His plan or wishes announced, it became useless and improper to offer suggestions leading to a different course. All that I could ask was that the policy of the campaign should be one of defensive tactics; that we should work so as to force the enemy to attack us, in such good position as we might find in our own country, so well adapted to that purpose—which might assure us of a grand triumph. To this he readily assented as an important and material adjunct to his general plan." Lee later claimed he "had never made any such promise, and had never thought of doing any such thing," but in his official report after the battle, Lee also noted, "It had not been intended to fight a general battle at such a distance from our base, unless attacked by the enemy.

Chapter 3: July 1, 1863

Without question, the most famous battle of the Civil War took place outside of the small town of Gettysburg, Pennsylvania, which happened to be a transpotation hub, serving as the center of a wheel with several roads leading out to other Pennsylvanian towns. Lee was unaware of Meade's position when an advanced division of Hill's Corps marched toward Gettysburg on the morning of July 1.

The battle began with John Buford's Union cavalry forces skirmishing against the advancing division of Heth's just outside of town. Buford intentionally fought a delaying action that was meant to allow John Reynolds' I Corps to reach Gettysburg and engage the Confederates, which eventually set the stage for a general battle.

Buford

    The I Corps was led by Pennsylvanian General John F. Reynolds, an effective general that had been considered for command of the entire army in place of Hooker and was considered by many the best general in the army. Since Lee had invaded Pennsylvania, many believe that Reynolds was even more active and aggressive than he might have otherwise been. In any event, Reynolds was personally at the front positioning two brigades, exhorting his men, "Forward men! Forward for God's sake, and drive those fellows out of the woods."

As he was at the front positioning his men, Reynolds fell from his horse, having been hit by a bullet behind the ear that killed him almost instantly. With his death, command of the I Corps fell upon Maj. Gen. Abner Doubleday, the Civil War veteran wrongly credited for inventing baseball. Despite the death of the corps commander, the I Corps successfully managed to drive the Confederates in their sector back, highlighted by sharp fighting from the Iron Brigade, a brigade comprised of Wisconsin, Indiana, and Michigan soldiers from the "West". In an unfinished railroad cut, the 6th Wisconsin captured the 2nd Mississippi, and regimental commander Rufus Dawes reported, "The officer replied not a word, but promptly handed me his sword, and his men, who still held them, threw down their muskets. The coolness, self possession, and discipline which held back our men from pouring a general volley saved a hundred lives of the enemy, and as my mind goes back to the fearful excitement of the moment, I marvel at it."

Reynolds

Around noon, the battle hit a lull, in part because Confederate division commander Henry Heth was under orders to avoid a general battle in the absence of the rest of the Army of Northern Virginia. At that point, however, the Union had gotten the better of the fighting, and the Confederate army was concentrating on the area, with more soldiers in Hill's corps in the immediate vicinity and Ewell's corps marching from the north toward the town.

As the Union's I Corps held the line, General Oliver O. Howard and his XI Corps came up on the right of the I Corps, eager to replace the stain the XI Corps had suffered at Chancellorsville thanks to Stonewall Jackson. As a general battle began to form northwest of town, news was making its way back to Meade several miles away that Reynolds had been killed, and that a battle was developing.

Meade had been drawing up a proposed defensive line several miles away from Gettysburg near Emmitsburg, Maryland, but when news of the morning's fighting reached him, Meade sent II Corps commander Winfield Scott Hancock ahead to take command in the field, putting him in temporary command of the "left wing" of the army consisting of the I, II, III and XI Corps. Meade also charged Hancock with determining whether to fight the general battle near Gettysburg or to pull back to the line Meade had been drawing up. Hancock would not be the senior officer on the field (Oliver Howard outranked him), so the fact that he was ordered to take command of the field demonstrates how much Meade trusted him.

As Hancock headed toward the fighting, and while the Army of the Potomac's I and XI Corps engaged in heavy fighting, they were eventually flanked from the north by Ewell's Confederate Corps, which was returning toward Gettysburg from its previous objective. For the XI Corps, it was certainly reminiscent of their retreat at Chancellorsville, and they began a disorderly retreat through the streets of the small town. Fighting broke out in various places throughout the town, while some Union soldiers hid in and around houses for the duration of the battle. Gettysburg's citizens also fled in the chaos and fighting.

After a disorderly retreat through the town itself, the Union men began to dig in on high ground to the southeast of the town. When Hancock met up with Howard, the two briefly argued over the leadership arrangement, until Howard finally acquiesced. Hancock told the XI Corps commander, "I think this the strongest position by nature upon which to fight a battle that I ever saw." When Howard agreed, Hancock replied, "Very well, sir, I select this as the battle-field."

As the Confederates sent the Union corps retreating, Lee arrived on the field and saw the importance of the defensive positions the Union men were taking up along Cemetery Hill and Culp's Hill. Late in the afternoon, Lee sent discretionary orders to Ewell that Cemetery Hill be taken "if practicable", but ultimately Ewell chose not to attempt the assault. Lee's order has been criticized because it left too much discretion to Ewell, leaving historians to speculate on how the more aggressive Stonewall Jackson would have acted on this order if he had lived to command this wing of Lee's army, and how differently the second day of battle would have proceeded with Confederate possession of Culp's Hill or Cemetery Hill. Discretionary orders were customary for General Lee because Jackson and Longstreet, his other principal subordinate, usually reacted to them aggressively and used their initiative to act quickly and forcefully. Ewell's decision not to attack, whether justified or not, may have ultimately cost the Confederates the battle. Edwin Coddington, widely considered the historian who wrote the greatest history of the battle, concluded, "Responsibility for the failure of the Confederates to make an all-out assault on Cemetery Hill on July 1 must rest with Lee. If Ewell had been a Jackson he might have been able to regroup his forces quickly enough to attack within an hour after the Yankees had started to retreat through the town. The likelihood of success decreased rapidly after that time unless Lee were willing to risk everything."

With so many men engaged and now taking refuge on the high ground, Meade, who was an engineer like Lee, abandoned his previous plan to draw up a defensive line around Emmittsburg a few miles to the south. After a council of war, the Army of the Potomac decided to defend at Gettysburg.

Day 1 by itself would have been one of the 25 biggest battles of the Civil War, and it was a tactical Confederate victory. Union casualties were almost 9,000, and the Confederates suffered slightly more than 6,000. But the battle had just started, and thanks to the actions of Meade and Hancock, the largest battle on the North American continent would take place on the ground of their choosing.

Chapter 4: July 2, 1863

By the morning of July 2, Major General Meade had put in place what he thought to be the optimal battle strategy. Positioning his now massive Army of the Potomac in what would become known as the "fish hook", he'd established a line configuration that was much more compact and maneuverable than Lee's, which allowed Meade to shift his troops quickly from inactive parts of the line to those under attack without creating new points of vulnerability. Moreover, Meade's army was taking a defensive stance on the high ground anchored by Culp's Hill, Cemetery Hill, and Cemetery Ridge. Meade also personally moved the III Corps under Maj. General Daniel Sickles into position on the left of the line.

On the morning of July 2, Meade was determined to make a stand at Gettysburg, and Lee was determined to strike at him. That morning, Lee decided to make strong attacks on both Union flanks while feinting in the middle, ordering Ewell's corps to attack Culp's Hill on the Union right while Longstreet's corps would attack on the Union left. Lee hoped to seize Cemetery Hill, which would give the Confederates the high ground to harass the Union supply lines and command the road to Washington, D.C. Lee also believed that the best way to do so would be to use Longstreet's corps to launch an attack up the Emmitsburg Road, which he figured would roll up the Union's left flank, presumed to be on Cemetery Hill. Lee was mistaken, due in part to the fact Stuart and his cavalry couldn't perform reconnaissance. In fact, the Union line extended farther south than Cemetery Hill, with the II Corps positioned on Cemetery Ridge and the III Corps nearly as far south as the base of Little Round Top and Round Top. Moreover, Ewell protested that this battle plan would demoralize his men, since they'd be forced to give up the ground they had captured the day before.

Lee's Plan for July 2

Longstreet's Assault

As it turned out, both attacks ordered by Lee would come too late. Though there was a controversy over when Lee ordered Longstreet's attack, Longstreet's march got tangled up and caused several hours of delay. Lost Cause advocates attacking Longstreet would later claim his attack was supposed to take place as early as possible, although no official Confederate orders gave a time for the attack. Lee gave the order for the attack around 11:00 a.m., and it is known that Longstreet was reluctant about making it; he still wanted to slide around the Union flank, interpose the Confederate army between Washington D.C. and the Army of the Potomac, and force Meade to attack them. Between Longstreet's delays and the mixup in the march that forced parts of his corps to double back and make a winding march, Longstreet's men weren't ready to attack until about 4:00 p.m.

Longstreet's biographer, Jeffrey Wert, wrote, "Longstreet deserves censure for his performance on the morning of July 2. He allowed his disagreement with Lee's decision to affect his conduct. Once the commanding general determined to assail the enemy, duty required Longstreet to comply with the vigor and thoroughness that had previously characterized his generalship. The concern for detail, the regard for timely information, and the need for preparation were absent." Edwin Coddington, whose history of the Gettysburg Campaign still continues to be considered the best ever written, described Longstreet's march as "a comedy of errors such as one might expect of inexperienced commanders and raw militia, but not of Lee's ' War Horse' and his veteran troops." Coddington considered it "a dark moment in Longstreet's career as a general."

Writing about July 2, Longstreet criticized Lee, insisting once again that the right move was to move around the Union flank. "The opportunity for our right was in the air. General Halleck saw it from Washington. General Meade saw and was apprehensive of it. Even General Pendleton refers to it in favorable mention in his official report. Failing to adopt it, General Lee should have gone with us to his right. He had seen and carefully examined the left of his line, and only gave us a guide to show the way to the right, leaving the battle to be adjusted to formidable and difficult grounds without his assistance. If he had been with us, General Hood's messengers could have been referred to general Headquarters, but to delay and send messengers five miles in favor of a move that he had rejected would have been contumacious. The opportunity was with the Confederates from the assembling on Cemetery Hill. It was inviting of their preconceived plans. It was the object of and excuse for the invasion as a substitute for more direct efforts for the relief of Vicksburg. Confederate writers and talkers claim that General Meade could have escaped without making aggressive battle, but that is equivalent to confession of the inertia that failed to grasp the opportunity."

As Longstreet's men began their circuitous march, Union III Corps commander Dan Sickles took it upon himself to advance his entire corps one half mile forward to a peach orchard, poising himself to take control of higher ground. Some historians assert that Sickles had held a grudge against Meade for taking command from his friend Joseph Hooker and intentionally disregarded orders. It has also been speculated by some historians that Sickles moved forward to occupy high ground in his front due to the devastation unleashed against the III Corps at Chancellorsville once Confederates took high ground and operated their artillery on Hazel Grove. Sickles and

Meade would feud over the actions on Day 2 in the years after the war, after Sickles (who lost a leg that day) took credit for the victory by disrupting Lee's attack plans. Historians have almost universally sided with Meade, pointing out that Sickles nearly had his III Corps annihilated during Longstreet's attack.

Sickles

Whatever the reasoning for Sickles' move, this unauthorized action completely undermined Meade's overall strategy by effectively isolating Sickles' corps from the rest of the Union line and exposing the Union left flank in the process. By the early afternoon of July 2, nothing but the fog of war was preventing the Confederates from turning and crushing Sickles' forces, then moving to outflank the entire Union Army.

With General George Meade once again in command, General Hancock and the II Corps was positioned on Cemetery Ridge, roughly in the center of the Union line. Since Lee intended to strike at both Union flanks, theoretically Hancock's men should very well not have been engaged at all on the second day of the battle. But as a result of the fact Sickles had moved his men so far out of position, it created a major gap in the Union line and brought the III Corps directly into Longstreet's path. It was 4:00 p.m. by the time Longstreet's two divisions were in position for the attack, and they were taken completely by surprise whent hey found the III Corps in front of them on the Emmitsburg Road. Division commander John Bell Hood lobbied Longstreet to change up the plan of attack, but at this late time in the day Longstreet refused to modify Lee's orders.

Thus, in the late afternoon, the fighting on Day 2 began in earnest, and Longstreet's assault commenced by smashing into Sickles III Corps, engaging them in a peach orchard, wheat field, and Devil's Den, an outcropping of boulders that provided the Confederates prime cover.

When it became obvious that Sickles' III Corps was in dire straits, the chaos in that sector acted like a vacuum that induced both sides to pour more men into the vicinity. Moreover, when Sickles was injured by a cannonball that nearly blew off his leg, command of the III Corps fell upon II Corps commander Hancock as well. As Meade tried to shuffle reinforcements to his left, Hancock sent in his II Corps' First Division (under Brig. General John C. Caldwell) to reinforce the III Corps in the wheat field. The fighting in the wheat field was so intense that Caldwell's division would be all but annihilated during the afternoon.

At the same time, men from Confederate General A. P. Hill's corps made their advance toward the Union center, forcing the Army of the Potomac to rally defenses and rushed unit to critical spots to patch the holes. With Hill in his front and Longstreet's attack to his left, Hancock was in the unenviable position of having to attempt to resist Confederate advances spread out over a few miles, at least until more and more reserves could be rushed over from the other side of the Union line to the army's left flank. At one point, Hancock ordered a regiment to make what was essentially a suicidal bayonet charge into the face of Hill's Confederates on Cemetery Ridge. Hancock sent the First Minnesota to charge a Confederate brigade four times its size. One of the Minnesota volunteers, one William Lochren later said, "Every man realized in an instant what the order meant -- death or wounds to us all; the sacrifice of the regiment to gain a few minutes time and save the position, and probably the battlefield -- and every man saw and accepted the necessity of the sacrifice."[8] While extremely costly to the regiment (the Minnesotans suffered 87% casualties, the worst of any regiment at Gettysburg), this heroic sacrifice bought time to organize the defensive line and kept the battle from turning in favor of the Confederates. Hancock would write of them, "I cannot speak too highly of this regiment and its commander in its attack, as well as in its subsequent advance against the enemy, in which it lost three-fourths of the officers and men engaged."

As Longstreet's assault on the Union left continued, his line naturally got more and more entangled as well. As Longstreet's men kept moving to their right, they reached the base of Little Round Top and Round Top, two rocky hills south of Gettysburg proper, at the far left. When Meade's chief engineer, Brig. General Gouverneur Warren, spotted the sun shining off the bayonets of Longstreet's men as they moved toward the Union left, it alerted the Army of the Potomac of the need to occupy Little Round Top, high ground that commanded much of the field.

With Warren having alerted his superiors to the importance of Little Round Top, Strong Vincent's brigade moved into position, under orders from Warren to "hold this ground at any costs," As part of Strong Vincent's brigade, Chamberlain's 20th Maine was on the left of the line, and thus Chamberlain's unit represented the extreme left of the Army of the Potomac's line.

In front of Vincent's brigade was General Evander Law's advancing Alabama Brigade (of Hood's Division). Law ordered 5 regiments to take Little Round Top, the 4th, 15th, and 47th Alabama, and the 4th and 5th Texas, but they had already marched more than 20 miles just to reach that point. They were now being asked to charge up high ground on a muggy, hot day.

Nevertheless, the Confederates made desperate assaults against Little Round Top, even after being repulsed by the Union defenders several times. In the middle of the fighting, after he saw Confederates trying to push around his flank, Chamberlain stretched his line until his regiment was merely a single-file line, and he then had to order his left (southernmost) half to swing back, thus forming an angle in their line in an effort to prevent a flank attack. Despite suffering heavy losses, the 20th Maine held through two subsequent charges by the 15th Alabama and other Confederate regiments for nearly 2 hours.

---

[8]   Davis, Kenneth C. *The Civil War: Everything You Need to Know About America's Greatest Conflict but Never Learned.* Page 301.

Chamberlain

Even after repulsing the Confederates several times, Chamberlain and his regiment faced a serious dilemma. With casualties mounting and ammunition running low, in desperation, Chamberlain *claimed* to have ordered his left wing to initiate an all-out, pivoting bayonet charge. With the 20th Maine charging ahead, the left wing wheeling continually to make the charging line swing like a hinge, thus creating a simultaneous frontal assault and flanking maneuver, they ultimately succeeded in not only taking the hill, but capturing 100 Confederate soldiers in the process. Chamberlain suffered two slight wounds in the battle, one when a shot ricocheted off his sword scabbard and bruised his thigh, another when his right foot was struck by a piece of shrapnel. With this success, Chamberlain was credited with preventing the Union flank from being penetrated and keeping the Confederates from pouring in behind Union lines.

Ultimately, it was the occupation and defense of Little Round Top that saved the rest of the Union line at Gettysburg. Had the Confederates commanded that high ground, it would have been able to position artillery that could have swept the Union lines along Cemetery Ridge and Cemetery Hill, which would have certainly forced the Army of the Potomac to withdraw from their lines. Chamberlain would be awarded the coveted Congressional Medal of Honor for "daring heroism and great tenacity in holding his position on the Little Round Top against repeated assaults, and carrying the advance position on the Great Round Top", and the 20th Maine's actions that day became one of the most famous attacks of the Battle of Gettysburg and the Civil War as a whole.

But did it really happen that way? Though historians have mostly given Chamberlain the credit for the order to affix bayonets and make the charge down Little Round Top, and Chamberlain received the credit from Sharaa's *The Killer Angels* and the movie *Gettysburg*, some recent researchers have claimed that Lt. Holman S. Melcher initiated the charge. According to

Chamberlain however, Melcher had requested permission to make an advance to help some of his wounded men, only to be told by Chamberlain that a charge was about to be ordered anyway.

While Chamberlain's men held the extreme left, the rest of Vincent's brigade struggled desperately to the right, and Vincent himself would be mortally wounded in the fighting. The Confederates had advanced as far as Devil's Den, but Warren continued to bring reinforcements to Little Round Top to hold off Confederate attempts on the high ground. For the rest of the battle, even after the Confederates were repulsed from Little Round Top, their snipers in Devil's Den made the defenders of Little Round Top miserable. Confederate sharpshooters stationed around Devil's Den mortally wounded General Stephen Weed, whose New York brigade had arrived as reinforcements, and when his friend, artilleryman Lt. Charles Hazlett leaned over to comfort Weed or hear what he was trying to say, snipers shot Hazlett dead as well.

The fighting on the Union left finally ended as night fell. George Sykes, the commander of the V Corps, later described Day 2 in his official report, "Night closed the fight. The key of the battle-field was in our possession intact. Vincent, Weed, and Hazlett, chiefs lamented throughout the corps and army, sealed with their lives the spot intrusted to their keeping, and on which so much depended.... General Weed and Colonel Vincent, officers of rare promise, gave their lives to their country."

Ewell's Attack

Ewell's orders from Lee had been to launch a demonstration on the Union right flank during Longstreet's attack, which started at about 4:00 p.m. as well, and in support of the demonstration by Hill's corps in the center. For that reason, Ewell would not launch his general assault on Culp's Hill and Cemetery Hill until 7:00 p.m.

While the Army of the Potomac managed to desperately hold on the left, Ewell's attack against Culp's Hill on the other end of the field met with some success in pushing the Army of the Potomac back. However, the attack started so late in the day that nightfall made it impossible for the Confederates to capitalize on their success. Due to darkness, a Confederate brigade led by George H. Steuart was unaware that they were firmly beside the Army of the Potomac's right flank, which would have given them almost unlimited access to the Union army's rear and its supply lines and line of communication, just 600 yards away. the main line of communication for the Union army, the Baltimore Pike, only 600 yards to their front. Col. David Ireland and the 137th New York desperately fought to preserve the Union army's flank, much the same way Chamberlain and the 20th Maine had on the other side, and in the process the 137th lost a third of their men.

Ewell's men would spend the night at the base of Culp's Hill and partially up the hill, in positions that had been evacuated by Union soldiers after Meade moved some of them to the left to deal with Longstreet's attack. It would fall upon the Confederates to pick up the attack the next morning.

That night, Meade held another council of war. Having been attacked on both flanks, Meade and his top officers correctly surmised that Lee would attempt an attack on the center of the line the next day. Moreover, captured Confederates and the fighting and intelligence of Day 2 let it be known that the only Confederate unit that had not yet seen action during the fighting was George Pickett's division of Longstreet's corps.

Chapter 5: July 3, 1863

Lee's Plan

If July 2 was Longstreet's worst day of the Civil War, July 3 was almost certainly Robert E. Lee's. After the attack on July 2, Longstreet spent the night continuing to plot potential movements around Little Round Top and Big Round Top, thinking that would again get the Confederate army around the Union's flank. Longstreet himself did not realize that a reserve corps of the Union army was poised to block that maneuver.

Longstreet did not meet with Lee on the night of July 2, so when Lee met with him the following morning he found Longstreet's men were not ready to conduct an early morning attack, which Lee had wanted to attempt just as he was on the other side of the lines against Culp's Hill. With Pickett's men not up, however, Longstreet's corps couldn't make such an attack. Lee later wrote that Longstreet's "dispositions were not completed as early as was expected."

On the morning of July 3, the Confederate attack against Culp's Hill fizzled out, but by then Lee had already planned a massive attack on the Union center, combined with having Stuart's cavalry attack the Union army's lines in the rear. A successful attack would split the Army of the Potomac at the same time its communication and supply lines were severed by Stuart, which would make it possible to capture the entire army in detail.

There was just one problem with the plan, as Longstreet told Lee that morning: no 15,000 men who ever existed could successfully execute the attack. The charge required marching across an open field for about a mile, with the Union artillery holding high ground on all sides of the incoming Confederates. Longstreet ardently opposed the attack, but, already two days into the battle, Lee explained that because the Army of the Potomac was here on the field, he must strike at it. Longstreet later wrote that he said, "General Lee, I have been a soldier all my life. It is my opinion that no fifteen thousand men ever arrayed for battle can take that position."[9] Longstreet proposed instead that their men should slip around the Union forces and occupy the high ground, forcing Northern commanders to attack them, rather than vice versa.

Realizing the insanity of sending 15,000 men hurtling into all the Union artillery, Lee planned to use the Confederate artillery to try to knock out the Union artillery ahead of time. Although old friend William Pendleton was the artillery chief, the artillery cannonade would be supervised by Porter Alexander, Longstreet's chief artillerist, who would have to give the go-ahead to the charging infantry because they were falling under Longstreet's command.

Longstreet was certain of failure, but Pickett and the men preparing to make the charge were confident in their commanders and themselves. As Stuart was in the process of being repulsed, just after 1:00 p.m. 150 Confederate guns began to fire from Seminary Ridge, hoping to incapacitate the Union center before launching an infantry attack. Confederate brigadier Evander Law said of the artillery bombardment, "The cannonade in the center ... presented one of the most magnificent battle-scenes witnessed during the war. Looking up the valley towards Gettysburg, the hills on either side were capped with crowns of flame and smoke, as 300 guns, about equally divided between the two ridges, vomited their iron hail upon each other."

Alexander discussed the early part of the cannonading, including some that he had not ordered:

"A little before noon there sprung up upon our left a violent cannonade which was prolonged for fully a half-hour, and has often been supposed to be a part of that ordered to precede Pickett's charge. It began between skirmishers in front of Hill's corps over the occupation of a house. Hill's artillery first took part in it, it was said, by his order. It was most unwise, as it consumed uselessly a large amount of his ammunition, the lack of which was much felt in the subsequent fighting. Not a single gun of our corps fired a shot, nor did the enemy in our front.

When the firing died out, entire quiet settled upon the field, extending even to the skirmishers in front, and also to the enemy's rear; whence behind their lines opposing us we had heard all the morning the noise of Johnson's combats.

My 75 guns had all been carefully located and made ready for an hour, while the infantry brigades were still not yet in their proper positions, and I was waiting for the signal to come from Longstreet, when it occurred to me to send for the nine howitzers under Richardson, that they might lead in the advance for a few hundred yards before coming into action. Only after the cannonade had opened did I learn that the guns had been removed and could not be found. It afterward appeared that Pendleton had

---

[9]   Gaffney, P. and D. Gaffney. *The Civil War: Exploring History One Week at a Time*. Page 282.

withdrawn four of the guns, and that Richardson with the other five, finding himself in the line of the Federal fire during Hill's cannonade, had moved off to find cover. I made no complaint, believing that had these guns gone forward with the infantry they must have been left upon the field and perhaps have attracted a counter-stroke after the repulse of Pickett's charge.

Meanwhile, some half-hour or more before the cannonade began, I was startled by the receipt of a note from Longstreet as follows: —

'Colonel: If the artillery fire does not have the effect to drive off the enemy or greatly demoralize him, so as to make our effort pretty certain, I would prefer that you should not advise Pickett to make the charge. I shall rely a great deal upon your judgment to determine the matter and shall expect you to let Gen. Pickett know when the moment offers.'

Until that moment, though I fully recognized the strength of the enemy's position, I had not doubted that we would carry it, in my confidence that Lee was ordering it. But here was a proposition that I should decide the question. Overwhelming reasons against the assault at once seemed to stare me in the face. Gen. Wright of Anderson's division was standing with me. I showed him the letter and expressed my views. He advised me to write them to Longstreet, which I did as follows:—

'General: I will only be able to judge of the effect of our fire on the enemy by his return fire, as his infantry is little exposed to view and the smoke will obscure the field. If, as I infer from your note, there is any alternative to this attack, it should be carefully considered before opening our fire, for it will take all the artillery ammunition we have left to test this one, and if result is unfavorable we will have none left for another effort. And even if this is entirely successful, it can only be so at a very bloody cost.'

To this note, Longstreet soon replied as follows: —

'Colonel: The intention is to advance the infantry if the artillery has the desired effect of driving the enemy's off, or having other effect such as to warrant us in making the attack. When that moment arrives advise Gen. Pickett and of course advance such artillery as you can use in aiding the attack.'"

At daylight Pickett had advanced his division to a spot "into a field near a branch," a few hundred yards behind the main Confederate line on Seminary Ridge. Forming battlelines, his men advanced east a few hundred yards before being ordered to lie down and wait. Advancing again through Spangler's Woods, they were again directed to lay down—this time behind the crest on which the Confederate artillery batteries were perched. Jocking for position to form the right wing of the afternoon's assault, Pickett then had his men form two lines, with Brigadier

Generals James Kemper and Richard Garnett in the first line, right to left, and Brigadier General Lewis Armistead to the rear. As a result, Pickett's men were forced to lay down during a ferocious artillery bombardment from both sides that certainly had to unnerve his men, but Pickett continued a dangerous ride along the lines as Union shells burst all around him, shouting to his men, "Up, men, and to your posts! Don't forget today that you are from Old Virginia."[10] One of the men in Kemper's brigade of Pickett's division recalled, "The first shot or two flew harmlessly over our heads; but soon they began to get the range, and then came--well, what General Gibbon, on the other side, called "pandemonium." First there was an explosion in the top of our friendly tree, sending a shower of limbs upon us. In a second there was another, followed by a piercing shriek, which caused Patton to spring up and run to see what was the matter. Two killed outright and three frightfully wounded, he said on his return."

East Cavalry Field

As Longstreet had predicted, from the beginning the plan was an abject failure. As Stuart's cavalry met its Union counterparts near East Cavalry Field, a young cavalry officer named George Custer convinced division commander Brig. General David McMurtrie Gregg to allow his brigade to stay and fight, even while Custer's own division was stationed to the south out of the action.

---

[10] Vectorsite.net, "July 1863 (3): Don't Forget Today That You Are From Old Virginia."

The fighting at East Cavalry Field turned out to be Custer's best known action of the Civil War, and it was his brigade that bore the brunt of the casualties in repulsing Stuart's cavalry. Right as the Confederates were starting the artillery bombardment ahead of Pickett's Charge, Stuart's men met Gregg's on the field.

After Stuart's men sent Union skirmishers scurrying, Gregg ordered Custer to counterattack with the 7th Michigan Cavalry Regiment. Custer led the charge personally, exhorting his men with the rallying cry, "Come on you Wolverines!" In the ensuing melee, which featured sabers and close range shooting, Custer had his horse shot out from under him, at which point he took a bugler's horse and continued fighting. Ultimately, his men sent Stuart's cavalry retreating, forcing Stuart to order in reinforcements.

Custer

Stuart's reinforcements sent the 7th Michigan in retreat, but now Custer rallied the 1st Michigan regiment to charge in yet another counterattack, with the same rallying cry, ""Come on you Wolverines!" Both sides galloped toward each other and crashed head on, engaging in more fierce hand-to-hand combat. Eventually, the Union held the field and forced Stuart's men to retreat.

Custer's brigade lost over 200 men in the attack, the highest loss of any Union cavalry brigade at Gettysburg, but he had just valiantly performed one of the most successful cavalry charges of the war. Custer wasn't exactly humble about his performance, writing in his official report after the battle, "I challenge the annals of warfare to produce a more brilliant or successful charge of cavalry."

Pickett's Charge

As Stuart was in the process of being repulsed, just after 1:00 p.m. 150 Confederate guns began to fire from Seminary Ridge, hoping to incapacitate the Union center before launching an infantry attack, but they mostly overshot their mark. The artillery duel could be heard from dozens of miles away, and all the smoke led to Confederate artillery constantly overshooting their targets. Realizing that the artillery was meant for them as a way of softening them up for an infantry charge, Hancock calmly rode his horse up and down the line of the II Corps, both inspiring and assuring his men with his own courage and resolve. During the massive Confederate artillery bombardment that preceded the infantry assault, Hancock was so conspicuous on horseback reviewing and encouraging his troops that one of his subordinates pleaded with him that "the corps commander ought not to risk his life that way." Hancock reportedly replied, "There are times when a corps commander's life does not count."

At some point before the charge, Pickett apparently managed to somehow hastily write a letter to his wife Sallie:

"At early dawn, darkened by the threatening rain, Armistead, Garnett, Kemper and your Soldier held a heart-to-heart powwow.

All three sent regards to you, and Old Lewis pulled a ring from his little finger and making me take it, said, "Give this little token, George, please, to her of the sunset eyes, with my love, and tell her the 'old man' says since he could not be the lucky dog he's mighty glad that you are."

Dear old Lewis—dear old "Lo," as Magruder always called him, being short for Lothario. Well, my Sally, I'll keep the ring for you, and some day I'll take it to John Tyler and have it made into a breastpin and set around with rubies and diamonds and emeralds. You will be the pearl, the other jewel. Dear old Lewis!

Just as we three separated to go our different ways after silently clasping hands, our fears and prayers voiced in the "Good luck, old man," a summons came from Old Peter, and I immediately rode to the top of the ridge where he and Marse Robert were making a reconnaissance of Meade's position. "Great God!" said Old Peter as I came up. "Look, General Lee, at the insurmountable difficulties between our line and that of the Yankees—the steep hills, the tiers of artillery, the fences, the heavy skirmish line—and then we'll have to fight our infantry against their batteries. Look at the ground we'll have to charge over, nearly a mile of that open ground there under the rain of their canister and shrapnel."

"The enemy is there, General Longstreet, and I am going to strike him," said Marse Robert in his firm, quiet, determined voice.

About 8 o'clock I rode with them along our line of prostrate infantry. They had been told to lie down to prevent attracting attention, and though they had been forbidden to cheer they voluntarily arose and lifted in reverential adoration their caps to our beloved commander as we rode slowly along. Oh, the responsibility for the lives of such men as these! Well, my darling, their fate and that of our beloved Southland will be settled ere your glorious brown eyes rest on these scraps of penciled paper—your Soldier's last letter, perhaps.

Our line of battle faces Cemetery Ridge. Our detachments have been thrown forward to support our artillery which stretches over a mile along the crests of Oak Ridge and Seminary Ridge. The men are lying in the rear, my darling, and the hot July sun pours its scorching rays almost vertically down upon them. The suffering and waiting are almost unbearable.

....

Well, my sweetheart, at one o'clock the awful silence was broken by a cannon-shot and then another, and then more than a hundred guns shook the hills from crest to base, answered by more than another hundred—the whole world a blazing volcano, the whole of heaven a thunderbolt—then darkness and absolute silence—then the grim and gruesome, low-spoken commands—then the forming of the attacking columns. My brave Virginians are to attack in front. Oh, may God in mercy help me as He never helped before!

I have ridden up to report to Old Peter. I shall give him this letter to mail to you and a package to give you if—Oh, my darling, do you feel the love of my heart, the prayer, as I write that fatal word?

Now, I go; but remember always that I love you with all my heart and soul, with every fiber of my being; that now and forever I am yours—yours, my beloved. It is almost three o'clock. My soul reaches out to yours—my prayers. I'll keep up a skookum tumtum for Virginia and for you, my darling."

Eventually, Union artillery chief Henry Hunt cleverly figured that if the Union cannons stopped firing back, the Confederates might think they successfully knocked out the Union batteries. On top of that, the Union would be preserving its ammunition for the impending charge that everyone now knew was coming. When they stopped, Lee, Alexander, and others mistakenly concluded that they'd knocked out the Union artillery.

A short time later, the Confederates were prepared to step out for the charge that bears Pickett's name, even though he commanded only about a third of the force and was officially under Longstreet's direction. Today historians typically refer to the charge as the Pickett-Pettigrew-Trimble Assault or Longstreet's Assault to be more technically correct. Since A.P. Hill was sidelined with illness, Pettigrew's and Trimble's divisions were delegated to Longstreet's authority as well. To make matters worse, Hill's sickness resulted in organizational snafus. Without Hill to assign or lead troops, some of his battle-weary soldiers of the previous two days were tapped to make the charge while fresh soldiers in his corps stayed behind.

Porter Alexander described the drama-filled moments during which he advised Pickett to begin the charge:

"It was just 1 P. M. by my watch when the signal guns were fired and the cannonade opened. The enemy replied rather slowly at first, though soon with increasing rapidity. Having determined that Pickett should charge, I felt impatient to launch him as soon as I could see that our fire was accomplishing anything. I guessed that a half-hour would elapse between my sending him the order and his column reaching close quarters. I dared not presume on using more ammunition than one hour's firing would consume, for we were far from supplies and had already fought for two days. So I determined to send Pickett the order at the very first favorable sign and not later than after 30 minutes firing.

At the end of 20 minutes no favorable development had occurred. More guns had been added to the Federal line than at the beginning, and its whole length, about two miles, was blazing like a volcano. It seemed madness to order a column in the middle of a hot July day to undertake an advance of three-fourths of a mile over open ground against the centre of that line.

But something had to be done. I wrote the following note and despatched it to Pickett at 1.25:—

'General: If you are to advance at all, you must come at once or we will not be able to support you as we ought. But the enemy's fire has not slackened materially and there are still 18 guns firing from the cemetery.'

I had hardly sent this note when there was a decided falling off in the enemy's fire, and as I watched I saw other guns limbered up and withdrawn. We frequently withdrew from fighting Federal guns in order to save our ammunition for their infantry. The enemy had never heretofore practised such economy. After waiting a few minutes and seeing that no fresh guns replaced those withdrawn, I felt sure that the enemy was feeling the punishment, and at 1.40 I sent a note to Pickett as follows:—

'For God's sake come quick. The 18 guns have gone. Come quick or my ammunition will not let me support you properly.'

This was followed by two verbal messages to the same effect by an officer and sergeant from the nearest guns. The 18 guns had occupied the point at which our charge was to be directed. I had been incorrectly told it was the cemetery. Soon only a few scattered Federal guns were in action, and still Pickett's line had not come forward, though scarcely 300 yards behind my guns.

I afterward learned what had followed the sending of my first note. It reached Pickett in Longstreet's presence. He read it and handed it to Longstreet. Longstreet read and stood silent. Pickett said, 'General, shall I advance?' Longstreet knew that it must be done, but was unwilling to speak the words. He turned in his saddle and looked away. Pickett saluted and said, 'I am going to move forward, sir,' and galloped off.

Longstreet, leaving his staff, rode out alone and joined me on the left flank of the guns. It was doubtless 1.50 or later, but I did not look at my watch again. I had grown very impatient to see Pickett, fearing ammunition would run short, when Longstreet joined me. I explained the situation. He spoke sharply,— 'Go and stop Pickett where he is and replenish your ammunition.' I answered: 'We can't do that, sir. The train has but little. It would take an hour to distribute it, and meanwhile the enemy would improve the time.'

Longstreet seemed to stand irresolute (we were both dismounted) and then spoke slowly and with great emotion: 'I do not want to make this charge. I do not see how it can succeed. I would not make it now but that Gen. Lee has ordered it and is expecting it.'

I felt that he was inviting a word of acquiescence on my part and that if given he would again order, 'Stop Pickett where he is.' But I was too conscious of my own youth and inexperience to express any opinion not directly asked. So I remained silent while Longstreet fought his battle out alone and obeyed his orders."

Thus, about 15,000 Confederates stepped out in sight and began their charge with an orderly march starting about a mile away, no doubt an inspiring sight to Hancock and the Union men directly across from the oncoming assault. Pickett launched his attack as ordered, but within five minutes the men came to the top of a low rise where his line came into full view of Union defenses. Though Pickett was seen galloping to the left to steady his men there, and one aide is said to remember him personally ordering the division to "double-quick" at the end of the advance, his exact whereabouts during the latter stages of the assault are unknown.

As the Confederate line advanced, Union cannon on Cemetery Ridge and Little Round Top began blasting away, with Confederate soldiers continuing to march forward. One Union soldier later wrote, "We could not help hitting them with every shot . . . a dozen men might be felled by one single bursting shell."[11] By the time Longstreet's men reached Emmitsburg Road, Union artillery switched to firing grapeshot (tin cans filled with iron and lead balls), and as the Confederate troops continued to approach the Union center, Union troops positioned behind the wall cut down the oncoming Confederates, easily decimating both flanks. And while some of the men did mange to advance to the Union line and engage in hand-to-hand combat, it was of little consequence.

After about 20 minutes, the Confederates had managed to cross the shallow valley but then hit the stone fence shielding Union soldiers (in some places, two-men deep). And although Pickett's men were finally able to reach and breach the Union line on the ridge, what followed next has been categorically described as a "blood bath." While some of the men did manage to advance to the Union line and engage in hand-to-hand combat, it was of little consequence. In the midst of the fighting, as he was conferring with one of his brigadier generals, General Hancock suddenly felt a searing pain in his thigh. He had just been severely wounded when a bullet struck the pommel of his saddle and entered his inner right thigh, along with wood splinters and a large bent nail. Helped from his horse by his aides, he removed the saddle nail himself and applied a tourniquet, colorfully swearing at his own men while demanding that they not let him bleed to death. Nevertheless, he refused to remove himself to the rear until the offensive had concluded.

One of the Virginians who marched straight into Hancock's II Corps was Pickett's brigadier Lewis A. Armistead, who famously led his brigade with his hat atop his sword, serving as a visual cue for his men. They actually breached the II Corps' line, making it about as far as any Confederate got. In the fighting, Armistead was mortally wounded and captured, dying days later. One of the men in his brigade would write about the charge after the war:

"When the advance commenced Armistead placed himself in front of the colors of the Fifty-third Regiment, and from that point watched and directed the advance until within a short distance of the enemy's line. When approximating the advance line General Kemper rode up to him and said, "General, hurry up, my men can stand no more."

He quietly turned to the officer commanding his battalion of direction and said, "Colonel, double quick." The double quick soon quickened into a run, the run into a charge, Armistead all the time in front of his line of battle, and when the desperate effort came and the final rush for the rock fence was made he dew his sword, put his hat on the end of it, called upon his men to follow, rushed over the rock fence and was shot just as he reached the enemy's guns between the two lines in the bloody angle, thus sealing with his life's blood the high water mark of the rebellion.

---

[11]   Gaffney, P. and D. Gaffney. *The Civil War: Exploring History One Week at a Time*. Page 283.

As Armistead was carried from the field he met Hancock as he was hurrying to the front. They recognized each other, and Hancock dismounted and grasped his hand and told him how sorry he was to see him wounded. Armistead returned his kindly expression and told him the wound was mortal and that he had on his person some things that he wish to entrust to him to be returned when opportunity presented to his people in Virginia. Hancock accepted the commission and tried to persuade Armistead to look upon the bright side, that he probably was not so seriously hurt as he feared, excused himself by saying he was compelled to hurry to the front, left Armistead, promising to see him the next day. In a short time he was wounded himself and they never met again.

This was related to me as I lay on the ground back of the battle line where hundreds of wounded were carried after the fight, by one of Hancock's staff, who rode up just about dusk and found a number of men congregated about me. When he found I was a badly wounded "Johnny Reb" Colonel he dismounted, drove everybody away that I might have fresh air, and commenced a conversation.

When he found that I was of Armistead's Brigade, he said, "Armistead, Armistead. I have just left him, he is mortally wounded," and then related the above, and said, "I will have you taken care of," etc.

Armistead lingered through the 4th and died on the 5th, leaving an example of patriotism, heroism and devotion to duty which ought to be handed down through the ages."

Kemper's brigade hardly had it any easier as it moved forward, and Kemper would be seriously injured and captured at the height of the fighting. One of his men wrote about the charge after the war:

The devoted little column moved to the assault, with Garnett, and Kemper in front, and Armistead behind in close supporting distance. Soon after clearing our batteries it was found necessary to change direction to the left. While conducting the movement, which was made in perfect order under a galling flank fire from the Round Top, General Pickett, for the second time, cautioned me to be sure and keep the proper interval with General Garnett; Armistead was expected to catch up and extend the line to the left. Then we swept onward again, straight for the Golgotha of Seminary Ridge, half a mile distant, across the open plain. As we neared the Emmettsburg road, along which, behind piles of rails, the enemy's strong line of skirmishers was posted, General Kemper called to me to give attention to matters on the left, while he went to see what troops those were coming up behind us. Glancing after him, I caught a glimpse of a small body of men, compact and solid as a wedge, moving swiftly to the left oblique, as if aiming to uncover Garnett's Brigade. They were Armistead's people, and as Kemper cantered down their front on his mettlesome sorrel they greeted him with a rousing cheer, which I know made his gallant heart leap for joy. At the same moment I saw a disorderly crowd of men breaking for the rear, and Pickett, with Stuart Symington, Ned Baird, and others, vainly trying to stop the rout. And now the guns of Cushing and Abbott double-stocked by General Gibbon's express order, reinforced the terrific fire of the infantry behind the stone fence, literally riddling the orchard on the left of the now famous Cordori house, through which my regiment and some of the others passed.

   Within a few steps of the stone fence, while in the act of shaking hands with General Garnett and congratulating him on being able to be with his men (he had been seriously ill a few days before), I heard some one calling me, and turning my head, saw that it was Captain Fry. He was mounted, and blood streaming from his horse's neck. Colonel Terry had sent him to stop the rush to left. The enemy in force (Stannard's Vermonters) had penetrated to our rear. He told me that Kemper had been struck down, it was feared mortally. With the help of Colonel Carrington, of the Eighteenth, and Major Bentley, of the Twenty-fourth, I hastily gathered a small band together and faced them to meet the new danger. After that everything was a wild kaleidoscopic whirl. A man near me seemed to be keeping a tally of the dead for my especial benefit. First it was Patton, then Collcote, then Phillips, and I know not how many more. Colonel Williams was knocked out of the saddle by a ball in the shoulder near the brick-house, and in falling was killed by his sword…Seeing the men as they fired, throw down their guns and pick up others from the ground, I followed suit, shooting into a flock of blue coats that were pouring down from the right, I noticed how close their flags were together. Probably they were the same people whom Hood and McLaws had handled so roughly the day before. "Used up," as General Meade said of them. Suddenly there was a hissing sound, like the hooded cobra's whisper of death, a deafening explosion, a sharp pang of pain somewhere, a momentary blank, and when I got on my feet again there were splinters of bone and lumps of flesh sticking to my clothes. Then I remembered seeing lank Tell Taliaferro, adjutant of the Twenty-fourth, jumping like a kangaroo and rubbing his crazy bone and blessing the Yankees in a way that did credit to old Jube Early's onetime law partner, and handsome Ocey White, the boy lieutenant of Company A, taking off his hat to show me where a ball had raised a whelk on his scalp and carried away one of his pretty flaxen curls, and lastly, "Old Buck" Terry, with a peculiarly sad smile on his face, standing with poor George and Val Harris and others, between the colors of the Eleventh and Twenty-fourth, near where now is the pretty monument of colonel Ward, of Massachusetts. I could not hear what he said, but he was pointing rearwards with his sword, and I knew what that meant.

   As I gave one hurried glance over the field we had traversed, the thought in my mind was repeated at my side, "Oh! Colonel, why don't they support us?" It was Walker, General Kemper's orderly, unhorsed, but still unscathed and undaunted, awkward, ungainly, hard-featured, good-natured, simple-minded, stout-hearted Walker, one of the Eleventh boys, I believe; only a private doing his duty with might and main and recking no more of glory than the ox that has won the prize at a cattle show. At the storming of the Redan when Wyndham's forlorn hope tumbled into the ditch and couldn't get out, owing to the scarcity of ladders, and the few they had were too short, the men huddled together dazed and bewildered, and were mowed down like dumb beasts by the Muscovite rifles, because there were no officers left to lead them. There was a notable exception, an Irishman, scrambling up the scrap, he shouted, "Come up, boys, follow the captain." The captain fell, but Pat went on to immortality. It was not so that day at Gettysburg.

Meanwhile, Pickett's brigadier Richard Garnett, whose courage had been impugned and challenged by Stonewall Jackson unfairly in 1862, had suffered a previous leg injury and insisted on riding his horse during the charge, despite the obvious fact that riding a horse clearly indicated he was an officer. Garnett was killed during the charge, and it's unknown where he fell or where he was buried. One of the men in Garnett's brigade, C.S. Peyton of the 19th Virginia, reported on the brigade's participation in his post-battle report:

MAJOR: In compliance with instructions from division headquarters, I have the honor to report the part taken by this brigade in the late battle near Gettysburg, Pa., July 3.

Notwithstanding the long and severe marches made by the troops of this brigade, they reached the field about 9 a.m.. in high spirits and in good condition. At about 12 m. we were ordered to take position behind the crest of the hill on which the artillery, under Colonel [E. Porter] Alexander, was planted, where we lay during a most terrific cannonading, which opened at 1.30 p.m., and was kept up without intermission for one hour.

During the shelling, we lost about 20 killed and wounded. Among the killed was Lieutenant-Colonel [John T.] Ellis, of the Nineteenth Virginia, whose bravery as a soldier, and his innocence, purity, and integrity as a Christian, have not only elicited the admiration of his own command, but endeared him to all who knew him.

At 2.30 p.m., the artillery fire having to some extent abated, the order to advance was given, first by Major-General Pickett in person, and repeated by General Garnett with promptness, apparent cheerfulness, and alacrity. The brigade moved forward at quick time. The ground was open, but little broken, and from 800 to 1,000 yards from the crest whence we started to the enemy's line. The brigade moved in good order, keeping up its line almost perfectly, notwithstanding it had to climb three high post and rail fences, behind the last of which the enemy's skirmishers were first met and immediately driven in. Moving on, we soon met the advance line of the enemy, lying concealed in the grass on the slope, about 100 yards in front of his second line, which consisted of a stone wall about breast-high, running nearly parallel to and about 30 paces from the crest of the hill, which was lined with their artillery.

The first line referred to above, after offering some resistance, was completely routed, and driven in confusion back to the stone wall. Here we captured some prisoners, which were ordered to the rear without a guard. Having routed the enemy here, General Garnett ordered the brigade forward, which it promptly obeyed, loading and firing as it advanced.

Up to this time we had suffered but little from the enemy's batteries, which apparently had been much crippled previous to our advance, with the exception of one posted on the mountain, about 1 mile to our right, which enfiladed nearly our entire line with fearful effect, sometimes as many as 10 men being killed and wounded by the bursting of a single shell. From the point it had first routed the enemy, the brigade moved rapidly forward toward the stone wall, under a galling fire both from artillery and infantry, the artillery using grape and canister. We were now within about 75 paces of the wall, unsupported on the right and left, General Kemper being some 50 or 60 yards behind and to the right, and General Armistead coming up in our rear.

General Kemper's line was discovered to be lapping on ours, when, deeming it advisable to have the line extended on the right to prevent being flanked, a staff officer rode back to the general to request him to incline to the right. General Kemper not being present (perhaps wounded at the time), Captain [W. T.] Fry, of his staff, immediately began his exertions to carry out the request, but, in consequence of the eagerness of the men in pressing forward, it was impossible to have the order carried out.

Our line, much shattered, still kept up the advance until within about 20 paces of the wall, when, for a moment, it recoiled under the terrific fire that poured into our ranks both from their batteries and from their sheltered infantry. At this moment, General Kemper came up on the right and General Armistead in rear, when the three lines, joining in concert, rushed forward with unyielding determination and an apparent spirit of laudable rivalry to plant the Southern banner on the walls of the enemy. His strongest and last line was instantly gained; the Confederate battle-flag waved over his defenses, and the fighting over the wall became hand to hand, and of the most desperate character; but more than half having already fallen, our line was found too weak to rout the enemy. We hoped for a support on the left (which had started simultaneously with ourselves), out hoped in vain. Yet a small remnant remained in desperate struggle, receiving a fire in front, on the right, and on the left, many even climbing over the wall, and fighting the enemy in his own trenches until entirely surrounded; and those who were not killed or wounded were captured, with the exception of about 300 who came off slowly, but greatly scattered, the identity of every regiment being entirely lost, and every regimental commander killed or wounded.

The brigade went into action with 1,287 men and about 140 officers, as shown by the report of the previous evening, and sustained a loss, as the list of casualties will show, of 941 killed, wounded, and missing, and it is feared, from all the information received, that the majority (those reported missing) are either killed or wounded.

It is needless, perhaps, to speak of conspicuous gallantry where all behaved so well. Each and every regimental commander displayed a cool bravery and daring that not only encouraged their own commands, but won the highest admiration from all those who saw them. They led their regiments in the fight, and showed, by their conduct, that they only desired their men to follow where they were willing to lead. But of our cool, gallant, noble brigade commander it may not be out of place to speak. Never had the brigade been better handled, and never has it done better service in the field of battle. There was scarcely an officer or man in the command whose attention was not attracted by the cool and handsome bearing of General Garnett, who, totally devoid of excitement or rashness, rode immediately in rear of his advancing line, endeavoring by his personal efforts, and by the aid of his staff, to keep his line well closed and dressed. He was shot from his horse while near the center of the brigade, within about 25 paces of the stone wall. This gallant officer was too well known to need further mention.

In making the above report, I have endeavored to be as accurate as possible, but have had to rely mainly for information on others, whose position gave them better opportunity for witnessing the conduct of the entire brigade than I could have, being with, and paying my attention to, my own regiment.

After the charge, there was debate (and later controversy) over where Pickett was as his brigadiers were falling at the front of their brigades. One of Pickett's staff men discussed the way communications were going from the front back to leaders like Longstreet further to the rear:

> I found General Longstreet sitting on a fence alone; the fence ran in the direction we were charging. Pickett's column had passed over the hill on our side of the Emmettsburg road, and could not then be seen. I delivered the message as sent by General Pickett. General Longstreet said: "Where are the troops that were placed on your flank ?" and I answered: "Look over your shoulder and you will see them." He looked and saw the broken fragments. Just then an officer rode at half-speed, drawing up his horse in front of the General, and saying: "General Longstreet, General Lee sent me here, and said you would place me in a position to see this magnificent charge. I would not have missed it for the world." General Longstreet answered: "I would, Colonel Freemantle, the charge is over. Captain Bright, ride to General Pickett, and tell

hin what you have heard me say to Colonel Freemantle." At this moment our men were near to but had not crossed the Emmettsburg road. I started and when my horse had made two leaps, General Longstreet called: "Captain Bright!" I checked my horse, and turned half around in my saddle to hear, and this was what he said: "Tell General Pickett that Wilcox's Brigade is in that peach orchard (pointing), and he can order him to his assistance."

When I reached General Pickett he was at least one hundred yards behind the division, having been detained in a position from which he could watch and care for his left flank. He at once sent Captain Baird to General Wilcox with the order for him to come in; then he sent Captain Symington with the same order, in a very few moments, and last he said: "Captain Bright, you go,' and I was about the same distance behind Symington that he was behind Baird. The fire was so dreadful at this time that I believe that General Pickett thought not more than one out of the three sent would reach General Wilcox.

When I rode up to Wilcox he was standing with both hands raised waving and saying to me, "I know, I know." I said, "But, General, I must deliver my message." After doing this I rode out of the peach orchard, going forward where General Pickett was watching his left. Looking that way myself, I saw moving out of the enemy's line of battle, in head of column, a large force; having nothing in their front, they came around our flank as described above. Had our left not deserted us these men would have hesitated to move in head of column, confronted by a line of battle. When I reached General Pickett I found him too far down towards the Ennmettshurg road to see these flanking troops, and he asked of me the number. I remember answering 7,000, but this proved an over estimate. Some of our men had been faced to meet this new danger, and so doing somewhat broke the force of our charge on the left. Probably men of the 1st Virginia will remember this.

Charging to the left of Pickett's men, Trimble and Pettigrew were both wounded in the fighting, with Trimble losing a leg and Pettigrew suffering a minor wound to the hand. One of the generals in Pettigrew's part of the assault wrote about their participation:

In the numerous accounts of the battle of Gettysburg heretofore published, the writers have generally referred to the last effort made by the Confederate troops as "Pickett's charge," and in almost every instance have conveyed the idea that no troops but Pickett's division took an active part in that fierce and tremendous struggle. Disclaiming any intention to detract in the least from the glory won on that day by the gallant Virginia division, or its heroic commander, who had then been for more than twenty years one of my most valued friends, I may be permitted to say that some injustice has been done to the division commanded by General Pettigrew.

As colonel of the Thirteenth Alabama infantry, I was attached to Archer's brigade of Heth's division. That brigade opened the battle on the morning of July 1st, and during the fighting which immediately ensued General Heth was wounded, and the command of the division devolved upon Brigadier-General Pettigrew. General Archer was captured, and I succeeded him in command of the brigade.

During the forenoon of the 3d, while our division was resting in line behind the ridge and skirt of woods which masked us from the enemy, Generals Lee, Longstreet and A. P. Hill rode up, and, dismounting, seated themselves on the trunk of a fallen tree some fifty or sixty paces from where I sat on my horse at the right of our division. After an apparently careful examination of a map, and a consultation of some length, they remounted and rode away. Staff officers and couriers began to move briskly about, and a few minutes after General Pettigrew rode up and informed me that after a heavy cannonade we would assault the position in our front, and added: "They will of course return the fire with all the guns they have; we must shelter the men as best we can, and make them lie down." At the same time he directed me to see General Pickett at once and have an understanding as to the dress in the advance. I rode to General Pickett, whose division was formed on the right of and in line with ours. He appeared to be in excellent spirits, and, after a cordial greeting and a pleasant reference to our having been together in work of that kind at Chapultipec, expressed great confidence in the ability of our troops to drive the enemy after they had been "demoralized by our artillery." General Garnett, who commanded his left brigade, having joined us, it was agreed that he would dress on my command. I immediately returned and informed General Pettigrew of this agreement. It was then understood that my command should be considered the centre, and that in the assault both divisions should allign themselves by it. Soon after the two divisions moved forward about a hundred paces, and the men lay down behind our line of batteries. The cannonade which followed has been often and justly described as the most terrible of the war. In it my command suffered a considerable loss. Several officers were killed and wounded, with a number of the rank and file. I received a painful wound on the right shoulder from a fragment of shell. After lying inactive under that deadly storm of hissing and exploding missiles, it seemed a relief to go forward to the desperate assault. At a signal from Pettigrew I called my command to attention. The men sprang up with cheerful alacrity, and the long line advanced. "Stormed at with shot and shell," it moved steadily on, and even when grape, canister, and musket balls began to rain upon it the gaps were quickly closed and the allignment preserved. Strong as was the position of the enemy, it seemed that such determination could not fail. I heard Garnett give a command to his men which, amid the rattle of musketry, I could not distinguish. Seeing my look or gesture of inquiry, he called our, "I am dressing on you!" A few seconds after he fell dead. A moment later- and after Captain Williams and Colonel George had been wounded by my side- a shot through the thigh prostrated me. I was so confident of victory that to some of my men who ran up to carry me off I shouted, "Go on; it will not last five minutes longer!" The men rushed forward into the smoke, which soon became so dense that I could see little of what was going on before me. But a moment later I heard General Pettigrew, behind me, calling to some of his staff to "rally them on the left." The roll of musketry was then incessant, and I believe that the Federal troops- probably blinded by the smoke- continued a rapid fire for some minutes after none but dead and wounded remained in their front. At length the firing ceased, and cheer after cheer from the enemy announced the failure of our attack. I was of course left a prisoner.

As evidence of how close was the fighting at that part of the line, I saw a Federal soldier with an ugly wound in his shoulder, which he told me he received from the spear on the end of one of my regimental colors; and I remembered having that morning observed and laughingly commented on the fact that the color-bearer of the Thirteenth Alabama had attached to his staff a formidable-looking lance head. All of the five regimental colors of my command reached the line of the enemy's works, and many of my men and officers were killed or wounded after passing over it. I believe the same was true of other brigades in General Pettigrew's command.

It is probable that Pickett's division, which up to that time had taken no part in the battle, was mainly relied upon for the final assault; but whatever may have been the first plan of attack, the division under Pettigrew went into it as part of the line of battle, and from the commencement of the advance to the closing death grapple, his right brigade was the directing one. General Pettigrew, who I know was that day in the thickest of the fire, was killed in a skirmish a few days later. No more earnest and gallant officer served in the Confederate army.

According to Longstreet, it was Pickett who finally called retreat; after about an hour, nearly 6,500 Confederates were dead or wounded, five times that of the Union, with all 13 regimental commanders in Pickett's division killed or wounded. As Pickett's men began to stream back in a broken and disorderly, Pickett's staff member recalled one of the most famous exchanges of the battle:

I informed the General that no help was to be expected from the artillery, but the enemy were closing around us, and nothing could now save his command. He had remained behind to watch and protect that left, to put in first help expected from infantry supports, then to break the troops which came around his flank with the artillery; all had failed. At this moment our left (Pickett's Division) began to crumble and soon all that was left came slowly back, 5,000 in the morning, 1,600 were put in camp that night, 3,400 killed, wounded and missing.

We moved back, and when General Pickett and I were about 300 yards from the position from which the charge had started, General Robert E. Lee, the Peerless, alone, on Traveler, rode up and said: "General Pickett, place your division in rear of this hill, and be ready to repel the advance of the enemy should they follow up their advantage." (I never heard General Lee call them the enemy before; it was always those or these people). General Pickett, with his head on his breast, said: "General Lee, I have no division now, Armistead is down, Garnett is down, and Kemper is mortally wounded."

Then General Lee said: "Come, General Pickett, this has been my fight and upon my shoulders rests the blame. The men and officers of your command have written the name of Virginia as high to-day as it has ever been written before." (Now talk about "Glory enough for one day," why this was glory enough for one hundred years.)

In the aftermath of the repulse of Pickett's Charge, General Longstreet stated, "General Lee came up as our troops were falling back and encouraged them as well as he could; begged them to reform their ranks and reorganize their forces . . . and it was then he used the expression . . . 'It was all my fault; get together, and let us do the best we can toward saving which is left to us.'"[12] Longstreet never resisted an opportunity to distance himself from failure and direct it towards someone else, even Lee.

Today Pickett's Charge is remembered as the American version of the Charge of the Light Brigade, a heroic but completely futile march that had no chance of success. In fact, it's remembered as Pickett's Charge because Pickett's Virginians wanted to claim the glory of getting the furthest during the attack in the years after the war. The charge suffered about a 50% casualty rate while barely making a dent in the Union line before retreating in disorder back across the field. Pickett's post-battle report was apparently so bitter that Lee ordered it destroyed.

Though the charge was named Pickett's Charge by newspapers for the purpose of praising Pickett's Virginians for making the furthest progress, Pickett felt the charge had tarnished his career, and he remained upset that his name remained associated with the sharply repulsed attack. Furthermore, Pickett himself has received much criticism (both then and to this day) for surviving the battle unscathed, having established his final position well to the rear of his troops, though any charges of cowardice are strongly contradicted by his record earlier in the Civil War and in Mexico.

After the battle, Pickett wrote to Sallie offering a few details about the fateful charge. Since his official report of the battle has never been found, his letters home were his only words about the events:

"MY letter of yesterday, my darling, written before the battle, was full of hope and

---

[12] Davis, Kenneth C. *The Civil War: Everything You Need to Know About America's Greatest Conflict but Never Learned.* Page 306.

cheer; even though it told you of the long hours of waiting from four in the morning, when Gary's pistol rang out from the Federal lines signaling the attack upon Culp's Hill, to the solemn eight-o'clock review of my men, who rose and stood silently lifting their hats in loving reverence as Marse Robert, Old Peter and your own Soldier reviewed them—on then to the deadly stillness of the five hours following, when the men lay in the tall grass in the rear of the artillery line, the July sun pouring its scorching rays almost vertically down upon them, till one o'clock when the awful silence of the vast battlefield was broken by a cannon-shot which opened the greatest artillery duel of the world. The firing lasted two hours. When it ceased we took advantage of the blackened field and in the glowering darkness formed our attacking column just before the brow of Seminary Ridge.

I closed my letter to you a little before three o'clock and rode up to Old Peter for orders. I found him like a great lion at bay. I have never seen him so grave and troubled. For several minutes after I had saluted him he looked at me without speaking. Then in an agonized voice, the reserve all gone, he said:

"Pickett, I am being crucified at the thought of the sacrifice of life which this attack will make. I have instructed Alexander to watch the effect of our fire upon the enemy, and when it begins to tell he must take the responsibility and give you your orders, for I can't."

While he was yet speaking a note was brought to me from Alexander. After reading it I handed it to him, asking if I should obey and go forward. He looked at me for a moment, then held out his hand. Presently, clasping his other hand over mine without speaking he bowed his head upon his breast. I shall never forget the look in his face nor the clasp of his hand when I said:—"Then, General, I shall lead my Division on." I had ridden only a few paces when I remembered your letter and (forgive me) thoughtlessly scribbled in a corner of the envelope, "If Old Peter's nod means death then good-by and God bless you, little one," turned back and asked the dear old chief if he would be good enough to mail it for me. As he took your letter from me, my darling, I saw tears glistening on his cheeks and beard. The stern old war-horse, God bless him, was weeping for his men and, I know, praying too that this cup might pass from them. I obeyed the silent assent of his bowed head, an assent given against his own convictions,—given in anguish and with reluctance.

My brave boys were full of hope and confident of victory as I led them forth, forming them in column of attack, and though officers and men alike knew what was before them,—knew the odds against them,—they eagerly offered up their lives on the altar of duty, having absolute faith in their ultimate success. Over on Cemetery Ridge the Federals beheld a scene never before witnessed on this continent,—a scene which has never previously been enacted and can never take place again—an army forming in line of battle in full view, under their very eyes—charging across a space nearly a mile in length over fields of waving grain and anon of stubble and then a smooth expanse— moving with the steadiness of a dress parade, the pride and glory soon to be crushed by an overwhelming heartbreak.

. . . .

Well, it is all over now. The battle is lost, and many of us are prisoners, many are dead, many wounded, bleeding and dying. Your Soldier lives and mourns and but for you, my darling, he would rather, a million times rather, be back there with his dead, to sleep for all time in an unknown grave."

Days later, Pickett wrote yet another tense letter back to Sallie, in which his angst can be felt:

General Lee's letter has been published to the division in general orders and received with appreciative satisfaction. The soldiers, one and all, love and honor Lee, and his sympathy and praise are always very dear to them. Just after the order was published I heard one of the men, rather rough and uncouth and not, as are most of the men, to the manner born, say, as he wiped away the tears with the back of his hand, "Dag-gone him, dag-gone him, dag-gone his old soul, I'm blamed ef I wouldn't be dag-gone willin' to go right through it all and be killed again with them others to hear Marse Robert, dag-gone him, say over again as how he grieved bout'n we-all's losses and honored us for we-all's bravery! Darned ef I wouldn't." Isn't that reverential adoration, my darling, to be willing to be "killed again" for a word of praise?

It seems selfish and inhuman to speak of Love—haunted as I am with the unnecessary sacrifice of the lives of so many of my brave boys. I can't think of anything but the desolate homes in Virginia and the unknown dead in Pennsylvania. At the beginning of the fight I was so sanguine, so sure of success! Early in the morning I had been assured by Alexander that General Lee had ordered that every brigade in his command was to charge Cemetery Hill; so I had no fear of not being supported. Alexander also assured me of the support of his artillery which would move ahead of my division in the advance. He told me that he had borrowed seven twelve-pound howitzers from Pendleton, Lee's Chief of Artillery, which he had put in reserve to accompany me.

In the morning I rode with him while he, by Longstreet's orders, selected the salient angle of the wood in which my line was formed, which line was just on the left of his seventy-five guns. At about a quarter to three o'clock, when his written order to make the charge was handed to me, and dear Old Peter after reading it in sorrow and fear reluctantly bowed his head in assent, I obeyed, leading my three brigades straight on the enemy's front. You never saw anything like it. They moved across that field of death as a battalion marches forward in line of battle upon drill, each commander in front of his command leading and cheering on his men. Two lines of the enemy's infantry were driven back; two lines of guns were taken—and no support came. Pendleton, without Alexander's knowledge, had sent four of the guns which he had loaned him to some other part of the field, and the other three guns could not be found. The two brigades which were to have followed me had, poor fellows, been seriously engaged in the fights of the two previous days. Both of their commanding officers had been killed, and while they had been replaced by gallant, competent officers, these new leaders were unknown to the men.

Ah, if I had only had my other two brigades a different story would have been flashed to the world. It was too late to retreat, and to go on was death or capture. Poor old Dick Garnett did not dismount, as did the others of us, and he was killed instantly, falling from his horse. Kemper, desperately wounded, was brought from the field and subsequently, taken prisoner. Dear old Lewis Armistead, God bless him, was mortally wounded at the head of his command after planting the flag of Virginia within the enemy's lines. Seven of my colonels were killed, and one was mortally wounded. Nine of my lieutenant colonels were wounded, and three lieutenant colonels were killed. Only one field officer of my whole command, Colonel Cabell, was unhurt, and the loss of my company officers was in proportion.

I wonder, my dear, if in the light of the Great Eternity we shall any of us feel this was for the best and shall have learned to say, "Thy will be done."

No castles to-day, sweetheart. No, the bricks of happiness and the mortar of love must lie untouched in this lowering gloom. Pray, dear, for the sorrowing ones."

Farnsworth's Charge

Pickett's Charge is the most memorable charge of July 3, but it wasn't the only fateful one made that day. As the Union cavalry repulsed Stuart, cavalry officer Hugh Judson Kilpatrick gave the order for some of his cavalry to charge north into the Confederates' right flank, Evander Law's brigade (which had opposed Chamberlain the day before). It's believed that the order was given as part of a plan by Meade to possibly follow up a repulse of Pickett's Charge with a flank attack that might lead to a rolling up of the Confederate line.

However, Kilpatrick was ordering the attack just as Pickett's infantry was starting the charge, not during its repulse, and he ordered an attack to be made piecemeal instead of one united assault.

West of Emmitsburg Road, Merrit's cavalry dismounted and began an attack on the Confederate flank, only to run into a brigade of Georgians, which easily repulsed the attack. The plan then called for Elon Farnsworth to attack, but this time Kilpatrick ordered a mounted cavalry charge. By now, with Merrit's attack having failed, the Confederate infantry was positioned behind a stone fence with wooden fence rails piled high above it to prevent horses from being able to jump into their lines. In essence, the Union cavalry would have to make a mounted charge, dismount right at the battle line, and then attempt a concerted attack. Historians have since accused Kilpatrick of shaming Farnsworth into making the suicidal chare, and Farnsworth allegedly told his superior, "General, if you order the charge I will lead it, but you must take the awful responsibility."

Farnsworth's charge began with a charge by the 1st West Virginia Cavalry that immediately devolved into confusion once they came under heavy fire. Eventually they dismounted near the wall, where they engaged in hand-to-hand fighting with sabers, rifles, and even rocks. The second part of the attack came from the 18th Pennsylvania, supported by companies of the 5th New York, but they were immediately repulsed.

Next, it fell upon the 400 man 1st Vermont Cavalry to charge forward, heading into a slaughter. As they rode forward, one lieutenant in an Albama regiment yelled, "Cavalry, boys, cavalry! This is no fight, only a frolic, give it to them!" All three battalions of the 1st Vermont were quickly repulsed. With that, the final attack was to be led by Farnsworth himself, which came upon the 15th Alabama. In the middle of the charge, Farnsworth fell dead from his horse, hit by 5 bullets. Kilpatrick's poorly designed attack resulted in Farnsworth and his men making a "Charge of the Light Brigade", and as it turned out, they would end up being the last major action of the Battle of Gettysburg.

Chapter 6: Controversy over Lee's Retreat

From a military perspective, Meade had made efficient use of his subordinates (particularly Generals John F. Reynolds and Winfield S. Hancock) during this three-day, course-changing battle, ultimately executing some of the most effective battleline strategies of the War. In short, Meade had successfully commanded the forces that repulsed Lee's Army and effectively won what most historians consider the battle that changed the course of the Civil War and ultimately resulted in a Confederate defeat.

While nobody questions that Meade's strategy at Gettysburg was strong, he was heavily criticized by contemporaries for not pursuing Lee's army more aggressively as it retreated. Chief-of-staff Daniel Butterfield, who would call into question Meade's command decisions and courage at Gettysburg, accused Meade of not finishing off the weakened Lee. Meade would later state that as his army's new commander, he was uncertain of his troops' capabilities and strength, especially after a battle that had just resulted in over 20,000 Union casualties. Moreover, heavy rains made pursuit almost impossible on July 4, and Lee actually invited an attack during the retreat, hoping Meade would haphazardly attack strongly fortified positions.

Though historians now mostly credit Meade with making proper decisions in the wake of the battle, Lincoln was incredibly frustrated when Lee successfully retreated south. On July 14, Lincoln drafted a letter that he ultimately put away and decided not to send to Meade, who never read it during his lifetime:

"I have just seen your despatch to Gen. Halleck, asking to be relieved of your command, because of a supposed censure of mine. I am very--very--grateful to you for the magnificent success you gave the cause of the country at Gettysburg; and I am sorry now to be the author of the slightest pain to you. But I was in such deep distress myself that I could not restrain some expression of it. I had been oppressed nearly ever since the battles at Gettysburg, by what appeared to be evidences that yourself, and Gen. Couch, and Gen. Smith, were not seeking a collision with the enemy, but were trying to get him across the river without another battle. What these evidences were, if you please, I hope to tell you at some time, when we shall both feel better. The case, summarily stated is this. You fought and beat the enemy at Gettysburg; and, of course, to say the least, his loss was as great as yours. He retreated; and you did not, as it seemed to me, pressingly pursue him; but a flood in the river detained him, till, by slow degrees, you were again upon him. You had at least twenty thousand veteran troops directly with you, and as many more raw ones within supporting distance, all in addition to those who fought with you at Gettysburg; while it was not possible that he had received a single recruit; and yet you stood and let the flood run down, bridges be built, and the enemy move away at his leisure, without attacking him. And Couch and Smith! The latter left Carlisle in time, upon all ordinary calculation, to have aided you in the last battle at Gettysburg; but he did not arrive. At the end of more than ten days, I believe twelve, under constant urging, he reached Hagerstown from Carlisle, which is not an inch over fifty-five miles, if so much. And Couch's movement was very little different.

Again, my dear general, I do not believe you appreciate the magnitude of the misfortune involved in Lee's escape. He was within your easy grasp, and to have closed upon him would, in connection with our other late successes, have ended the war. As it is, the war will be prolonged indefinitely. If you could not safely attack Lee last Monday, how can you possibly do so South of the river, when you can take with you very few more than two thirds of the force you then had in hand? It would be unreasonable to expect, and I do not expect you can now effect much. Your golden opportunity is gone, and I am distressed immeasurably because of it.

I beg you will not consider this a prosecution, or persecution of yourself As you had learned that I was dissatisfied, I have thought it best to kindly tell you why."

Still, Meade was promoted to brigadier general in the regular army and was officially awarded the Thanks of Congress, which commended Meade "... and the officers and soldiers of [the Army of the Potomac], for the skill and heroic valor which at Gettysburg repulsed, defeated, and drove back, broken and dispirited, beyond the Rappahannock, the veteran army of the rebellion."

Hancock was unquestionably one of the Union heroes at Gettysburg, but his recognition was slow in coming. In the months after the battle, the U.S. Congress thanked Meade and Howard without listing Hancock. Eventually, Major General Hancock later received the Thanks of the U. S. Congress for "gallant, meritorious, and conspicuous share in that great and decisive victory."

As usual, Hancock shared the credit with his men, writing in his post-battle report:

"To speak of the conduct of the troops would seem to be unnecessary, but still it may be justly remarked that this corps sustained its well-earned reputation on many fields, and that the boast of its gallant first commander, the late Maj. Gen. E. V. Sumner, that the Second Corps had "never given to the enemy a gun or color," holds good now as it did under the command of my predecessor, Major-General Couch. To attest to its good conduct and the perils through which it has passed, it may be stated that its losses in battle have been greater than those of any other corps in the Army of the Potomac, or probably in the service, notwithstanding it has usually been numerically weakest."

Chapter 7: Who's to Blame?

Lee?

From almost the moment the Civil War ended, Gettysburg has been widely viewed as one of the decisive turning points of the Civil War. As renowned Civil War historian described Gettysburg, "It might be less of a victory than Mr. Lincoln had hoped for, but it was nevertheless a victory—and, because of that, it was no longer possible for the Confederacy to win the war. The North might still lose it, to be sure, if the soldiers or the people should lose heart, but outright defeat was no longer in the cards." While some still dispute that labeling, Lee's Army of Northern Virginia was never truly able to take the strategic offensive again for the duration of the war.

Naturally, if Gettysburg marked an important turning point in the Civil War, then to the defeated South it represented one of the last true opportunities the South had to win the war. After the South had lost the war, the importance of Gettysburg as one of the "high tide" marks of the Confederacy became apparent to everyone, making the battle all the more important in the years after it had been fought. Former Confederate comrades like Longstreet and Jubal Early would go on to argue who was responsible for the loss at Gettysburg (and thus the war) in the following decades. Much of the debate was fueled by those who wanted to protect Lee's legacy, especially because Lee was dead and could not defend himself in writing anymore. However, on July 3, Lee insisted on taking full blame for what occurred at Gettysburg, telling his retreating men, "It's all my fault." Historians have mostly agreed, placing the blame for the disastrous Day 3 on Lee's shoulders.

Porter Alexander would later call it Lee's "worst day" of the war and further explained:

"There was one single advantage conferred by our exterior lines, and but one, in exchange for many disadvantages. They gave us the opportunity to select positions for our guns which could enfilade the opposing lines of the enemy. Enfilading fire is so effective that no troops can submit to it long. Illustrations of this fact were not wanting in the events of this day. What has been called the shank of the Federal fish-hook, extending south from the bend at Cemetery Hill toward Little Round Top, was subject to enfilade fire from the town and its flanks and suburbs. That liability should have caused special examination by our staff and artillery officers, to discover other conditions which might favor an assault. There were and are others still easily recognizable on the ground. The salient angle is acute and weak, and within about 500 yards of its west face is the sheltered position occupied by Rodes the night of July 2d, which has already been mentioned.

From nowhere else was there so short and unobstructed an approach to the Federal line, and one so free from flank fire. On the northeast, at but little greater distance, was the position whence Early's two brigades the evening before had successfully carried the east face of the same salient. Within the edge of the town between these two positions was abundant opportunity to accumulate troops and to establish guns at close ranges.

As long as Gettysburg stands and the contour of its hills remains unchanged, students of the battle-field must decide that Lee's most promising attack from first to last was upon Cemetery Hill, by concentrated artillery fire from the north and assaults from the nearest sheltered ground between the west and northeast.

That this was not realized at the time is doubtless partly due to the scarcity of trained staff and reconnoitring officers, and partly to the fact that Ewell had discontinued and withdrawn the pursuit on the afternoon of the 1st, when it was about to undertake this position. Hence the enemy's pickets were not driven closely into their lines, and the vicinity was not carefully examined. Not a single gun was established within a thousand yards, nor was a position selected which enfiladed the lines in question.

Quite by accident, during the cannonade preceding Pickett's charge, Nelson's battalion of Ewell's corps fired a few rounds from a position which did enfilade with great effect part of the 11th corps upon Cemetery Hill, but the fire ceased on being sharply replied to. Briefly the one weak spot of the enemy's line and the one advantage possessed by ours were never apprehended."

Ironically, though he had no use for post-war politics, Lee's legacy was crafted and embroiled in it. While Lee accepted the South's loss, unreconstructed rebels continued to "fight" the Civil War with the pen, aiming to influence how the war was remembered. Much of this was accomplished by the Southern Historical Society, whose stated aim was the homogenization of Southern white males. But longstanding feuds between former generals found their way into the papers, and the feuds were frequently based on regional differences. These former Confederates looked to their idealized war heroes as symbols of their suffering and struggle. Based in Richmond, the Society's ideal Southern white male embodied the "Virginian" essence of aristocracy, morality and chivalry. The Society's ideal male, of course, was Robert E. Lee. David Blight credits the Society for creating a "Lee cult" that dominates public perception to this day. Writing about this perception of Lee, Charles Osbourne described the perception as "an edifice of myth built on the foundation of truth…the image became an icon."

Still, Lee was far from perfect, despite the attempts of the Southern Historical Society to defend his war record as fault free, at the expense of some of his subordinates. Given that the Confederacy lost the war, some historians have pointed out that Lee was often too eager to engage in offensive warfare. After all, Lee scored large and smashing victories at places like Chancellorsville that deprived him of more manpower against opponents that could afford casualties more than he could. Moreover, for the engineer who used tactics to successfully defend against typical Civil War tactics, he all too often engaged in the same futile offensive tactics himself, none more costly than Pickett's Charge.

Longstreet?

However, after the war, former Confederates would not accept criticism of Lee, and blame for the loss at Gettysburg was thus placed upon other scapegoats. Although it was not immediately apparent where the blame rested for such a devastating loss, not long after the Battle of Gettysburg two names kept surfacing: cavalry leader General "Jeb" Stuart and General James Longstreet; Stuart blamed for robbing Lee of the "eyes" he needed to know of Union movement, and Longstreet for delaying his attack on Round Top Hills the second day and acting too slowly in executing the assault on the Union left flank.

Long before Gettysburg, Longstreet was characterized by his men and commanders as "congenitally resistant to hurry himself,"[13] resistant to change of orders (even from his supreme commander, Lee), and disliked to overextend his men (once bivouacked, he allowed his men to

---

[13] Dowdey, Clifford. *Lee's Last Campaign: The Story of Lee & His Men against Grant--1864*. Page 134.

prepare three-days' rations before breaking camp, even when they were supposed to stick to a timetable). In fact, his designation as Lee's "old reliable" appears to have been bestowed by someone who had never actually worked with him or had to rely upon him.

Similarly, Longstreet's clash with A. P. Hill, then Jackson, Hood and Toombs, were indicative of his unwillingness to accept that he was not the center of attention; not the one destined for greatness. And, of course, as the War progressed, Longstreet's propensity to find fault (and start feuds) with Lafayette McLaws (who he tried to have court-martialed), Evander Law (who he tried to have arrested), Charles Field, and ultimately, Lee himself, was highly indicative of the self-possessed illusion Longstreet was living (and fighting) under. While always quick to reprimand any subordinate who questioned his orders, he clearly hesitated to resist orders from his superiors on occasions. In his Gettysburg account, Longstreet had the impudence to blame Lee for "not changing his plans" based on Longstreet's "want of confidence in them."

After General Robert E. Lee died in October of 1870, a group of ex-Confederates led by General Jubal Early (who had led a division in Ewell's corps at Gettysburg) publicly criticized Longstreet for ignoring orders and delaying his attack on the second day of the Battle on July 2, 1863. But while many former Confederates held Longstreet accountable for not following orders, Early took it one step further, arguing that Longstreet -- not Lee -- was responsible for the Confederate defeat (deemed a "tactical disaster" by most) that by most accounts was the beginning of the end for the Confederacy.

In his memoirs, however, Longstreet defended himself, saying that the blistering post-War attacks concerning Gettysburg were merely "payback for supporting Black suffrage", thus shifting the blame back to Lee. He wrote, "[Lee] knew that I did not believe that success was possible . . . he should have put an officer in charge who had more confidence in his plan."[14] He went on to say that Lee should have given the responsibility to Early, thus justifying his insubordination.

On the other hand, Longstreet's reputation has mostly been on the upswing in the past few decades, due in no small part to Michael Shaara's 1974 novel *The Killer Angels*, which portrayed Longstreet in a more flattering light. That novel was the basis for the 1993 film *Gettysburg*, which has also helped rehabilitate Longstreet's legacy and helped make clear to the public how instrumental he was during the war. In 1982, Thomas L. Connolly and Barbara L. Bellows published *God and General Longstreet*, which took the Lost Cause proponents like Early to task for their blatant fabrications (such as the one that Lee ordered Longstreet to attack in the early morning of Day 2 of Gettysburg), helping make clear the extent of historical revision propagated by the Lost Cause. In doing so, they cast Longstreet as a sympathetic victim of circumstances

---

[14] Gaffney, P., and D. Gaffney. *The Civil War: Exploring History One Week at a Time.* Page 442.

and sectional and political hostility.

It's also important to note that Lee himself never made any post-War statements to suggest that he held Longstreet responsible for the Confederacy's demise.

Stuart?

Outwardly, Stuart was the embodiment of reckless courage, magnificent manhood, and unconquerable virility; a man who could wear--without drawing suspicion of instability--the flamboyant adornments of a classic cavalier. It was once written that his black plume and hat caught up with a golden star, seemed the proper frame for a knightly face. In that same vein, people were always aware that Stuart was engaging in public relations even then, and Civil War historian Jeff Wert captured it well: "Stuart had been the Confederacy's knight-errant, the bold and dashing cavalier, attired in a resplendent uniform, plumed hat, and cape. Amid a slaughterhouse, he had embodied chivalry, clinging to the pageantry of a long-gone warrior. He crafted the image carefully, and the image befitted him. He saw himself as the Southern people envisaged him. They needed a knight; he needed to be that knight." Stuart, in effect, was the very essence of the Lost Cause.

It has been widely presumed that those same vainglorious traits led Stuart on a glory-seeking mission near the end of June 1863, which badly damaged Lee's abilities in Pennsylvania and directly led to the Army of Northern Virginia stumbling into a general battle Lee wished to avoid. Though credited with devoting his full attention to the Confederate cause upon his arrival, many historians attribute the catastrophic loss to the absence of Stuart and his cavalry. Immediately becoming the most devastating event of Stuart's military career, in his official report General Lee's wrote, " . . . the absence of the cavalry rendered it impossible to obtain accurate information. By the route [we] pursued, the Federal Army was interposed between [my] command and our main body, preventing any communication with [Stuart] until his arrival at Carlisle. The march toward Gettysburg was conducted more slowly than it would have been had the movements of the Federal Army been known." Some of Stuart's subordinates would come to his defense after the war, and Lee deserves some blame for allowing his subordinates so much discretion, which may have worked with Stonewall Jackson but backfired spectacularly with Ewell and Stuart. After the war, Stuart's subordinate, General Thomas L. Rosser stated what many were already convinced of, "On this campaign, [Stuart] undoubtedly, make the fatal blunder which lost us the battle of Gettysburg."[15]

The Army of the Potomac?

To a great extent, the Confederates' search for scapegoats is a product of the fact that they were

---

[15] Wert, Jeffry D. *Cavalryman of the Lost Cause: A Biography of J.E.B. Stuart*. Page 300.

so used to being successful that a defeat had to be explained by a Southern failure, not a Northern success.

In casting about for Southern deficiencies, it is often overlooked that Meade and his top subordinates fought a remarkably efficient battle. Meade created an extremely sturdy defensive line anchored on high ground, he held the interior lines by having his army spread out over a smaller area, and he used that ability to shuffle troops from the right to the left on July 2. Moreover, Meade was able to rely on his corps commanders, especially Hancock, to properly use their discretion. Before the battle, Lee reportedly said that Meade "would commit no blunders on my front and if I make one ... will make haste to take advantage of it." If he said it, he was definitely right.

Perhaps none other than George Pickett himself put it best. When asked (certainly ad nauseam) why Pickett's Charge had failed, Pickett is said to have tersely replied, "I've always thought the Yankees had something to do with it."

Meade Bibliography

Catton, Bruce. *Grant Takes Command*. New York: Little, Brown and Company, 1968.
This Hallowed Ground. Great Britain: Wordsworth, 1998.

Civil War Women website, "Margaretta Sergeant Meade" accessed via: http://www.civilwarwomenblog.com/2009/06/margaretta-sergeant-meade.html 07.25.2012.

Davis, Kenneth C. *The Civil War: Everything You Need to Know About America's Greatest Conflict but Never Learned*. New York: William Morrow and Company, Inc., 1996.

Eicher, John H., and David J. Eicher. *Civil War High Commands*. Stanford, CA: Stanford University Press, 2001.

Gaffney, P., and D. Gaffney. *The Civil War: Exploring History One Week at a Time*. New York: Hyperion, 2011.

General Meade Society of Philadelphia website: http://www.civilwar.com/news/recent-postings/150484-the-general-meade-society-of-philadelphia.html accessed 07.20. 2012.

Historynet.com, "Day One at Chancellorsville" accessed via: http://www.historynet.com/day-one-at-chancellorsville-march-96-americas-civil-war-feature.htm 07.24.2012.

Lanning, Michael Lee. *The Civil War 100*. Illinois: Sourcebooks, Inc., 2006.

Meade George G. Jr. *The Life and Letters of George Gordon Meade*. 2 Vols. New York, 1913, accessed via: http://www.rocemabra.com/~roger/tagg/generals/general01.html 07.18.2012.

McPherson, James M. *Ordeal by Fire: The Civil War and Reconstruction*. New York: McGraw- Hill, 2001.

Porter, Horace. *Campaigning with Grant*. New York: Bonanza Books, 1961.

Sell, Bill. *Civil War Chronicles: Leaders of the North and South*. New York: MetroBooks, 1996.

Stevens, Joseph E. *1863: The Rebirth of a Nation*. New York: Bantam Books, 1999.

Hancock Bibliography

Catton, Bruce. *Grant Takes Command*. New York: Little, Brown and Company, 1968.

Davis, Kenneth C. *The Civil War: Everything You Need to Know About America's Greatest Conflict but Never Learned*. New York: William Morrow and Company, Inc., 1996.

Gaffney, P., and D. Gaffney. *The Civil War: Exploring History One Week at a Time*. New York: Hyperion, 2011.

Goodrich, Frederick Elizur. *Life of Winfield Scott Hancock, Major-General, U. S. A.* Boston: B. B. Russell, 1886. Accessed via: http://books.google.com/books?id=g1B9CIlrGbwC&pg=PA23&source=gbs_toc_r&cad=4#v=onepage&q&f=false 07.13.2012.

Kopel, David, et al. "The Hero of Gettysburg: Winfield Scott Hancock's shot straight." *National Review Online*, accessed via http://old.nationalreview.com/comment/kopel200407020018.asp 07.15.2012.

Lanning, Michael Lee. *The Civil War 100*. Illinois: Sourcebooks, Inc., 2006.

McPherson, James M. *Ordeal by Fire: The Civil War and Reconstruction*. New York: McGraw- Hill, 2001.

Porter, Horace. *Campaigning with Grant*. New York: Bonanza Books, 1961.

Tagg, Larry. *The Generals of Gettysburg*. Campbell, CA: Savas Publishing, 1998.

Tucker, Glenn. *Hancock the Superb*. Indianapolis: Bobbs-Merrill Co., 1960.

Chamberlain Bibliography

Bowdoin College Archives, accessed via: http://learn.bowdoin.edu/joshua-lawrence-chamberlain/ 06.27.2012.

Davis, Kenneth C. *The Civil War: Everything You Need to Know About America's Greatest Conflict but Never Learned*. New York: William Morrow and Company, Inc., 1996.

Desjardin, Thomas A. *Stand Firm Ye Boys from Maine: The 20th Maine and the Gettysburg Campaign*. Thomas Publications, 1995.

"Why People Admire Joshua Lawrence Chamberlain." Accessed via http://www.joshua.lurker00.com/jlcadmirers.htm 06.30.2012.

Gaffney, P., and D. Gaffney. *The Civil War: Exploring History One Week at a Time*. New York: Hyperion, 2011.

Lanning, Michael Lee. *The Civil War 100*. Illinois: Sourcebooks, Inc., 2006.

Sell, Bill. *Civil War Chronicles: Leaders of the North and South*. New York: MetroBooks, 1996.

Wallace, Willard M. *Soul of the Lion: A Biography of General Joshua L. Chamberlain*. Gettysburg, PA: Stan Clark Military Books, 1991.

Lee Bibliography

Freeman, Douglas Southall. *R.E. Lee: A Biography*, 1934-5.

Blount, Jr., Roy. *Robert E. Lee*. New York: Penguin Books, 2003.

Connelly, Thomas L. *The Marble Man: Robert E. Lee and His Image in American Society*. New York: Alfred A. Knopf, 1977.

Dowdey, Clifford (editor). *The Wartime Papers of R. E. Lee*. New York: Bramhall House, 1961.

Fellman, Michael. *The Making of Robert E. Lee*. New York: Random House, 2000.

Flood, Charles. *Lee: The Last Years*. New York: Houghton, 1981.

Horn, Stanley F. (editor). *The Robert E. Lee Reader*. New York: Konecky & Konecky, 1949.

Nagel, Paul C. *The Lee's of Virginia*. New York: Oxford University Press, 1990.

Pryor, Elizabeth Brown (October 29, 2009). "Robert Edward Lee (ca. 1806-1870)," *Encyclopedia Virginia*. Retrieved March 11, 2012.

Thomas, Emory M. *Robert E. Lee: A Biography*. New York: W. W. Norton & Company, 1995.

Van Doren Stern, Philip. *Robert E. Lee: The Man and the Soldier*. New York: Bonanza Books, 1963.

Longstreet Bibliography

Alexander, Edward P. (Gary W. Gallagher, editor). *Fighting for the Confederacy: The Personal Recollections of General Edward Porter Alexander*. Chapel Hill: University of North Carolina Press, 1989.

Catton, Bruce. *This Hallowed Ground*. New York: Doubleday & Company, Inc., 1956.

Davis, Kenneth C. *The Civil War: Everything You Need to Know About America's Greatest Conflict but Never Learned*. New York: William Morrow and Company, Inc., 1996.

Dowdey, Clifford. *Lee's Last Campaign: The Story of Lee & His Men against Grant--1864*. Lincoln: University of Nebraska Press, 1988.

Gaffney, P., and D. Gaffney. *The Civil War: Exploring History One Week at a Time*. New York: Hyperion, 2011.

Garrison, Webb. *Civil War Curiosities*. Nashville: Rutledge Hill Press, 1994.

Lanning, Michael Lee. *The Civil War 100*. Illinois: Sourcebooks, Inc., 2006.

Neely, Mark E., Holzer, Harold & Boritt, Gabor S. *The Confederate Image*. Chapel Hill: The University of North Carolina Press, 1987.

Phillips, Kevin. *The Cousins' Wars*. New York: Basic Books, 1999.

Rhea, Gordon C. *The Battle of the Wilderness May 5-6, 1864*. Baton Rouge: Louisiana State University Press, 1994.

Sanger, Donald B., & Thomas Robson Hay. *James Longstreet, I: Soldier*. Baton Rouge: Louisiana State University Press, 1952.

Sell, Bill. *Civil War Chronicles: Leaders of the North and South*. New York: MetroBooks, 1996.

Stepp, John, W. and Hill, William I. (editors). *Mirror of War, The Washington Star Reports the Civil War*. The Evening Star Newspaper Co., 1961.

Tagg, Larry. *The Generals of Gettysburg*. CA: Savas Publishing, 1998.

Wert, Jeffry D. *General James Longstreet: The Confederacy's Most Controversial Soldier: A Biography*. New York: Simon & Schuster, 1993.

Stuart Bibliography

Catton, Bruce. *This Hallowed Ground: The Story of the Union Side of the Civil War*. New York: Doubleday & Company, 1955.

Davis, Burke. *Jeb Stuart: The Last Cavalier*. New York: Random House, 1957.

Eaton, Clement. *Jefferson Davis*. New York: The Free Press, 1977.

Eicher, John H. & David, J. *Civil War High Commands*. Stanford: Stanford University Press, 2001.

Escott, Paul D. "The Uses of Gallantry: Virginians and the Origins of J. E. B. Stuart's Historical Image," *The Virginia Magazine of History and Biography*, Vol 103, No 1, 1995. Accessed via Jstor:
http://www.jstor.org/discover/10.2307/4249485?uid=3739600&uid=2&uid=4&uid=3739256&sid=21100770232471 05.05.2012.

Garrison, Webb. *Civil War Curiosities*. Nashville: Rutledge Hill Press, 1994.

Howard, O. O. (Oliver Otis), *Autobiography of Oliver Otis Howard, Major General, United States Army*. New York: The Baker & Taylor Company, 1907. Accessed via http://archive.org/details/autobiographyofo01howarich 05.07.2012.

Lanning, Michael Lee. *The Civil War 100*. Illinois: Sourcebooks, Inc., 2006.

Lee, Robert E., Jr. *Recollections and Letters of General Robert E. Lee by Captain E. Lee, His Son*. Retrieved via http://www.quillspirit.org/ebooks/Letters_of_General_R_E_Lee/6.php 05.06.2012.

Mosby, John Singleton. *The Memoirs of Colonel John S. Mosby*. Boston: Little, Brown, and Company, 1917. Accessed via http://docsouth.unc.edu/fpn/mosby/menu.html 05.05.2012.

Philips, David. *Crucial Land Battles*. New York: MetroBooks, 1996.

Sears, Stephen W. *Chancellorsville*. Boston: Houghton Mifflin, 1996.
   Gettysburg. Boston: Houghton Mifflin, 2003.

Sifakis, Stewart, "Who Was Who In The Civil War." Accessed via: http://www.civilwarhome.com/stuartbi.htm 05.07.2012.

Stuart Family Archives: http://archiver.rootsweb.ancestry.com/th/read/STUART/2006-04/1144035927 Accessed 05.04.2012.

Stepp, John W. & Hill, William I. (editors), *Mirror of War, the Washington Star Reports the Civil War*. The Evening Star Newspaper Company, 1961.

Thomas, Emory M. *Bold Dragoon: The Life of J.E.B. Stuart*. Norman: University of Oklahoma Press, 1986.

Wert, Jeffry D. *Cavalryman of the Lost Cause: A Biography of J.E.B. Stuart*. New York: Simon & Schuster, 2008.

Wright, C. M. "Flora Cooke Stuart (1836–1923)." Retrieved via Encyclopedia Virginia: http://www.EncyclopediaVirginia.org/Stuart_Flora_Cooke_1836-1923 on 05.06.2012.

The Battle of Chickamauga

Chapter 1: The Summer of 1863

Of all the commanders who led armies during major battles of the Civil War, historians have by and large agreed that the most inept generals to face each other were the Union's William Rosecrans and the Confederacy's Braxton Bragg. The two generals' armies, the Union Army of the Cumberland and the Confederate Army of Tennessee, had already fought at the Battle of Stones River (Battle of Murfreesboro) at the end of 1862, inflicting massive casualties on each other without gaining an advantage.

Rosecrans and Bragg

During the first half of 1863, the two armies maneuvered around Chattanooga, Tennessee, one of the important railroad hubs of the theater. With Ulysses S. Grant laying siege to Vicksburg and trying to close off the Mississippi River, the Lincoln Administration hoped that a decisive campaign by Bragg in southern Tennessee would lay the groundwork for the capture of Atlanta, one of the Confederacy's most important cities.

That very thought terrorized the minds of Confederate officials and generals, even some of those fighting in the East. Early in 1863, Robert E. Lee's principal subordinate, James Longstreet, had advocated letting him take his corps west to try to relieve Vicksburg or conduct a campaign in Tennessee that would force Grant to stop his siege or send some of his men elsewhere. Lee had not wanted to detach any soldiers from his own army, given that it was badly outnumbered by the Union Army of the Potomac, but after the fall of Vicksburg and the defeat at Gettysburg, the situation had changed. Longstreet explained in his memoirs:

> "To me the emergency seemed so grave that I decided to write the Honorable Secretary of War (excusing the informality under the privilege given in his request in May) expressing my opinion of affairs in that military zone. I said that the successful march of General Rosecrans's army through Georgia would virtually be the finishing stroke of the war; that in the fall of Vicksburg and the free flow of the Mississippi River the lungs of the Confederacy were lost; that the impending march would cut through the heart of the South, and leave but little time for the dissolution; that to my mind the remedy was to order the Army of Northern Virginia to defensive work, and send detachments to reinforce the army in Tennessee; to call detachments of other commands to the same service, and strike a crushing blow against General Rosecrans before he could receive reinforcing help; that our interior lines gave the opportunity, and it was only by the skilful use of them that we could reasonably hope to equalize our power to that of the better-equipped adversary; that the subject had not been mentioned to my commander, because like all others he was opposed to having important detachments of his army so far beyond his reach; that all must realize that our affairs were languishing, and that the only hope of reviving the waning cause was through the advantage of interior lines."

Longstreet

After the fall of Vicksburg, the Confederate high command had reached the same opinion, and during the end of July and into August they went about strengthening Bragg's Army of Tennessee. Bragg had about 50,000 men that summer, but Davis added the Department of East Tennessee, which included nearly 18,000 men under Maj. Gen. Simon B. Buckner, into Bragg's Department of Tennessee. Meanwhile, plans were set in motion to detach Longstreet's corps from Lee's Army of Northern Virginia and transfer it to Tennessee by rail.

As Bragg's army was being reinforced, there was another matter that Jefferson Davis had to work through: the internal squabbles among his generals. Bragg's previous campaigns (and their lack of successes) had led to harsh criticism from some of the men now nominally under his command, including the equally incompetent Lt. Gen. Leonidas Polk, as well as William Hardee and Simon Bolivar Buckner. In his official report to the Confederate government after the battle, Bragg hinted at how the mutual disdain among the senior officers in his department led to arguments over orders that summer:

"On August 20, it was ascertained certainly that the Federal army from Middle Tennessee, under General Rosecrans, had crossed the mountains to Stevenson and Bridgeport. His force of effective infantry and artillery amounted to fully 70,000, divided into four corps. About the same time General Burnside advanced from Kentucky toward Knoxville, East Tennessee, with a force estimated by the general commanding that department at over 25,000.

In view of the great superiority of numbers brought against him General Buckner concluded to evacuate Knoxville, and with a force of about 5,000 infantry and artillery and his cavalry took position in the vicinity of Loudon. Two brigades of his command (Frazer's, at Cumberland Gap, and Jackson's, in Northeast Tennessee) were thus severed from us.

The enemy having already obtained a lodgment in East Tennessee by another route, the continued occupation of Cumberland Gap became very hazardous to the garrison and comparatively unimportant to us. Its evacuation was accordingly ordered, but on the appeal of its commander, stating his resources and ability for defense, favorably indorsed by Major-General Buckner, the orders were suspended on August 31. The main body of our army was encamped near Chattanooga, while the cavalry force, much reduced and enfeebled by long service on short rations, was recruiting in the vicinity of Rome, Ga."

Hardee, in command of one of Bragg's corps, despised Bragg so greatly that he requested for a transfer out of Bragg's department in July and was replaced by D.H. Hill, brother-in-law to Stonewall Jackson and a close friend to both James Longstreet and Joseph E. Johnston. Although his military ability was well respected, he was underutilized during the second half of the Civil War due to his own falling out with Lee. Longstreet would later incur the wrath of some of his former Confederate comrades by writing that Hill was not given command of a corps in the Army of Northern Virginia because he wasn't a Virginian, which was considered an implicit criticism of Lee. Hill and Longstreet were both substantial command upgrades and among the best generals the Confederacy had, and by the time Chickamauga was over they would both harbor an intense dislike of Bragg as well.

Hill would write an account of the battle after the war that was published in the seminal *Battles & Leaders of the Civil War* series, and in it he recounted his first meeting with Bragg in years:

"On the 19th of July I reported to General Bragg at Chattanooga. I had not seen him since I had been the junior lieutenant in his battery of artillery at Corpus Christi, Texas, in 1845. The other two lieutenants were George H. Thomas and John F. Reynolds. We four had been in the same mess there. Reynolds had been killed at Gettysburg twelve days before my new assignment. Thomas, the strongest and most pronounced Southerner of the four, was now Rosecrans's lieutenant. It was a strange casting of lots that three messmates of Corpus Christi should meet under such changed circumstances at Chickamauga.

My interview with General Bragg at Chattanooga was not satisfactory. He was silent and reserved and seemed gloomy and despondent. He had grown prematurely old since I saw him last, and showed much nervousness. His relations with his next in command (General Polk) and with some others of his subordinates were known not to be pleasant. His many retreats, too, had alienated the rank and file from him, or at least had taken away that enthusiasm which soldiers feel for the successful general, and which makes them obey his orders without question, and thus wins for him other successes. The one thing that a soldier never fails to understand is victory, and the commander who leads him to victory will be adored by him whether that victory has been won by skill or by blundering, by the masterly handling of a few troops against great odds, or by the awkward use of over whelming numbers."

Hill's account suggests that the issues between Bragg and his subordinates were so well-known that it was already coloring the attitudes of men who had not yet served under him. It's likely that the only reason this situation was allowed to fester for as long as it did is because Bragg and Jefferson Davis had been close friends since their days at West Point decades earlier. Davis's loyalty to his friends presented similar problems, as he had very obvious favorites among his generals, like Lee, Bragg, and Albert Sidney Johnston. At the same time, he constantly bickered with other generals in the field, notably Joseph E. Johnston, and the discord hurt the Southern cause, especially in the West. Even after Davis reluctantly removed Bragg from command out West, he would bring Bragg to Richmond to serve as a military advisor.

While the discord among the generals clearly didn't help matters, the reinforcements gave Bragg a numbers advantage over Rosecrans, a rare situation for a Confederate army during the war. With that, Bragg was determined to take offensive operations in late August and early September, as he had been urged to do by the Confederate government.

Bragg's account noted that one of the reasons he wanted to delay moving forward was because the geographical terrain made advancing difficult, and he had hoped that it would be Rosecrans who would be forced to move forward in that same area. Sure enough, Rosecrans was hoping to avoid doing just that, but he was also being pressed to conduct offensive operations by his government. Rosecrans would thus have to march his army through the Cumberland Plateau, which would disrupt his supply lines due to poor roads and a lack of resources in the vicinity, and when he was ordered forward by Henry "Old Brains" Halleck, the general-in-chief, he described the order as being full of "recklessness, conceit and malice."

Rosecrans had managed to outmaneuver Bragg earlier in 1863 without much fighting, and he hoped to do so again in the summer. His ambitious plan called for using part of his army to pin down Bragg north of Chattanooga while the rest of his army crossed the Tennessee River well downstream and then had space to march forward on a wide front and encircle Bragg in Chattanooga or compel him to evacuate.

Rosecrans had outlined an overly ambitious marching strategy, which was made all the more bewildering by the fact that he detailed the complex difficulties associated with the movements in his post-battle report:

"It is evident from this description of the topography that to reach Chattanooga, or penetrate the country south of it, on the railroad, by crossing the Tennessee below Chattanooga was a difficult task. It was necessary to cross the Cumberland Mountains, with subsistence, ammunition, at least a limited supply of forage, and a bridge train; to cross Sand or Raccoon Mountains into Lookout Valley, then Lookout Mountain, and finally the lesser ranges, Missionary Ridge, if we went directly to Chattanooga, or Missionary Ridge, Pigeon Mountain, and Taylor s Ridge, if we struck the railroad at Dalton or south of it. The Valley of the Tennessee River, though several miles in breadth between the bases of the mountains, below Bridgeport, is not a broad, alluvial farming country, but full of barren oak ridges, sparsely settled, and but a small part of it under cultivation…

The first step was to repair the Nashville and Chattanooga Railroad, to bring forward to Tullahoma, McMinnville, Decherd, and Winchester needful forage and subsistence, which it was impossible to transport from Murfreesborough to those points over the horrible roads which we encountered on our advance to Tullahoma. The next was to extend the repairs of the main stem to Stevenson and Bridgeport, and the Tracy City branch, so that we could place supplies in depot at those points, from which to draw after we had crossed the mountains…

The crossing of the river required that the best points should be chosen, and means provided for the crossing. The river was reconnoitered, the pontoons and trains ordered forward as rapidly as possible, hidden from view in rear of Stevenson and prepared for use. By the time they were ready the places of crossing had been selected and dispositions made to begin the operation.

It was very desirable to conceal to the last moment the points of crossing, but as the mountains on the south side of the Tennessee rise in precipitous rocky bluffs to the height of 800 or 1,000 feet, completely overlooking the whole valley and its coves, this was next to impossible."

As Rosecrans was attempting the multiple crossings and aiming to concentrate his army again after doing so, the amount of time it took allowed more Confederate reinforcements to arrive from Mississippi. Adding to his challenges, there were only three suitable roads that could be used to link the several corps of his armies back together, leaving the isolated elements of his army dangerously exposed. When Bragg became aware of these dispositions, he evacuated from Chattanooga and fell back for the purpose of crushing that part of the Army of the Cumberland to his south, which included Alexander McCook's XX Corps and George H. Thomas's XIV Corps. Badly mistaking Bragg's movement as a general retreat further back into Atlanta, a joyous Rosecrans telegraphed Washington on September 9, "Chattanooga is ours without a struggle and East Tennessee is free."

Thomas

In actuality, Bragg had pulled the Army of Tennessee 20 miles back to LaFayette, which would allow him to potentially fall on the two isolated Union corps, who were way too far away from the rest of the Army of the Cumberland to receive support from them in the case of an attack. After Thomas Crittenden's XXI Corps occupied Chattanooga, Rosecrans ignored Thomas's advice to delay an advance on Bragg's army until the three Union corps could get within supporting range of each other and secure their supply lines. Instead, Rosecrans ordered one of his cavalry divisions to raid the Confederate supply lines at Resaca, have McCook's XX Corps swing further south across Lookout Mountain, push Crittenden's corps south in chase of Bragg, and move Thomas forward to LaFayette.

In other words, Rosecrans was unwittingly marching Thomas's 23,000 men straight at Bragg's entire army, just as Bragg was concentrating there for the purposes of attacking an isolated corps.

Chapter 2: Davis's Cross Roads

Given Rosecrans's orders, Thomas's corps began marching toward Dug Gap in column formation, with James Negley's division in the vanguard 12 hours ahead of the next closest division. Bragg was already aware of this forward movement on September 9, and he immediately took steps to attack Negley's division near Davis's Cross Roads by hopefully having Thomas Hindman's division march into Negley's rear near McLemore's Cove as Negley unwittingly pressed forward, thereby separating Negley from the rest of Thomas's corps:

"During the 9th it was ascertained that a column, estimated at from 4,000 to 8,000, had crossed Lookout Mountain into the cove by way of Stevens' and Cooper's Gaps. Thrown off his guard by our rapid movement, apparently in retreat, when in reality we had concentrated opposite his center, and deceived by the information from deserters and others sent into his lines, the enemy pressed on his columns to intercept us and thus exposed himself in detail.

Major-General Hindman received verbal instructions on the 9th to prepare his division to move against this force, and was informed that another division from Lieutenant-General Hill's command, at La Fayette, would join him. That evening the following written orders were issued to Generals Hindman and Hill:"

The first of several examples of incompetence among Confederate officers took place on the morning of September 10. Bragg had coordinated Hindman's division to march southwest into Negley's flank and rear as Patrick Cleburne's division of D.H. Hill's corps opposed Negley in front. As Negley kept unwittingly walking into the trap, around the time his division reached Davis's Cross Roads he heard about Hindman's movement threatening his left flank and rear and thus pulled back to take up a defensive position around McLemore's Cove, where Hindman could not flank him.

That countermarch was made possible by the fact that Cleburne's division never marched that day, which would lead to finger pointing between Bragg and D.H. Hill. Writing after the war, Hill blamed Bragg, insisting not only that the orders arrived too late but that Cleburne was ill and their proposed march would have been obstructed by physical obstacles anyway:

"As the failure of Bragg to beat Rosecrans in detail has been the subject of much criticism, it may be well to look into the causes of the failure. So far as the commanding general was concerned, the trouble with him was : first, lack of knowledge of the situation; second, lack of personal supervision of the execution of his orders. No general ever won a permanent fame who was wanting in these and elements of success, knowledge of his own and his enemy's condition, and personal superintendence of operations on the field.

The failure to attack Negley's division in the cove on September 10th, was owing to Bragg's ignorance of the condition of the roads, the obstructions at Dug Gap, and the position of the enemy."

D.H. Hill

While Hill dithered, Hindman had come within 4 miles of Negley's division but became concerned about attacking without Cleburne's division attacking in front as well. Even after being reinforced with more men from Buckner's corps, Hindman refused to make the attack on the afternoon of the 10th.

Infuriating Bragg even further, despite Hill's claims about Cleburne being sick, Cleburne was apparently well enough to order his division to start clearing the felled timber around Dug Gap and get ready to advance once he heard Hindman commence an attack on the 11th, but there seemed to have been some confusion at Hindman's headquarters over whether he was supposed to attack on the 11th. Hindman had already advised against making his attack on the 10th, only to have that advice rejected by Bragg, so naturally his attack on the 11th would be half-hearted as well. By the time the Confederates had finally coordinated an attack on Negley, a second division of the corps had reached them and taken up a defensive position, making an orderly retreat possible with a rearguard covering against Hindman's skirmishers.

Rosecrans seemed to more fully understand the situation and his dire predicament after the near disaster at Davis's Cross Roads, writing:

"On the 10th, Negley's division advanced to within a mile of Dug Gap, which he found heavily obstructed, and Baird's division came up to his support on the morning of the 11th. Negley became satisfied that the enemy was advancing upon him, in heavy force, and perceiving that if he accepted battle in that position he would probably be cut off, he fell back after a sharp skirmish, in which General Baird's division participated, skillfully covering and securing their trains, to a strong position in front of Stevens' Gap. On the 12th, Reynolds and Brannan, under orders to move promptly, closed up to the support of these two advanced divisions.

During the same day General McCook had reached the vicinity of Alpine, and, with infantry and cavalry, had reconnoitered the Broom-town Valley to Summerville, and ascertained that the enemy had not retreated on Rome, but was concentrating at La Fayette.

Thus it was ascertained that the enemy was concentrating all his forces, both infantry and cavalry, behind the Pigeon Mountain, in the vicinity of La Fayette, while the corps of this army were at Gordon's Mills, Bailey's Cross-Roads, at the foot of Stevens' Gap, and at Alpine, a distance of 40 miles, from flank to flank, by the nearest practicable roads, and 57 miles by the route subsequently taken by the Twentieth Army Corps. It had already been ascertained that the main body of Johnston's army had joined Bragg, and an accumulation of evidence showed that the troops from Virginia had reached Atlanta on the 1st of the month, and that re-enforcements were expected soon to arrive from that quarter. It was therefore a matter of life and death to effect the concentration of the army."

Chapter 3: Concentrating the Army of the Cumberland

The day after Negley avoided disaster in the south, Rosecrans began drawing up orders to link up his army. On September 12, he ordered McCook's XX Corps and his cavalry to march northeast and link up with Thomas's corps near Stevens Gap, and together they would continue marching northeast to link back up with Crittenden. As it turned out, the sheer distance between McCook and Rosecrans near Chattanooga meant it would take an entire day just for that order to reach McCook. It would then take at least three more days of hard marching to successfully link the three corps back up together.

Bragg's attempt to bag Negley's division had been a disappointment, but he still hoped to strike out at the isolated Union corps in detail, including Crittenden's corps. One of Bragg's cavalry corps, commanded by the legendary Nathan Bedford Forrest, reported Crittenden's southern movement toward Lee and Gordon's Mill, inducing Bragg to order Polk to make an attack with two of the corps under his command.

Forrest

On the night of September 12, Polk sent the order:

"Lieutenant-General POLK:

GENERAL: I inclose you a dispatch from General Pegram. This presents you a fine opportunity of striking Crittenden in detail, and I hope you will avail yourself of it at daylight to-morrow. This division crushed, and the others are yours. We can then turn again on the force in the cove. Wheeler's cavalry will move on Wilder, so as to cover your right. I shall be delighted to hear of your success."

Once again, the attack Bragg envisioned failed to materialize, this time because Bragg himself was unfamiliar with the dispositions of Crittenden's corps. Bragg had ordered Polk's men to certain points previously that would have made it impossible to reach Lee and Gordon's Mill in time to attack Crittenden before the entire corps had passed that point. This was lost on Bragg, who was infuriated at the time and complained in his post-battle report:

"Early on the 13th, I proceeded to the front, ahead of Buckner's command, to find that no advance had been made on the enemy, and that his forces had formed a junction and recrossed the Chickamauga. Again disappointed, immediate measures were taken to place our trains and limited supplies in safe positions, when all our forces were concentrated along the Chickamauga, threatening the enemy in front."

D.H. Hill pinned the blame for Bragg's lack of knowledge on what he considered a very obvious mistake, juxtaposing him with Stonewall Jackson for good measure:

"During the active operations of a campaign the post of the commander-in-chief should be in the center of his marching columns, that he may be able to give prompt and efficient aid to whichever wing may be threatened. But whenever a great battle is to be fought, the commander must be on the field to see that his orders are executed and to take advantage of the ever-changing phases of the conflict. Jackson leading a cavalry fight by night near Front Royal in the pursuit of Banks, Jackson at the head of the column following McClellan in the retreat from Richmond to Malvern Hill, presents a contrast to Bragg sending, from a distance of ten miles, four consecutive orders for an attack at daylight, which he was never to witness.

Surely in the annals of warfare there is no parallel to the coolness and nonchalance with which General Crittenden marched and counter-marched for a week with a delightful unconsciousness that he was in the presence of a force of superior strength. On the 11 we find him with two divisions (Van Cleve's and Palmer's) at Ringgold, twenty miles from Chattanooga, and with his third (Thomas J. Wood's), ten miles from Ringgold, at Lee and Gordon's Mills where it remained alone and unsupported, until late in the , day of the 12th."

Over the next several days, Rosecrans began to concentrate his army relatively unmolested and try to bring them all safely back toward Chattanooga. For their part, Bragg and his commanders decided that attacking Rosecrans in or around Chattanooga was their best available option. By the time that decision was made, the two divisions of Longstreet's corps that had been detached were just days away from arriving by rail.

On September 17, McCook's corps and Thomas's corps had linked back up, but Bragg tried to strike out north on September 18 toward Chattanooga, hoping to force a battle with Rosecrans or take the valuable city unopposed. If the Army of the Cumberland did put up a fight, Bragg figured his men would be well-positioned to turn their left flank, but in so doing he issued complex orders that would require a nearly impossible degree of coordination at 4 distinct crossing points of the Chickamauga creek.

"HEADQUARTERS ARMY OF TENNESSEE,

In the Field, Leet's Tan-yard, September 18, 1863.

1. Johnson's column (Hood's), on crossing at or near Reed's Bridge, will turn to the left by the most practicable route and sweep up the Chickamauga, toward Leo and Gordon's Mills.

2. Walker, crossing at Alexander's Bridge, will unite in this move and push vigorously on the enemy's flank and rear in the same direction.

3. Buckner, crossing at Thedford's Ford, will join in the movement to the left, and press the enemy up the stream from Polk's front at Lee and Gordon's Mills.

4. Polk will press his forces to the front of Lee and Gordon's Mills, and if met by too much resistance to cross will bear to the right and cross at Dalton's Ford, or at Thedford's, as may be necessary, and join in the attack wherever the enemy may be.

5. Hill will cover our left flank from an advance of the enemy from the cove, and by pressing the cavalry in his front ascertain if the enemy is re-enforcing at Lee and-Gordon's Mills, in which event he will attack them in flank.

6. Wheeler's cavalry will hold the gaps in Pigeon Mountain and cover our rear and left and bring up stragglers.

7. All teams, &c., not with troops should go toward Ringgold and Dalton, beyond Taylor's Ridge. All cooking should be done at the trains. Rations, when cooked, will be forwarded to the troops.

8. The above movements wall be executed with the utmost promptness, vigor, and persistence."

Naturally, these movements were full of delays on the morning of the 18th, not to mention the presence of Union cavalry in the area. Bragg later reported, "The resistance offered by the enemy's cavalry and the difficulties arising from the bad and narrow country roads caused unexpected delays in the execution of these movements. Though the commander of the right column was several times urged to press forward, his crossing was not effected until late in the afternoon."

Rosecrans correctly predicted what Bragg was attempting and moved to counter it by quickly bringing up Thomas on Crittenden's left:

> "Evidence accumulated during the day of the 18th that the enemy was moving to our left. Minty's cavalry and Wilder's mounted brigade encountered the enemy's cavalry at Reed's and Alexander's Bridges, and toward evening were driven into the Rossville road. At the same time the enemy had been demonstrating for 3 miles up the Chickamauga. Heavy clouds of dust had been observed 3 or 4 miles beyond the Chickamauga, sweeping to the northeast.
>
> In view of all these facts, the necessity became apparent that General Thomas must use all possible dispatch in moving his corps to the position assigned it. He was

therefore directed to proceed with all dispatch, and General McCook to close up to Crawfish Spring as soon as Thomas' column was out of the way. Thomas pushed forward uninterruptedly during the night, and at daylight the head of his column had reached Kelly's house on the La Fayette road, where Baird's division was posted. Brannan followed, and was posted on Baird's left, covering the roads leading to Reed's and Alexander's Bridges.

General Thomas ordered Brannan with two brigades to reconnoiter in that direction and attack any small force he should meet. The advance brigade, supported by the rest of the division, soon encountered a strong body of the enemy, attacked it vigorously, and drove it back more than half a mile, where a very strong column of the enemy was found, with the evident intention of turning our left and gaining possession of the La Fayette road between us and Chattanooga."

After the delays and dealing with the advanced Union defenders, several of Bragg's divisions had successfully pushed across the Chickamauga. By now, however, Thomas and Crooks were within supporting distance of Crittenden's corps. D.H. Hill faulted Bragg for being too late to make his attack orders:

"Had this order been issued on any of the four preceding days, it would have found Rosecrans wholly unprepared for it, with but a single infantry division (Wood's) guarding the crossings of the Chickamauga, and that at one point only, Lee and Gordon's - the fords north of it being watched by cavalry . Even if the order had been given twenty-four hours earlier, it must have been fatal to Rosecrans in the then huddled and confused grouping of his forces.

All that was effected on the 18th was the sending over of Walker's small corps of a little more than 5000 men near Alexander's Bridge, and Bushrod Johnson's division of 3600 men at Reed's Bridge, farther north. These troops drove off Wilder's mounted infantry from the crossings immediately south of them, so as to leave undisputed passage for Bragg's infantry, except in the neighborhood of Lee and Gordon's."

Chapter 4: September 19

Bragg's attack hadn't been carried out as expeditiously as he had hoped, but because he was unaware of the location of Thomas's corps, he planned for yet another attack on what he believed to be the Union's left flank during the morning of the 19th:

"The movement was resumed at daylight on the 19th, and Buckner's corps, with Cheatham's division, of Polk's, had crossed and formed, when a brisk engagement commenced with our cavalry under Forrest on the extreme right about 9 o'clock. A brigade from Walker was ordered to Forrest's support, and soon after Walker was ordered to attack with his whole force. Our line was now formed, with Buckner's left resting on the Chickamauga about 1 mile below Lee and Gordon's Mills. On his right came Hood with his own and Johnson's divisions, with Walker on the extreme right, Cheatham's division being in reserve, the general direction being a little east of north. The attack ordered by our right was made by General Walker in his usual gallant style, and soon developed a largely superior force opposed."

Fighting on the morning of September 19

Ironically, the first fighting of what became the Battle of Chickamauga involved Forrest's cavalry skirmishing with advanced pickets from Army of the Cumberland's Reserve Corps, commanded by Gordon Granger and stationed a couple of miles north. While those forces skirmished, it provided the Confederates evidence of the fact that the Union's left flank was not nearly as far south as Bragg had assumed it was. As the Union pickets were withdrawn north, the commander of their brigade, Daniel McCook, reported to Thomas that he assumed the fighting meant a Confederate infantry brigade was across the Chickamauga and potentially isolated. Unsure of whether McCook's report was accurate, Thomas sent orders to one of his division commanders, John Brannan, to try to find the brigade and destroy it. Thomas later reported:

> "I directed General Brannan to post a brigade, within supporting distance of Baird, on the road to Alexander's Bridge, and with his other two brigades to reconnoiter the road leading to Reed's Bridge to see if he could locate the brigade reported by Colonel McCook, and, if a favorable opportunity occurred, to capture it. His dispositions were made according to instructions by 9 a.m."

McCook, of course, had skirmished with Forrest's Confederate cavalry, not a vulnerable infantry brigade. As the Union division advanced in a battle line, Forrest fought a delaying action by dismounting his cavalry troopers while requesting reinforcements from Bragg and William Walker, the commander of the two-division corps just south of Forrest's troopers. While Walker was ordering one of his brigades forward around 9:00 a.m., Bragg interpreted the advance of Brannan's division as being a major attack on his right flank, so he began the process of scrambling more and more men to his right. Thus, Thomas thought he was dealing with a Confederate brigade and had sent a division, while Bragg thought he was dealing with a major offensive by Rosecrans. Bragg later reported, "The enemy, whose left was at Lee and Gordon's Mills when our movement commenced, had rapidly transferred forces from his extreme right, changing his entire line, and seemed disposed to dispute with all his ability our effort to gain the main road to Chattanooga, in his rear. Lieutenant-General Polk was ordered to move his remaining division across at the nearest ford, and to assume the command in person on our right. Hill's corps was also ordered to cross below Lee and Gordon's Mills and join the line on the right."

By the time those movements were being made by the Confederates, the fighting between Walker's brigade and Forrest's cavalry against Brannan's division had started in earnest. Even by this early point, it was clear that the terrain around the Chickamauga would play a major role in the nature of the fighting and the ability to control the armies. Historian Steven Woodworth aptly described its effects on the fighting:

> "The land between Chickamauga Creek and the LaFayette Road was gently rolling but almost completely wooded. ... In the woods no officer above brigadier could see all his command at once, and even the brigadiers often could see nobody's troops but their own and perhaps the enemy's. Chickamauga would be a classic 'soldiers battle,' but it would test officers at every level of command in ways they had not previously been tested. An additional complication was that each army would be attempting to fight a

shifting battle while shifting its own position...Each general would have to conduct a battle while shuffling his own units northward toward an enemy of whose position he could get only the vaguest idea. Strange and wonderful opportunities would loom out of the leaves, vines, and gunsmoke, be touched and vaguely sensed, and then fade away again into the figurative fog of confusion that bedeviled men on both sides. In retrospect, victory for either side would look simple when unit positions were reviewed on a neat map, but in Chickamauga's torn and smoky woodlands, nothing was simple."

As the fighting started raging between Brannan's division and the Confederates, it acted like a vacuum that began sucking in nearby units on both sides, as Thomas started ordering more of his men to relieve Brannan. Thomas reported:

"General Baird was directed to throw forward his right wing, so as to get more nearly in line with Brannan, but to watch well on his right flank. Soon after this disposition of those two divisions, a portion of Palmer's division, of Crittenden's corps, took position to the right of General Baird's division. About 10 o'clock Croxton's brigade of Brannan's division, posted on the road leading to Alexander's Bridge, became engaged with the enemy, and I rode forward to his position to ascertain the character of the attack. Colonel Croxton reported to me that he had driven the enemy nearly half a mile, but that he was then meeting with obstinate resistance. I then rode back to Baird's position, and directed him to advance to Croxton's support, which he did with his whole division, Starkweather's brigade in reserve, and drove the enemy steadily before him for some distance, taking many prisoners. Croxton's brigade, which had been heavily engaged for over an hour with greatly superior numbers of the enemy, and being nearly exhausted of ammunition, was then moved to the rear to enable the men to fill up their boxes; and Baird and Brannan, having united their forces, drove the enemy from their immediate front. General Baird then halted for the purpose of readjusting his line; and hearing from prisoners that the enemy were in heavy force on his immediate right, he threw back his right wing in order to be ready for an attack from that quarter."

As Baird's division was pushing the Confederates back, St. John R. Liddell's division arrived to reinforce the Confederate line, hitting Baird's right flank and routing them. However, as Baird's brigades were breaking for the rear, the advancing Confederates were stunned and stopped by Ferdinand Van Derveer's brigade of Brannan's division. These attacks and counterattacks had inflicted steady losses, but neither side was able to hold onto the advantage for long, which all but guaranteed that both sides would send more men that way to try to achieve a decisive breakthrough.

The fighting on the afternoon of September 19

The problem with this kind of fighting, as Hill noted, was that the reinforcements would go in piecemeal and make uncoordinated attacks, as opposed to reforming lines and making a general advance in larger force. Hill explained, "Unfortunately for the Confederates, there was no general advance, as there might have been along the whole line-an advance that must have given a more decisive victory on the 19th than was gained on the 20th. It was desultory fighting from right to left, without concert, and at inopportune times. It was the sparring of the amateur boxer, and not the crushing blows of the trained pugilist. From daylight on the 19th until after midday, there was a gap of two miles between Crittenden and Thomas, into which the Confederates could have poured, turning to right or left, and attacking in flank whichever commander was least prepared for the assault."

The closest the Confederates would come to a breakthrough would be in the center of the Union line during the early afternoon by men under the command of tenacious Texan John Bell Hood. A division commander in Longstreet's corps, Hood had been severely wounded at Gettysburg, recovering in time for the fighting at Chickamauga, and until Longstreet personally arrived later on the night of the 19th, Hood had command of the men in Longstreet's corps, which included his own division and Bushrod Johnson's division. As they advanced around 2:30, they began to steadily push the Union defenders back, thereby relieving a Confederate division under Alexander Stewart on their right, and for a moment they took control of the road to Chattanooga. However, a further advance was rebuffed by reinforcements in the form of four Union divisions, which pushed them back across the road, ensuring the Army of the Cumberland could keep using it to keep its own corps together.

Hood

The Union army subsequently launched a series of unsuccessful and uncoordinated counterattacks in that same sector, failing to push back the three Confederate divisions that had made about a mile of progress. Those attacks came to an end as night fell, but Bragg still intended to keep the fight going that night. Around 6:00 p.m., as it was getting dark, Bragg ordered Cleburne's division to shore up the Confederate army's right flank. Though the fighting in that sector had died down as Hood's men had pushed the action to the south, Cleburne now launched an attack that was hampered by the night and the heavily wooded underbrush. Cleburne called off the attack at 9:00 p.m., but not before having incurred about 30% casualties in his division.

The last attacks of September 19

At the end of the fighting on September 19, some of the Confederates felt they had won a victory, particularly Bragg and Hood. Bragg was also determined to take the fight to Rosecrans again the following day:

> "Night found us masters of the ground, after a series of very obstinate contests with largely superior numbers. From captured prisoners and others we learned with certainty that we had encountered the enemy's whole force, which had been moving day and

night since they first ascertained the direction of our march. Orders had been given for the rapid march to the field of all re-enforcements arriving by railroad, and three additional brigades from this source joined us early next morning. The remaining forces on our extreme left, east of the Chickamauga, had been ordered up early in the afternoon, but reached the field too late to participate in the engagement of that day. They were ordered into line on their arrival, and disposed for a renewal of the action early the next morning."

Naturally, Rosecrans saw things differently, reporting:

"The roar of battle hushed in the darkness of night, and our troops, weary with a night of marching and a day of fighting, rested on their arms, having everywhere maintained their positions, developed the enemy, and gained thorough command of the Rossville and Dry Valley roads to Chattanooga, the great object of the battle of the 19th of September.

The battle had secured us these objects. Our flanks covered the Dry Valley and Rossville roads, while our cavalry covered the Missionary Ridge and the Valley of Chattanooga Creek, into which latter place our spare trains had been sent on Friday, the 18th.

We also had indubitable evidence of the presence of Longstreet's corps and Johnston's forces, by the capture of prisoners from each, and the fact that at the close of the day we had present but two brigades which had not been opportunely and squarely in action, opposed to superior numbers of the enemy, assured us that we were greatly outnumbered, and that the battle the next day must be for the safety of the army and the possession of Chattanooga."

To a degree, both of them were partly wrong. Rosecrans had not been attacked by a greatly superior force, but he was right that the Army of the Cumberland certainly hadn't suffered any consequential setbacks either. Both men have been criticized for the nature of the attacks and the counterattacks, which inflicted thousands of casualties on each other through piecemeal actions that only involved individual brigades or divisions, as opposed to concerted attacks with multiple divisions or a corps.

Bragg has been particularly criticized by historians for the failure to win anything of substance on the 19th. Thomas Connelly, who wrote a history on the Confederate Army of Tennessee, asserted, "Bragg's inability to readjust his plans had cost him heavily. He had never admitted that he was wrong about the location of Rosecrans' left wing and that as a result he bypassed two splendid opportunities. During the day Bragg might have sent heavy reinforcements to Walker and attempted to roll up the Union left; or he could have attacked the Union center where he knew troops were passing from to the left. Unable to decide on either, Bragg tried to do both, wasting his men in sporadic assaults. Now his Army was crippled and in no better position than that morning. Walker had, in the day's fighting, lost over 20 per cent of his strength, while Stuart and Cleburne had lost 30 per cent. Gone, too, was any hope for the advantage of a surprise blow against Rosecrans."

On top of that, Bragg's previous defeats had sapped the morale of the Confederate army and their belief in his abilities, something Hood noticed on the night of the 19th. Hood later noted in his memoirs, "In the evening, according to my custom in Virginia under General Lee, I rode back to Army headquarters to report to the Commander-in-Chief the result of the day upon my part of the line. I there met for the first time several of the principal officers of the Army of Tennessee, and, to my surprise, not one spoke in a sanguine tone regarding the result of the battle in which we were then engaged. I found the gallant Breckinridge, whom I had known from early youth, seated by the root of a tree, with a heavy slouch hat upon his head. When, in the course of brief conversation, I stated that we would rout the enemy the following day, he sprang to his feet, exclaiming, 'My dear Hood, I am delighted to hear you say so. You give me renewed hope; God grant it may be so.'"

One thing may have gone right for the Confederates on the night of the 19th. As Longstreet and his men marched toward Bragg's army, they may have inadvertently run into the Union army. Longstreet explained the odd encounter in his memoirs:

> It was a bright moonlight night, and the woodlands on the sides of the broad highway were quite open, so that we could see and be seen. After a time we were challenged by an outlying guard, 'Who comes there?' We answered, 'Friends.' The answer was not altogether satisfying to the guard, and after a very short parley we asked what troops they were, when the answer gave the number of the brigade and of the division. As Southern brigades were called for their commanders more than by their numbers, we concluded that these friends were the enemy. There were, too, some suspicious obstructions across the road in front of us, and altogether the situation did not look inviting. The moon was so bright that it did not seem prudent to turn and ride back under the fire that we knew would be opened on us, so I said, loudly, so that the guard could hear, 'Let us ride down a little way to find a better crossing.' Riding a few rods brought us under cover and protection of large trees, sufficiently shading our retreat to enable us to ride quietly to the rear and take the road over which we had seen so many men and vehicles passing while on our first ride."

Surprisingly, by the time Longstreet and his men arrived around 11:00 p.m., Bragg was asleep. It was then that Longstreet learned he was being given command of the left wing of the army, leaving Hood in command of his corps, and that Leonidas Polk was given command of the right wing of the army.

Bragg's decision to reorganize his command structure ahead of the attack on the 20th has also come in for criticism, especially because it confused some of his own officers by adding another layer of command for orders. This was particularly a problem for the Confederates' right flank, which was manned by the corps of D.H. Hill. It was not until late that night that Hill even learned about the reorganization of the command structure, and that he had now been made one of Polk's subordinates. And if Hill is to be believed, the confusion that resulted in the reorganization led to him not receiving the attack orders that Bragg intended for him on the morning of the 20th:

> "[M]y chief-of-staff gave me a message from General Polk that my corps had been put under his command, and that he wished to see me at Alexander's Bridge. He said not a word to any of them about an attack at daylight, nor did he to General Breckinridge, who occupied the same room with him that night. I have by me written statements from General Breckinridge and the whole of my staff to that effect. General Polk had issued an order for an attack at daylight, and had sent a courier with a copy, but he had failed to find me. I saw the order for the first time nineteen years afterward in Captain Polk's letter to the Southern Historical Society."

Chapter 5: The Morning of September 20

"Taken as a whole, the performance of the Confederate right wing this morning had been one of the most appalling exhibitions of command incompetence of the entire Civil War." – Steven Woodworth

On the morning of the 20th, Bragg had anticipated that his right flank would be launching an attack on the Union left at daylight, only to discover nothing going on at daylight. Bragg reported:

> "Lieutenant-General Polk was ordered to assail the enemy on our extreme right at day-dawn on the 20th, and to take up the attack in succession rapidly to the left. The left wing was to await the attack by the right, take it up promptly when made, and the whole line was then to be pushed vigorously and persistently against the enemy throughout its extent.
>
> Before the dawn of day myself and staff were ready for the saddle, occupying a position immediately in rear of and accessible to all parts of the Free. With increasing anxiety and disappointment I waited until after sunrise without hearing a gun, and at length dispatched a staff officer to Lieutenant-General Polk to ascertain the cause of the delay and urge him to a prompt and speedy movement. This officer, not finding the general with his troops, and learning where he had spent the night, proceeded across Alexander's Bridge to the east side of the Chickamauga and there delivered my message.

Proceeding in person to the right wing, I found the troops not even prepared for the movement. Messengers were immediately dispatched for Lieutenant-General Polk, and he shortly after joined me. My orders were renewed, and the general was urged to their prompt execution, the more important as the ear was saluted throughout the night with the sounds of the ax and falling timber as the enemy industriously labored to strengthen his position by hastily constructed barricades and breastworks. A reconnaissance made in the front of our extreme right during this delay crossed the main road to Chattanooga and proved the important fact that this greatly desired position was open to our possession."

When Bragg found Hill around 8:00 a.m., Hill later claimed that was the first time he had heard of an attack order, after which he protested to Bragg that an attack would be unwise:

"Bragg rode up at 8 A. M. and inquired of me why I had not begun the attack at daylight. I told him that I was hearing then for the first time that such an order had been issued and had not known whether we were to be the assailants or the assailed. He said angrily, 'I found Polk after sunrise sitting down reading a newspaper at Alexander's Bridge, two miles from the line of battle, where he ought to have been fighting.' However, the essential preparations for battle had not been made up to this hour and, in fact, could not be made without the presence of the commander-in-chief. The position of the enemy had not been reconnoitered, our line of battle had not been adjusted, and par t of it was at right angles with the rest; there was no cavalry on our flanks, and no order had fixed the strength or position of the reserves."

The delay may have been fatal. Around 9:30 a.m., 4 hours after Bragg intended for the attack on the Union left to start, with Breckinridge's division and Cleburne's division of Hill's corps pushing forward. This was problematic for several reasons. First, Bragg intended that Cleburne and Breckinridge would be just the start of a coordinated series of attacks that would drive the Union's left flank to the south and southwest. Second, the delay allowed Thomas's men to dig in and erect breastworks that would greatly aid their defensive line, leading Bragg to complain that without the Confederates' delay, "our independence might have been won.

Perhaps most important of all, Bragg's attack was starting with a division that had fought late the previous night and had been sapped of nearly a third of its manpower. While Breckinridge's division had some success on the far right of the line and began pushing south along the LaFayette Road, the presence of Union breastworks had discouraged some of his men and the men in Cleburne's division. Cleburne's men went nowhere in front of several Union divisions, and the left wing of his division got mixed up with Stewart's division, which had marched to the right to close a gap in the Confederate line and inadvertently marched into the left wing of Cleburne's division. Since Stewart and Cleburne had their men tangled, Benjamin Cheatham's division, poised to advance after them, could not move forward with the Confederates in their front. Meanwhile, Hill's attempt to shore up the gap forming between Breckinridge and Cleburne was quickly savaged, and the gap remained in the line.

The Confederate attacks on the morning of September 20

By noon, the attack that Bragg had envisioned starting at dawn and rolling up the Union's left flank had completely fizzled out. Bragg could not hide his disgust in his official report, writing:

> "The reasons assigned for this unfortunate delay by the wing commander appear in part in the reports of his subordinates. It is sufficient to say they are entirely unsatisfactory. It also appears from these reports that when the action was opened on the right about 10 a.m. the troops were moved to the assault in detail and by

detachments, unsupported, until nearly all parts of the right wing were in turn repulsed with heavy losses.

Our troops were led with the greatest gallantry and exhibited great coolness, bravery, and heroic devotion. In no instance did they fail when called on to rally and return to the charge. But though invariably driving the enemy with slaughter at the points assailed, they were compelled in turn to yield to the greatly superior numbers constantly brought against them."

Chapter 6: The Union Blunder

The only good thing that can be said about the Confederates' attack on the morning of September 20 is that it set in motion a chain of miscommunications among Union officers that would ultimately produce one of the biggest blunders of the entire war.

When the attack started on the left flank, Thomas began requesting reinforcements from the generals and commands to his right. One of them was Brannan, and he sent a brigade north as reinforcements early in the morning only to be asked for more reinforcements around 10:00 a.m. At the same time, Brannan was aware that if he sent his entire division as reinforcements, it would leave a gap between Thomas Wood's division and Joseph Reynolds's division, so he initially talked the matter over with Reynolds, who suggested that Brannan withdraw his division but only after informing Rosecrans back at headquarters.

Brannan

Brannan wisely kept his division in the line, prudently waiting for Rosecrans to approve the decision and giving Rosecrans time to then reform the line and close up the gap. But somehow, Brannan's staff officer got the notion that Brannan's division was in the process of pulling out of the line and marching north as he rode back to Rosecrans. Rosecrans explained, "A message from General Thomas soon followed, that he was heavily pressed, Captain Kellogg, aide-de-camp, the bearer, informing me at the same time that General Brannan was out of line, and General Reynolds' right was exposed. Orders were dispatched to General Wood to close up on Reynolds, and word was sent to General Thomas that he should be supported, even if it took away the whole corps of Crittenden and McCook. General Davis was ordered to close on General Wood, and General McCook was advised of the state of affairs and ordered to close his whole command to the left with all dispatch."

The orders that Wood received were not what Rosecrans remembered, probably because Rosecrans did not actually review the orders before they reached Wood. Instead, his aide-de-camp, Frank Bond, wrote out the order to Wood: "The general commanding directs that you close up on Reynolds as fast as possible, and support him." Since Brannan's division was still in line, Wood could not "close up" on Reynolds's right because that spot was already filled. To "support" Reynolds meant that Wood should pull his division and organize in the rear of Reynolds's division. In other words, there was no way Wood could close up and support Reynolds at the same time unless Brannan's division had already moved out of the line.

Since it was impossible to close up on Reynolds, Wood decided to go ahead and support Reynolds, thereby pulling his division out of the Union line. Wood knew full well that he was creating a gap and thought the orders were strange, but he had already been chastised for not moving promptly after receiving orders earlier that day, so he accepted the orders. Historian Peter Cozzens noted the argument over the intent of the orders between Wood and one of the staffers:

"While Wood read the order, Starling began to explain its intent. Wood interrupted. Brannan was in position, he said, there was no vacancy between Reynold's division and his own. 'Then there is no order,' retorted Starling. There the matter should have ended. And with anyone but Tom Wood, it most assuredly would have. Rosecrans had upbraided Wood twice for failing to obey orders promptly...the dressing down just 90 minutes earlier in front of Wood's entire staff. The barbs of Rosecrans's invective pained the Kentuckian. Anger clouded his reason. No, he told Starling, the order was imperative, he would move at once."

Instead of verifying the intent with Rosecrans, whose headquarters were just 5 minutes away, Wood began to act. As he began pulling his division out of the line, Wood did not consult with his own corps commander (Crittenden) but with corps commander McCook, and though Wood later claimed McCook vowed to fill the gap, the gap essentially went unfilled. Wood was pulling out an entire division from the line, and it would only be partially filled by a single brigade.

Wood

Thus, unbeknownst to Rosecrans and McCook, a wide gap was being created right in the middle of the right wing of the Army of the Cumberland's line, and as fortune would have it, the delays brought about by Confederate confusion on their right resulted in Longstreet's left wing delaying its own attack until after 11:00. Having taken time to reform his battle lines, Longstreet had established an attacking force in 5 lines consisting of three divisions with his veterans from the Army of Northern Virginia. Bushrod Johnson's division was in front, and it was given the objective of advancing across the field of the Brotherton farm, the very part of the line that Wood's division was vacating.

Longstreet's attack

Longstreet has often been criticized for being slow to march and form his lines before an attack, but there's no question that this time it was incredibly fortuitous. The initial attackers struck the right flank of Wood's division was it was pulling out of the line and routed them, establishing the gap for nearly 15,000 Confederates to push through. Longstreet described the initial rout in his memoirs:

> "As we approached a second line, Johnson's division happened to strike it while in the act of changing position of some of the troops, charged upon and carried it, capturing some artillery, Hood's and Hindman's troops pressing in close connection. This attack forced the parts of the Twentieth and Twenty-first Corps from that part of the field,

back over Missionary Ridge, in disordered retreat, and part of Negley's division of the Fourteenth Corps by the same impulsion. As our right wing had failed of the progress anticipated, and had become fixed by the firm holding of the enemy's left, we could find no practicable field for our work except by a change of the order of battle from wheel to the left, to a swing to the right on my division under General Stewart."

Bushrod Johnson was awed by the sight of the Confederates streaming through the gap, writing, "The scene now presented was unspeakably grand. The resolute and impetuous charge, the rush of our heavy columns sweeping out from the shadow and gloom of the forest into the open fields flooded with sunlight, the glitter of arms, the onward dash of artillery and mounted men, the retreat of the foe, the shouts of the hosts of our army, the dust, the smoke, the noise of fire-arms—of whistling balls and grape-shot and of bursting shell—made up a battle scene of unsurpassed grandeur."

By pushing through the gap and wheeling to the right, Longstreet had effectively cut the Army of the Cumberland in two and now fell upon the left flank of Crittenden's corps. Shortly after Longstreet's wheel to the right started, the man in charge of his corps, Hood, was nearly killed. Hood explained, "With a shout along my entire front, the Confederates rushed forward, penetrated into the wood, over and beyond the enemy's breastworks, and thus achieved another glorious victory for our arms. About this time I was pierced with a Minie ball in the upper third of the right leg; I turned from my horse upon the side of the crushed limb and fell — strange to say, since I was commanding five divisions — into the arms of some of the troops of my old brigade, which I had directed so long a period, and upon so many fields of battle." Hood's leg would be amputated nearly at the hip.

As several Union brigades began heading to the rear, one of the brigades in Wood's division, commanded by Charles Harker, managed to stay intact enough to withdraw in an orderly fashion toward Horseshoe Ridge, a naturally strong defensive spot. Luckily for Harker and the Union, the Confederates in his front, brigades led by Joseph Kershaw and Benjamin G. Humphreys, were unsupported in their advance and were unable to dislodge the brigade from Horseshoe Ridge. In the chaos and confusion, the Confederate brigades closest to Kershaw and Humphreys had become scattered in their pursuit of retreating Union brigades.

By driving through the gap and wheeling to the right, Longstreet's left flank was exposed to some of the divisions in McCook's XX Corps, but the general chaos and panic resulted in most of that corps putting up almost no fight and evacuating the field to the west. With command structure having entirely broken down, brigadier-generals were left to their own devices, and those that tried to stay and fight were dispatched by some of the Confederate attackers who had not wheeled left so as to protect the flank.

Little Phil Sheridan's division was a textbook example of the difficulties Union generals had in maintaining order. As two of his brigades, led by William Lytle and Nathan Walworth, held their ground and actually repulsed the Confederate advance, his other two brigades had quickly broken and fled to the rear. When Lytle was killed leading his men, the leaderless brigade also quickly broke. Sheridan would describe his situation in his memoirs:

> "During these occurrences General Rosecrans passed down the road behind my line, and sent word that he wished to see me, but affairs were too critical to admit of my going to him at once, and he rode on to Chattanooga. It is to be regretted that he did not wait till I could join him, for the delay would have permitted him to see that matters were not in quite such bad shape as he supposed; still, there is no disguising the fact that at this juncture his army was badly crippled.
>
> Shortly after my division had rallied on the low hills already described, I discovered that the enemy, instead of attacking me in front, was wedging in between my division and the balance of the army; in short, endeavoring to cut me off from Chattanooga. This necessitated another retrograde movement, which brought me back to the southern face of Missionary Ridge, where I was joined by Carlin's brigade of Davis's division. Still thinking I could join General Thomas, I rode some distance to the left of my line to look for a way out, but found that the enemy had intervened so far as to isolate me effectually. I then determined to march directly to Rossville, and from there effect a junction with Thomas by the Lafayette road. I reached Rossville about 5 o'clock in the afternoon, bringing with me eight guns, forty-six caissons, and a long ammunition train, the latter having been found in a state of confusion behind the widow Glenn's when I was being driven back behind the Dry Valley road."

Rosecrans justified his leaving the field in his post-battle report:

> "At the moment of the repulse of Davis' division, I was standing in rear of his right, waiting the completion of the closing of McCook's corps to the left. Seeing confusion among Van Cleve's troops, and the distance Davis' men were falling back, and the tide of battle surging toward us, the urgency for Sheridan's troops to intervene became imminent, and I hastened in person to the extreme right, to direct Sheridan's movement on the flank of the advancing rebels. It was too late. The crowd of returning troops rolled back, and the enemy advanced. Giving the troops directions to rally behind the ridge west of the Dry Valley road, I passed down it accompanied by General Garfield, Major McMichael, Major Bond, and Captain Young, of my staff, and a few of the escort, under a shower of grape, canister, and musketry, for 200 or 300 yards, and attempted to rejoin General Thomas and the troops sent to his support, by passing to the rear of the broken portion of our lines, but found the routed troops far toward the left, and hearing the enemy's advancing musketry and cheers, I became doubtful whether the left had held its ground, and started for Rossville. On consultation and further reflection, however, I determined to send General Garfield there, while I went to

Chattanooga, to give orders for the security of the pontoon bridges at Battle Creek and Bridgeport, and to make preliminary dispositions either to forward ammunition and supplies, should we hold our ground, or to withdraw the troops into good position."

However, Sheridan's sentiment about Rosecrans's disappearance was echoed by Rosecrans biographer William Lamers, who wrote, "Whether he did or did not know that Thomas still held the field, it was a catastrophe that Rosecrans did not himself ride to Thomas, and send Garfield to Chattanooga. Had he gone to the front in person and shown himself to his men, as at Stone River, he might by his personal presence have plucked victory from disaster, although it is doubtful whether he could have done more than Thomas did. Rosecrans, however, rode to Chattanooga instead."

Around the same time, one of the Union's cavalry brigades, led by John T. Wilder, was prevented from trying to attack Longstreet's flank by Assistant Secretary of War Charles Dana, who had grown so discouraged by what he had seen that he demanded to be taken back to Chattanooga, where he could inform Washington of what was going on via telegraph. Wilder had to detach part of his command to escort Dana to the city, and that afternoon Dana hysterically telegraphed Washington, "My report today is of deplorable importance. Chickamauga is as fatal a name in our history as Bull Run."

Chapter 7: The Rock of Chickamauga

By about 1:00, Longstreet's men had pushed almost all of McCook's XX Corps and Crittenden's XXI Corps off the field, including the commanding general Rosecrans along with them. As the commander and his routed Union soldiers began a panicked retreat toward Chattanooga, Longstreet met with Bragg, and according to Longstreet the commanding general was indecisive at best:

"After caring for and sending him off, and before we were through with our lunch, General Bragg sent for me. He was some little distance in rear of our new position. The change of the order of battle was explained, and the necessity under which it came to be made. We had taken some thirty or more field-pieces and a large number of small-arms, and thought that we had cut off and put to disorder the Twentieth and Twenty-first Corps that had retreated through the pass of the Ridge by the Dry Valley road. He was informed of orders given General Johnson for my left, and General Buckner for a battery on the right. I then offered as suggestion of the way to finish our work that he abandon the plan for battle by our right wing, or hold it to defence, draw off a force from that front that had rested since the left wing took up the battle, join them with the left wing, move swiftly down the Dry Valley road, pursue the retreating forces, occupy the gaps of the Ridge behind the enemy standing before our right, and call that force to its own relief.

He was disturbed by the failure of his plan and the severe repulse of his right wing, and was little prepared to hear suggestions from subordinates for other moves or progressive work. His words, as I recall them, were: 'There is not a man in the right wing who has any fight in him.' From accounts of his former operations I was prepared for halting work, but this, when the battle was at its tide and in partial success, was a little surprising. His humor, however, was such that his subordinate was at a loss for a reopening of the discussion. He did not wait, nor did he express approval or disapproval of the operations of the left wing, but rode for his Headquarters at Reed's Bridge.

There was nothing for the left wing to do but work along as best it could. The right wing ceased its active battle as the left forced the enemy's right centre, and the account of the commanding general was such as to give little hope of his active use of it in supporting us. After his lunch, General Johnson was ordered to make ready his own and Hindman's brigades, to see that those of Hood's were in just connection with his right, and await the opening of our battery. Preston's division was pulled away from its mooring on the river bank to reinforce our worn battle. "

Longstreet was beside himself at Bragg's suggestion that the battle was not being won, but Bragg was (correctly) disappointed that his ability to destroy the entire Army of the Cumberland was out of reach because his right wing's inability to advance allowed them to flee toward Chattanooga. With Bragg all but refusing to order anything out of his right wing, the work was left for Longstreet's men to try to finish the job against Thomas's Corps, which still held its defensive line.

By now, Longstreet's attack was hours old, and even if the terrain had allowed his general officers to see their entire commands, the ensuing pursuits and chaos had broken down a lot of coordination. D.H. Hill noted how unique it was that Thomas and Longstreet had become the de facto commanding generals on the field, writing "Some of the severest fighting had yet to be done after 3 P. M. It probably never happened before for a great battle to be fought to its bloody conclusion with the commanders of each side away from the field of conflict. But the Federals were in the hands of the indomitable Thomas, and the Confederates were under their two heroic wing commanders Longstreet and Polk."

While Thomas's corps held the same lines from the morning, Thomas had been going about ordering the impromptu line on Horseshoe Ridge, which was attracting small pockets of Union soldiers and allowing them to reform there. Brannan's division began forming on the ridge, while Negley's division went about directing artillery. While some Union generals, like corps commander Crittenden, declined to stick around, others like Phil Sheridan found their way to Horseshoe Ridge to take part in the defensive stand. Thomas's line was also bolstered by Gordon Granger's Reserve Corps; after listening to gunfire for hours and receiving no orders from the absent Rosecrans, Granger took it upon himself to march to the sound and somehow managed to march past Forrest's cavalry. Longstreet would later complain that he was not even informed of Granger's arrival by anyone on the right of the Confederate army.

Eventually, Longstreet's advance on the right compelled Thomas to move the rest of his defensive line gradually back toward Horseshoe Ridge. Longstreet explained:

"We were pushed back through the valley and up the slope, until General Preston succeeded in getting his brigade under Trigg to the support. Our battery got up at last under Major Williams and opened its destructive fire from eleven guns, which presently convinced General Thomas that his position was no longer tenable. He drew Reynolds's division from its trenches near the angle, for assignment as rearguard. Lieutenant-Colonel Sorrel, of the staff, reported this move, and was sent with orders to General Stewart to strike down against the enemy's moving forces. It seems that at the same time Liddell's division of the extreme right of our right wing was ordered against the march of the reserves. Stewart got into part of Reynolds's line and took several hundred prisoners. Meanwhile, Reynolds was used in meeting the attack and driving back the division of General Liddell. That accomplished, he was ordered to position to cover the retreat. As no reports came to the left from the commanding general or from the right wing, the repulse of Liddell's division was thought to indicate the strong holding of the enemy along his intrenched front line, and I thought that we should wait to finish the battle on the morrow."

It was only after the battle that Longstreet learned that the line he thought was strongly entrenched was actually empty, which only made him more disgusted with Bragg: "It is hardly possible that the Confederate commander could have failed to find the enemy's empty lines along the front of his right wing, and called both wings into a grand final sweep of the field to the capture of Thomas's command; but he was not present, and the condition of affairs was embarrassing to the subordinate commanders."

The defense of Horseshoe Ridge

Now that Thomas had all of his men back on Horseshoe Ridge, they and the scattered remnants of the other two corps who had not fled made a defiant last stand against multiple Confederate attacks. Thomas reported:

"About 2 p.m., very soon after Captain Kellogg left me, hearing heavy firing to my right and rear through the woods, I turned in that direction and was riding to the slope of the hill in my rear to ascertain the cause. Just as I passed out of the woods bordering the State road, I met Captain Kellogg returning, who reported to me that in attempting to reach General Sheridan he had met a large force in an open corn-field to the rear of Reynolds' position, advancing cautiously, with a strong line of skirmishers thrown out to their front, and that they had fired on him and forced him to return. He had reported this to Colonel Harker, commanding a brigade of Wood's division, posted on a ridge a short distance to the rear of Reynolds' position, who also saw this force advancing, but, with Captain Kellogg, was of the opinion that they might be Sheridan's troops coming to our assistance. I rode forward to Colonel Harker's position, and told him that, although I was expecting Sheridan from that direction, if those troops fired on him, seeing his flag, he must return their fire and resist their farther advance. He immediately ordered his skirmishers to commence firing, and took up a position with his brigade on the crest of a hill a short distance to his right and rear, placing his right in connection with Brannan's division and portions of Beatty's and Stanley's brigades of Negley's division, which had been retired to that point from the left, as circumstantially narrated in the reports of General John Beatty and Colonel Stanley. I then rode to the crest of the hill referred to above. On my way I met General Wood, who confirmed me in the opinion that the troops advancing upon us were the enemy, although we were not then aware of the disaster to the right and center of our army. I then directed him to place his division on the prolongation of Brannan's, who, I had ascertained from Wood, was on the top of the hill above referred to, and to resist the farther advance of the enemy as long as possible. I sent my aide, Captain Kellogg, to notify General Reynolds that our right had been turned, and that the enemy was in his rear in force.

General Wood barely had time to dispose his troops on the left of Brannan before another of those fierce assaults, similar to those made in the morning on my lines, was made on him and Brannan combined, and kept up by the enemy throwing in fresh troops as fast as those in their front were driven back, until near nightfall. About the time that Wood took up his position, General Gordon Granger appeared on my left flank at the head of Steedman's division of his corps. I immediately dispatched a staff officer, Captain Johnson, Second Indiana Cavalry, of Negley's division, to him with orders to push forward and take position on Brannan's right, which order was complied with with the greatest promptness and alacrity. Steedman, moving his division into position with almost as much precision as if on drill, and fighting his way to the crest of the hill on Brannan s right, moved forward his artillery and drove the enemy down the southern slope, inflicting on him a most terrible loss in killed and wounded. This opportune arrival of fresh troops revived the flagging spirits of our men on the right, and inspired them with new ardor for the contest. Every assault of the enemy from that time until nightfall was repulsed in the most gallant style by the whole line."

One of Rosecrans's staff officers, James Garfield, met Thomas during the afternoon, and he informed Rosecrans, "Thomas is standing like a rock." After meeting with Thomas, Garfield went so far as to suggest that Rosecrans return to the field and bring back the rest of the army to take up the fight again tomorrow, insisting "our men not only held their ground, but in many points drove the enemy splendidly. Longstreet's Virginians have got their bellies full." But Rosecrans was a beaten man, with one account claiming that he was found weeping in Chattanooga that night. Lincoln telegraphed the commanding general, "Be of good cheer. ... We have unabated confidence in you and your soldiers and officers. In the main, you must be the judge as to what is to be done. If I was to suggest, I would say save your army by taking strong positions until Burnside joins you." Lincoln, of course, knew what was truly going on, and he confided to his secretary that Rosecrans seemed "confused and stunned like a duck hit on the head."

As night fell, Thomas was able to extricate the rest of the Union defenders to Rossville Gap nearer Chattanooga right from under the nose of Bragg's army. Phil Sheridan recounted seeing Thomas near Rossville Gap that night and noted how physically and mentally exhausted he seemed:

> "The General appeared very much exhausted, seemed to forget what he had stopped for, and said little or nothing of the incidents of the day. This was the second occasion on which I had met him in the midst of misfortune, for during the fight in the cedars at Stone River, when our prospects were most disheartening, we held a brief conversation respecting the line he was then taking up for the purpose of helping me. At other times, in periods of inactivity, I saw but little of him. He impressed me now as he did in the cedars, his quiet, unobtrusive demeanor communicating a gloomy rather than a hopeful view of the situation. This apparent depression was due no doubt to the severe trial through which he had gone in the last fortyeight hours, which strain had exhausted him very much both physically and mentally. His success in maintaining his ground was undoubtedly largely influenced by the fact that two-thirds of the National forces had been sent to his succor, but his firm purpose to save the army was the main-stay on which all relied after Rosecrans left the field. As the command was getting pretty well past, I rose to go in order to put my troops into camp. This aroused the General, when, remarking that he had a little flask of brandy in his saddle-holster, he added that he had just stopped for the purpose of offering me a drink, as he knew I must be very tired. He requested one of his staff-officers to get the flask, and after taking a sip himself, passed it to me. Refreshed by the brandy, I mounted and rode off to supervise the encamping of my division, by no means an easy task considering the darkness, and the confusion that existed among the troops that had preceded us into Rossville."

Thomas, on the other hand, had just earned the eternal nickname "The Rock of Chickamauga". While there is a never ending stream of acclaim going to generals like Grant, Lee, and Sherman, General Thomas has managed to fly under the radar, despite having an unusual background as a Southerner fighting for the Union and scoring almost inconceivable successes at Missionary Ridge, Franklin, and Nashville. Thomas also skillfully fought at Perryville, Stones River, and in Sherman's Atlanta Campaign, but he has remained best known for his defense at Chickamauga on September 20, 1863.

Thomas had one of the most stellar records of any officer in the war, was instrumental in the Union's ultimate victory in the Western theater, and scored the kinds of decisive victories that eluded more celebrated generals like Lee. So why does Thomas fly under the radar? A stern military man, Thomas eschewed self-promotion and aggrandizement, and though his methodical generalship was almost always successful, it sometimes annoyed General Ulysses S. Grant. With Grant's star rising as his relationship with Thomas was cooling, Thomas was on the wrong end of history. And when he died in 1870, Thomas had burned his papers and had not written memoirs or an account of his participation in the war, missing his final opportunity to directly leave his mark and define his own legacy instead of having others write it for him.

Chapter 8: The Aftermath of Chickamauga

The Battle of Chickamauga was the second deadliest battle of the Civil War with nearly 35,000 total casualties. The Army of the Cumberland had lost over 16,000, including nearly 5,000 being captured as a result of the panic of the 20th. Bragg's army lost even more, with 2,300 killed and over 14,500 wounded, losing nearly 18,500 all told. The casualties amounted to nearly 40% of both armies, a staggering number.

Like Longstreet, D.H. Hill was shocked that Bragg had no plans to pursue Rosecrans on the 21st:

> "Whatever blunders each of us in authority committed before the battles of the 19th and 20th, and during their progress, the great blunder of all was that of not pursuing the enemy on the 21st. The day was spent in burying the dead and gathering up captured stores. Forrest, with his usual promptness, was early in the saddle, and saw that the retreat was a rout. Disorganized masses of men were hurrying to the rear ; batteries of artillery were inextricably mixed with trains of wagons ; disorder and confusion pervaded the broken ranks struggling to get on. Forrest sent back word to Bragg that 'every hour was worth a thousand men.' But the commander-in-chief did not know of the victory until the morning of the 21st, and then he did not order a pursuit. Rosecrans spent the day and the night of the 21st in hurrying his trains out of town. A breathing-space was allowed him; the panic among his troops subsided, and Chattanooga - the objective point of the campaign - was held."

The day after Chickamauga ended, Rosecrans put his men to work digging defensive entrenchments around Chattanooga and waiting for Washington to send reinforcements. On September 23, Bragg's army arrived at the outskirts of Chattanooga and proceeded to seize control of the surrounding heights: Missionary Ridge (to the east), Lookout Mountain (to the southwest), and Raccoon Mountain (to the west). From these key vantage points, the Confederates could not only lob long-range artillery onto the Union entrenchments but also sweep the rail and river routes that supplied the Union army. Bragg planned to lay siege to the city and starve the Union forces into surrendering.

On September 29, U. S. Secretary of War Edwin M. Stanton ordered Union general Ulysses S. Grant, commander of the newly-created Military Division of the Mississippi, to go to

Chattanooga to bring all the territory from the Appalachian Mountains to the Mississippi River (including a portion of Arkansas) under a single command for the first time. Considering General Rosecrans's spotty record, Grant was given the option of replacing him with General Thomas. Hearing an inaccurate report that Rosecrans was preparing to abandon Chattanooga, Grant relieved Rosecrans of command and installed Thomas as commander of the Army of the Cumberland, telegraphing Thomas saying, "Hold Chattanooga at all hazards. I will be there as soon as possible." Without hesitation, Thomas replied, "We will hold the town till we starve."[16]

What followed were some of the most amazing operations of the Civil War. Grant relieved Rosecrans and personally came to Chattanooga to oversee the effort, placing General Thomas in charge of reorganizing the Army of the Cumberland. Meanwhile, Lincoln detached General Hooker and two divisions from the Army of the Potomac and sent them west to reinforce the garrison at Chattanooga. During a maneuver in which General Hooker had moved three divisions into Chattanooga Valley hoping to occupy Rossville Gap, Hooker's first obstacle was to bypass an artillery line the Confederates had established to block the movement of Union supplies. Initially, Grant merely used Hooker's men to establish the "Cracker Line", a makeshift supply line that moved food and resources into Chattanooga from Hooker's position on Lookout Mountain.

In November 1863, the situation at Chattanooga was dire enough that Grant took the offensive in an attempt to lift the siege. By now the Confederates were holding important high ground at positions like Lookout Mountain and Missionary Ridge. First Grant ordered General Sherman and four divisions of his Army of the Tennessee to attack Bragg's right flank, but the attempt was unsuccessful. Then, in an attempt to make an all out push, Grant ordered all forces in the vicinity to make an attack on Bragg's men.

On November 24, 1863 Maj. Gen. Hooker captured Lookout Mountain in order to divert some of Bragg's men away from their commanding position on Missionary Ridge. But the victory is best remembered for the almost miraculous attack on Missionary Ridge by part of General Thomas's Army of the Cumberland.

General Sheridan was part of a force sent to attack the Confederate midsection at nearby Missionary Ridge. According to several present, when Sheridan reached the base of Ridge, he stopped and toasted the Confederate gunners, shouting out, "Here's to you!"[17] In response, the Confederates sprayed his men with bullets, prompting Sheridan to quip, "That was ungenerous! I'll take your guns for that!" at which time he lit out, leading a spirited charge while screaming,

---

[16]   Cleaves, Freeman. *Rock of Chickamauga: The Life of General George H. Thomas*. Page 182.
[17]   Gaffney, P., and D. Gaffney. *The Civil War: Exploring History One Week at a Time*. Page 308.

"Chickamauga! Chickamauga!". The advance actually defied Grant's orders, since Grant, initially upset, had only ordered them to take the rifle pits at the base of Missionary Ridge, figuring that a frontal assault on that position would be futile and fatal. As Sheridan stormed ahead, General Grant caught the advance from a distance and asked General Thomas why he had ordered the attack. Thomas informed Grant that he hadn't; his army had taken it upon itself to charge up the entire ridge.

As it turned out, historians have often criticized Grant's orders, with acclaimed historian Peter Cozzens noting, "Grant's order to halt at the rifle pits at the base of the ridge was misunderstood by far too many of the generals charged with executing it. Some doubted the order because they thought it absurd to stop an attack at the instant when the attackers would be most vulnerable to fire from the crest and to a counterattack. Others apparently received garbled versions of the order." Sheridan later wrote, "Seeing the enemy thus strengthening himself, it was plain that we would have to act quickly if we expected to accomplish much, and I already began to doubt the feasibility of our remaining in the first line of rifle-pits when we should have carried them. I discussed the order with Wagner, Harker, and Sherman, and they were similarly impressed, so while anxiously awaiting the signal I sent Captain Ransom of my staff to Granger, who was at Fort Wood, to ascertain if we were to carry the first line or the ridge beyond. Shortly after Ransom started the signal guns were fired, and I told my brigade commanders to go for the ridge."

Regardless, to the amazement of Grant and the officers watching, the men making the attack scrambled up Missionary Ridge in a series of disorganized attacks that somehow managed to send the Confederates into a rout, thereby lifting the siege on Chattanooga. With that, the Army of the Cumberland had essentially conducted the most successful frontal assault of the war spontaneously. While Pickett's Charge, still the most famous attack of the war, was one unsuccessful charge, the Army of the Cumberland made over a dozen charges up Missionary Ridge and ultimately succeeded.

When the siege of Chattanooga was lifted, the Confederate victory at Chickamauga, the biggest battle in the Western Theater, had been rendered virtually meaningless. Not surprisingly, in the wake of Chickamauga there were recriminations among the generals involved on both sides. Chickamauga ensured Thomas continued to lead the Army of the Cumberland for the rest of the war, while the tension between Bragg and his principal subordinates bordered on outright mutiny. Longstreet discussed the unbelievable sequence of events within the Army of Tennessee's high command over the next month:

"After moving from Virginia to try to relieve our comrades of the Army of Tennessee, we thought that we had cause to complain that the fruits of our labor had been lost, but it soon became manifest that the superior officers of that army themselves felt as much aggrieved as we at the halting policy of their chief, and were calling in letters and petitions for his removal. A number of them came to have me write the President for them. As he had not called for my opinion on military affairs since the Johnston conference of 1862, I could not take that liberty, but promised to write to the Secretary of War and to General Lee, who I thought could excuse me under the strained condition of affairs. About the same time they framed and forwarded to the President a petition praying for relief.2 It was written by General D. H. Hill (as he informed me since the war).

While the superior officers were asking for relief, the Confederate commander was busy looking along his lines for victims. Lieutenant-General Polk was put under charges for failing to open the battle of the 20th at daylight; Major-General Hindman was relieved under charges for conduct before the battle, when his conduct of the battle with other commanders would have relieved him of any previous misconduct, according to the customs of war, and pursuit of others was getting warm.

On the Union side the Washington authorities thought vindication important, and Major-Generals McCook and Crittenden, of the Twentieth and Twenty-first Corps, were relieved and went before a Court of Inquiry; also one of the generals of division of the Fourteenth Corps.

The President came to us on the 9th of October and called the commanders of the army to meet him at General Bragg's office. After some talk, in the presence of General Bragg, he made known the object of the call, and asked the generals, in turn, their opinion of their commanding officer, beginning with myself. It seemed rather a stretch of authority, even with a President, and I gave an evasive answer and made an effort to turn the channel of thought, but he would not be satisfied, and got back to his question. The condition of the army was briefly referred to, and the failure to make an effort to get the fruits of our success, when the opinion was given, in substance, that our commander could be of greater service elsewhere than at the head of the Army of Tennessee. Major-General Buckner was called, and gave opinion somewhat similar. So did Major-General Cheatham, who was then commanding the corps recently commanded by Lieutenant-General Polk, and General D. H. Hill, who was called last, agreed with emphasis to the views expressed by others."

The problem for the Confederates who wanted to be done with Bragg is that he was friends with Jefferson Davis, as Longstreet was reminded when suggesting to Davis that Bragg be replaced by Joseph E. Johnston:

"In my judgment our last opportunity was lost when we failed to follow the success at Chickamauga, and capture or disperse the Union army, and it could not be just to the service or myself to call me to a position of such responsibility. The army was part of General Joseph E. Johnston's department, and could only be used in strong organization by him in combining its operations with his other forces in Alabama and Mississippi. I said that under him I could cheerfully work in any position. The suggestion of that name only served to increase his displeasure, and his severe rebuke.

I recognized the authority of his high position, but called to his mind that neither his words nor his manner were so impressive as the dissolving scenes that foreshadowed the dreadful end. He referred to his worry and troubles with politicians and non-combatants. In that connection, I suggested that all that the people asked for was success; with that the talk of politicians would be as spiders' webs before him."

Despite the negative feelings so many held about Bragg, Davis would not relieve him of command until late November 1863, well after the disastrous siege of Chattanooga was finished. By then, Bragg had successfully suspended Hindman and Polk for what he considered to be their failures during the Chickamauga campaign, and D.H. Hill was also suspended in early October.

With the failure to make anything out of the victory at Chickamauga, the Confederacy's best chance at somehow turning the tide in the West and possibly winning the war had been lost. As a result, Chickamauga became an extremely sore subject among the Confederates who had fought there, and historians still look at it as the South's last best chance in that theater.

D.H. Hill, who had played such a controversial role in the campaign, may have put it best:

There was no more splendid fighting in '61, when the flower of the Southern youth was in the field, than was displayed in those bloody days of September, '63. But it seems to me that the élan of the Southern soldier was never seen after Chickamauga - that brilliant dash which had distinguished him was gone forever. He was too intelligent not to know that the cutting in two of Georgia meant death to all his hopes. He knew that Longstreet's absence was imperiling Lee's safety, and that what had to be done must be done quickly. The delay in striking was exasperating to him; the failure to strike after the success was crushing to all his longings for an independent South. He fought stoutly to the last, but, after Chickamauga, with the sullenness of despair and without the enthusiasm of hope.

That 'barren victory' sealed the fate of the Southern Confederacy."

Bibliography

Cleaves, Freeman. Rock of Chickamauga: The Life of General George H. Thomas. Norman: University of Oklahoma Press, 1948.

Connelly, Thomas L. Autumn of Glory: The Army of Tennessee 1862–1865. Baton Rouge: Louisiana State University Press, 1971.

Cozzens, Peter. This Terrible Sound: The Battle of Chickamauga. Urbana: University of Illinois Press, 1992.

Knudsen, LTC Harold M. General James Longstreet: The Confederacy's Most Modern General. Tarentum, PA: Word Association Publishers, 2007.

Korn, Jerry, and the Editors of Time-Life Books. The Fight for Chattanooga: Chickamauga to Missionary Ridge. Alexandria, VA: Time-Life Books, 1985.

Lamers, William M. The Edge of Glory: A Biography of General William S. Rosecrans, U.S.A. Baton Rouge: Louisiana State University Press, 1961.

Tucker, Glenn. Chickamauga: Bloody Battle in the West. Dayton, OH: Morningside House, 1972.

Turchin, John Basil. Chickamauga. Chicago: Fergus Printing Co., 1888.

U.S. War Department, The War of the Rebellion: a Compilation of the Official Records of the Union and Confederate Armies. Washington, DC: U.S. Government Printing Office, 1880–1901.

Welsh, Douglas. The Civil War: A Complete Military History. Greenwich, CT: Brompton Books Corporation, 1981.

Woodworth, Steven E. Six Armies in Tennessee: The Chickamauga and Chattanooga Campaigns. Lincoln: University of Nebraska Press, 1998.

The Battle of the Wilderness

Chapter 1: Grant Comes East

Failing to secure the capture of any major northern cities, or the recognition of Great Britain or France, or the complete destruction of any northern armies, the Confederacy's last chance to survive the Civil War was the election of 1864. Democrats had been pushing an anti-war stance or at least a stance calling for a negotiated peace for years, so the South hoped that if a Democrat defeated President Lincoln, or if anti-war Democrats could retake the Congress, the North might negotiate peace with the South. In the election of 1862, anti-war Democrats made some gains in Congress and won the governorship of the State of New York. Confederates were therefore hopeful that trend would continue to the election of 1864.

Although the Army of the Potomac had been victorious at Gettysburg, Lincoln was still upset at what he perceived to be General George Meade's failure to trap Robert E. Lee's Army of Northern Virginia in Pennsylvania. When Lee retreated from Pennsylvania without much fight from the Army of the Potomac, Lincoln was again discouraged, believing Meade had a chance to end the war if he had been bolder. Though historians dispute that, and the Confederates actually invited attack during their retreat, Lincoln was constantly looking for more aggressive fighters to lead his men.

Lincoln's appreciation for aggressive fighters had made him a defender of Ulysses S. Grant as far back as 1862. In April 1862, Grant's army had won the biggest battle in the history of North America to date at Shiloh, with nearly 24,000 combined casualties among the Union and Confederate forces. Usually the winner of a major battle is hailed as a hero, but Grant was hardly a winner at Shiloh. The Battle of Shiloh took place before costlier battles at places like Antietam and Gettysburg, so the extent of the casualties at Shiloh shocked the nation. Moreover, at Shiloh the casualties were viewed as needless; Grant was pilloried for allowing the Confederates to take his forces by surprise, as well as the failure to build defensive earthworks and fortifications, which nearly resulted in a rout of his army. Speculation again arose that Grant had a drinking problem, and some even assumed he was drunk during the battle. Though the Union won, it was largely viewed that their success owed to the heroics of General William Tecumseh Sherman in rallying the men and Don Carlos Buell arriving with his army, and General Buell was happy to receive the credit at Grant's expense.

Grant

As a result of the Battle of Shiloh, General Halleck demoted Grant to second-in-command of all armies in his department, an utterly powerless position. And when word of what many considered a "colossal blunder" reached Washington, several congressmen insisted that Lincoln replace Grant in the field. Lincoln famously defended Grant, telling critics, "I can't spare this man. He fights."

Lincoln may have defended Grant, but he found precious few supporters, and the negative attention bothered Grant so much that it is widely believed he turned to alcohol again. While historians still debate that, what is known is that he considered resigning his commission, only to be dissuaded from doing so by General Sherman. While Grant was at the low point of his career, Sherman's career had been resurrected, and he was promoted to major-general the following month. With rumors that Grant was falling off the wagon with alcohol, Sherman tried to reassure Grant not to quit the war, telling him "some happy accident might restore you to favor and your true place." Sherman's appreciation of Grant's faith in his abilities cemented his loyalty and established a friendship between the two that would last a lifetime. In later years Sherman would say, "General Grant is a great general! He stood by me when I was crazy, and I stood by him when he was drunk; and now, sir, we stand by each other always."

Although Grant stayed in the army, it's unclear what position he would have held if Lincoln had not called Halleck to Washington to serve as general-in-chief in July 1862. At the same time, Halleck was given that position in large measure due to Grant's successes in the department under Halleck's command. Thankfully for the Union, Halleck's departure meant that Grant was reinstated as commander.

Lincoln's steadfastness ensured that Grant's victories out West continued to pile up, and after Vicksburg and Chattanooga, Grant had effectively ensured Union control of the states of Kentucky and Tennessee, as well as the entire Mississippi River. Thus, at the beginning of 1864, Lincoln put him in charge of all federal armies, a position that required Grant to come east.

Grant had already succeeded in achieving two of President Lincoln's three primary directives for a Union victory: the opening of the Mississippi Valley Basin, and the domination of the corridor from Nashville to Atlanta. If he could now seize Richmond, he would achieve the third.

Before beginning the Overland Campaign against Lee's army, Grant, Sherman and Lincoln devised a new strategy that would eventually implement total war tactics. Grant aimed to use the Army of the Potomac to attack Lee and/or take Richmond. Meanwhile, General Sherman, now in command of the Department of the West, would attempt to take Atlanta and strike through Georgia. In essence, having already cut the Confederacy in half with Vicksburg campaign, he now intended to bisect the eastern half.

On top of all that, Grant and Sherman were now intent on fully depriving the Confederacy of the ability to keep fighting. Sherman put this policy in effect during his March to the Sea by confiscating civilian resources and literally taking the fight to the Southern people. For Grant, it meant a war of attrition that would steadily bleed Lee's Army of Northern Virginia. To take full advantage of the North's manpower, in 1864 the Union also ended prisoner exchanges to ensure that the Confederate armies could not be bolstered by paroled prisoners.

By 1864, things were looking so bleak for the South that the Confederate war strategy was simply to ensure Lincoln lost reelection that November, with the hope that a new Democratic president would end the war and recognize the South's independence. With that, and given the shortage in manpower, Lee's strategic objective was to continue defending Richmond, while hoping that Grant would commit some blunder that would allow him a chance to seize an opportunity.

With that, the stage was set for the two most successful generals of the Civil War to finally face each other. Confederate Brigadier-General John B. Gordon, whose brigade would play a crucial role at the Battle of the Wilderness, aptly summarized the situation entering May 1864: "Grant had come from his campaigns in the Southwest with the laurels of Fort Donelson, Shiloh, Vicksburg, and Missionary Ridge on his brow. Lee stood before him with a record as military executioner unrivalled by that of any warrior of modern times. He had, at astoundingly short intervals and with unvarying regularity, decapitated or caused the official 'taking off' of the five previously selected commanders-in-chief of the great army which confronted him…This advance by General Grant inaugurated the seventh act in the 'On to Richmond' drama played by the armies of the Union."

Chapter 2: Entering the Wilderness

As usual, the Army of the Potomac had a large numbers advantage over Lee's Army of Northern Virginia, with Grant bringing an estimated 100,000 into the Wilderness to face Lee's 60,000. Although George Meade was nominally in command of the Union army, the fact that Grant marched with the army essentially meant that he would be making the overall decisions.

The Army of the Potomac was organized into three infantry corps, John Sedgwick's VI Corps, Winfield Scott Hancock's II Corps, and Gouverneur Warren's V Corps, along with a cavalry corps led by Phil Sheridan, who Grant brought east with him. Sedgwick was considered one of the most competent and aggressive corps commanders in the Union, and Hancock's heroics during the last two days of the Battle of Gettysburg more than demonstrated his ability to lead a corps. Warren had been a staff officer who alertly manned Little Round Top on the second day at Gettysburg, but he was relatively new to commanding a corps, and it would show. Ambrose Burnside's IX Corps was an independent command in the vicinity, but it would not fight in the Wilderness.

The Army of Northern Virginia started the Overland Campaign with the same structure as it had after losing Stonewall Jackson at Chancellorsville in May 1863. Lee's army was also divided into three corps commanded by James Longstreet, A.P. Hill and Richard S. Ewell. Longstreet was perhaps the best corps commander on either side during the Civil War, but Hill and Ewell struggled leading their corps at Gettysburg after having distinguished themselves in charge of smaller commands earlier in the war. The Confederate cavalry was led by their flamboyant but skilled cavalier, JEB Stuart, who was nearly as competent as he was vainglorious.

While the Union's advantage in manpower colored Grant's attritional strategy, on a tactical level it would not help the Army of the Potomac in the Wilderness because of the terrain. Grant explained why in his memoirs:

"The country over which the army had to operate, from the Rapidan to the crossing of the James River, is rather flat, and is cut by numerous streams which make their way to the Chesapeake Bay. The crossings of these streams by the army were generally made not far above tide-water, and where they formed a considerable obstacle to the rapid advance of troops even when the enemy did not appear in opposition. The country roads were narrow and poor. Most of the country is covered with a dense forest, in places, like the Wilderness and along the Chickahominy, almost impenetrable even for infantry except along the roads. All bridges were naturally destroyed before the National troops came to them."

Moreover, the Confederate soldiers' faith in their own abilities and General Lee ensured that they were constantly up to the challenge when facing the bigger Army of the Potomac. Gordon described the mood in camp that spring, "The reports of General Lee's scouts were scarcely necessary to our appreciation of the fact that the odds against us were constantly and rapidly increasing: for from the highland which bordered the southern banks of the Rapidan one could almost estimate the numbers that were being added to Grant's ranks by the growth of the city of tents spreading out in full view below. The Confederates were profoundly impressed by the situation, but they rejected as utterly unworthy of a Christian soldiery the doctrine that Providence was on the side of the heaviest guns and most numerous battalions."

When Grant began marching the army on May 4, he actually hoped to avoid a general battle against Lee in the Wilderness, given that the heavy forestry and thick underbrush would make infantry coordination impossible and artillery practically unusable. To avoid fighting on this ground, Grant needed to move the army southeast as quickly as he could, and he hoped to reach Spotsylvania Court House before fighting Lee.

As it turned out, Grant would fight Lee at Spotsylvania Court House, but it would be the second pitched battle of the campaign. The sheer size of the army made it difficult to move everything, especially its supplies. Grant's army was marching with just 10 days of rations, so a lot of live cattle had to be brought along to be butchered along the way, not to mention the thousands of wagons and ambulances as well. By some counts the rear of the marching army would've extended over 60 miles if marching down a single road. Grant wrote about all the work and necessities that went into provisioning his large army:

> "There never was a corps better organized than was the quartermaster's corps with the Army of the Potomac in 1864. With a wagon-train that would have extended from the Rapidan to Richmond, stretched along in single file and separated as the teams necessarily would be when moving, we could still carry only three days' forage and about ten to twelve days' rations, besides a supply of ammunition. To overcome all difficulties, the chief quartermaster, General Rufus Ingalls, had marked on each wagon the corps badge with the division color and the number of the brigade. At a glance, the particular brigade to which any wagon belonged could be told. The wagons were also marked to note the contents: if ammunition, whether for artillery or infantry; if forage, whether grain or hay; if rations, whether, bread, pork, beans, rice, sugar, coffee or whatever it might be. Empty wagons were never allowed to follow the army or stay in camp. As soon as a wagon was empty it would return to the base of supply for a load of precisely the same article that had been taken from it. Empty trains were obliged to leave the road free for loaded ones. Arriving near the army they would be parked in fields nearest to the brigades they belonged to. Issues, except of ammunition, were made at night in all cases. By this system the hauling of forage for the supply train was almost wholly dispensed with."

To alleviate the logistical issues, Grant intended to have his three corps march separately on two different roads toward their objective, as he explained in his memoirs:

> "The 5th corps, General Warren commanding, was in advance on the right, and marched directly for Germania Ford, preceded by one division of cavalry, under General J. H. Wilson. General Sedgwick followed Warren with the 6th corps. Germania Ford was nine or ten miles below the right of Lee's line. Hancock, with the 2d corps, moved by another road, farther east, directly upon Ely's Ford, six miles below Germania, preceded by Gregg's division of cavalry, and followed by the artillery. Torbert's division of cavalry was left north of the Rapidan, for the time, to picket the river and prevent the enemy from crossing and getting into our rear. The cavalry seized the two crossings before daylight, drove the enemy's pickets guarding them away, and by six o'clock A.M. had the pontoons laid ready for the crossing of the infantry and artillery. This was undoubtedly a surprise to Lee. The fact that the movement was unopposed proves this.
>
> Burnside, with the 9th corps, was left back at Warrenton, guarding the railroad from Bull Run forward to preserve control of it in case our crossing the Rapidan should be long delayed. He was instructed, however, to advance at once on receiving notice that the army had crossed; and a dispatch was sent to him a little after one P.M. giving the

information that our crossing had been successful.

The country was heavily wooded at all the points of crossing, particularly on the south side of the river. The battle-field from the crossing of the Rapidan until the final movement from the Wilderness toward Spottsylvania was of the same character. There were some clearings and small farms within what might be termed the battle-field; but generally the country was covered with a dense forest. The roads were narrow and bad. All the conditions were favorable for defensive operations."

Lee hadn't opposed the crossings because he had dispersed his army to prepare for several avenues of attack that Grant might choose. In fact, he anticipated that Grant would cross exactly how he did, using the Germanna and Ely Fords across the Rapidan River, but he hadn't concentrated his army until he knew for sure. As a result, Ewell's corps and Hill's corps were within marching distance of the Wilderness, but Longstreet was about 20 miles southwest near Gordonsville.

Grant's march intended to turn Lee's right flank, but once Lee realized which way Grant was marching on May 4, he began swiftly moving to meet the Union army in the Wilderness, since it was ideal for defense and negated the artillery advantage enjoyed by the Army of the Potomac. And as a result of the manner in which Grant's army was marching down separate roads, Lee was being given a chance to strike the Union's right flank instead of vice-versa. Ewell's corps and Hill's corps were close enough to fight in the Wilderness, but it would take a day for Longstreet's corps to come up.

Lee's intentions were assisted by the nature of the terrain, which allowed his two corps to march almost entirely undetected, as well as the Union's misuse of their cavalry. While cavalry was typically used to screen the infantry's advance and to conduct reconnaissance, Sheridan's cavalry was east of the army responding to a report that JEB Stuart's cavalry was near Fredericksburg, presumably with the intention of harassing the Union army's rear. The only problem was that the report was completely inaccurate; Stuart was actually southeast near Spotsylvania, where his cavalry would be in a position to ride north and intercept Warren's advancing V Corps.

As the armies' movements progressed on May 4, Grant and Meade had no clue that Lee's army was in close proximity, so they ultimately decided to camp near Chancellorsville, giving their gigantic wagon trains a chance to stay close. It had only taken a day for everything to fall Lee's way. Two of his corps were in position to intercept the Army of the Potomac from the west as it was marching south, and one of the Union army's three corps was marching on a separate road and wouldn't be able to immediately come to the other two corps' assistance in the event of a surprise attack.

Chapter 3: May 5

The armies' dispositions on the morning of May 5

Although Grant did not realize that Lee's army was closing in on his, he did have the wherewithal to face his army west when it wasn't marching south, aware that if an attack did come, it would come from that direction. Indeed, it wouldn't take long for the armies to run into each other on May 5.

As Warren's column started marching south around dawn on the 5th, it ran into Ewell's corps heading east on the Orange Turnpike toward him around 6:00 a.m. Shortly after that, Union cavalry reported Confederate infantry (Hill's Corps) marching in force east down the Orange Plank Road. In response, Grant immediately scrambled to form a battle line on both of Warren's flanks while preparing to attack whatever force was in his front, but with Hancock's II Corps too far away, Grant had to order up one of the divisions in Sedgwick's corps to advance and join Warren's left flank while the rest of the VI Corps formed on Warren's right flank:

> "My orders were given through General Meade for an early advance on the morning of the 5th. Warren was to move to Parker's store, and Wilson's cavalry—then at Parker's store—to move on to Craig's meeting-house. Sedgwick followed Warren, closing in on his right. The Army of the Potomac was facing to the west, though our advance was made to the south, except when facing the enemy. Hancock was to move south-westward to join on the left of Warren, his left to reach to Shady Grove Church.
>
> At six o'clock, before reaching Parker's store, Warren discovered the enemy. He sent word back to this effect, and was ordered to halt and prepare to meet and attack him.

Wright, with his division of Sedgwick's corps, was ordered, by any road he could find, to join on to Warren's right, and Getty with his division, also of Sedgwick's corps, was ordered to move rapidly by Warren's rear and get on his left. This was the speediest way to reinforce Warren who was confronting the enemy on both the Orange plank and turnpike roads."

Grant's aide, Theodore Lyman, would later describe just how difficult the Wilderness was to maneuver around near the Orange Plank Road: "The very worst of it is parallel with Orange plank and upper part of the Brock road. Here it is mostly a low, continuous, thick growth of small saplings, fifteen to thirty feet high and seldom larger than one's arm. The half-grown leaves added to the natural obscurity, and there were many places where a line of troops could with difficulty be seen at fifty yards. This was the terrain on which we were called to manoeuvre a great army."

As Grant's orders were put into motion and Warren started to prepare a battle line, Ewell's corps started going about digging in, building earthworks and fortifications to the west near Saunders Field, a small clearing in the dense woods near the Turnpike. Though Lee obviously wanted to block Grant's march and ensnare him in the Wilderness, he also didn't want to give battle himself until he could get Longstreet up. When Longstreet received orders to march, it was nearly 1:00 p.m. and his corps would have to march nearly 30 miles. Luckily for the Confederates, Hancock's II Corps would also not be in position to link up with Getty's division on Warren's left until the middle of the afternoon at the earliest.

Grant and Meade initially believed that Ewell's corps was not an entire corps but merely an advance guard, an assumption that was dispelled when Warren's men approached Saunders Field only to find the Confederates' defensive line extended past his right flank. Warren suggested to Meade that his assault on the Confederate line not take place until Sedgwick's VI Corps joined his right, but delays in their march eventually induced the frustrated Meade into ordering an attack at 1:00 p.m. regardless of Sedgwick's positioning.

The afternoon of May 5

It didn't take long for Warren's men to suffer for the decision. Although the clearing actually allowed for a cohesive line to form and advance, the outflanked Union soldiers experienced devastating enfilades from Confederate soldiers on their right, compelling Romeyn Ayres's brigade to halt its forward movement even as the brigades to their left kept moving forward. In fact, Joseph Bartlett's brigade managed to pierce the Confederate line by overrunning a Confederate brigade led by John M. Jones, who was killed during the fight. Unfortunately, this breakthrough could not be exploited due to the fact that the inability of Ayres to move his brigade forward opened up Bartlett's right flank to the same kind of enfilade that pinned down Ayres in the first place.

As the general fight continued, Lyman described what it was like behind the lines, as general officers from the various Union corps were trying to get their commands to their respective positions.

I found General Getty at the plank road (a spot I shall remember for some years) and gave him instructions. He told me the whole of Hill's Corps was in his front and the skirmishers only 300 yards from us. For all I could see they might have been in Florida, but the occasional wounded men who limped by, and the sorry spectacle of two or three dead, wrapped in their blankets, showed that some fighting had already taken place. I got back and reported a little before one o'clock, and had scarcely got there when B-r-r-r-r wrang went the musketry, in front of Griffin and of Wright, which for the next hour and a half was continuous — not by volley, for that is impossible in such woods; but a continuous crackle, now swelling and now abating, and interspersed with occasional cannon. Very soon the ambulances began to go forward for their mournful freight. A little before two, I was sent with an order to a cavalry regiment, close by. The pike was a sad spectacle indeed; it was really obstructed with trains of ambulances and with the wounded on foot; all had the same question, over and over again; 'How far to the 5th Corps' hospital?'"

Although Bartlett's advance was repulsed by the shooting on his right flank, the Iron Brigade continued advancing on the left. Although this was one of the hardest and most famous brigades of the entire war, it had been so badly devastated at Gettysburg that the brigade needed to be refilled with raw recruits, to the extent that the character of the Iron Brigade in 1864 was no longer what it was in 1862 and 1863. But for a time, it didn't seem like that would matter, because the Iron Brigade made a steady advance that sent a Confederate brigade under Cullen Battle into a disorderly retreat.

The Confederates were fortunate enough to have John B. Gordon's brigade behind the line. Indicative of the confusion that both sides were experiencing in the early fighting, Gordon's brigade found itself in position to reinforce the line simply because it had marched in the direction where the gunfire sounded heaviest. Gordon recalled the scene as his men were coming up to provide reinforcements:

"Alternate confidence and apprehension were awakened as the shouts of one army or the other reached our ears. So distinct in character were these shouts that they were easily discernible. At one point the weird Confederate 'yell' told us plainly that Ewell's men were advancing. At another the huzzas, in mighty concert, of the Union troops warned us that they had repelled the Confederate charge; and as these ominous huzzas grew in volume we know that Grant's lines were moving forward. Just as the head of my column came within range of the whizzing Miniés, the Confederate yells grew fainter, and at last ceased; and the Union shout rose above the din of battle. I was already prepared by this infallible admonition for the sight of Ewell's shattered forces retreating in disorder. The oft-repeated but spasmodic efforts of first one army and then the other to break through the opposing ranks had at last been ended by the sudden rush of Grant's compact veterans from the dense covert in such numbers that Ewell's attenuated lines were driven in confusion to the rear. These retreating divisions, like broken and receding waves, rolled back against the head of my column while we were still rapidly advancing along the narrow road. The repulse had been so sudden and the confusion so great that practically no resistance was now being made to the Union advance; and the elated Federals were so near me that little time was left to bring my men from column into line in order to resist the movement or repel it by countercharge."

Gordon

As his men were coming up, Gordon ran into Ewell himself, who told Gordon that the fate of the day rested on his men's shoulders. With that, Gordon ordered his men forward, producing what he called the "strangest" scene he saw during the Civil War:

. " At this moment of dire extremity I saw General Ewell, who was still a superb horseman, notwithstanding the loss of his leg, riding in furious gallop toward me, his thoroughbred charger bounding like a deer through the dense underbrush…'General Gordon, the fate of the day depends on you, sir,' he said. 'These men will save it, sir,' I replied, more with the purpose of arousing the enthusiasm of my men than with any well-defined idea as to how we were to save it. Quickly wheeling a single regiment into line, I ordered it forward in a countercharge, while I hurried the other troops into position. The sheer audacity and dash of that regimental charge checked, as I had hoped it would, the Union advance for a few moments, giving me the essential time to throw the other troops across the Union front. Swiftly riding to the centre of my line, I gave in person the order: 'Forward!' With a deafening yell which must have been heard miles away, that glorious brigade rushed upon the hitherto advancing enemy, and by the shock of their furious onset shattered into fragments all that portion of the compact Union line which confronted my troops.

At that moment was presented one of the strangest conditions ever witnessed upon a battle-field. My command covered only a small portion of the long lines in blue, and not a single regiment of those stalwart Federals yielded except those which had been struck by the Southern advance. On both sides of the swath cut by this sweep of the Confederate scythe, the steady veterans of Grant were unshaken and still poured their incessant volleys into the retreating Confederate ranks. My command had cut its way through the Union centre, and at that moment it was in the remarkably strange position of being on identically the same general line with the enemy, the Confederates facing in one direction, the Federals in the other. Looking down that line from Grant's right toward his left, there would first have been seen a long stretch of blue uniforms, then a short stretch of gray, then another still longer of blue, in one continuous line. The situation was both unique and alarming…

As soon as my troops had broken through the Union ranks, I directed my staff to halt the command; and before the Union veterans could recover from the shock, my regiments were moving at double-quick from the centre into file right and left, thus placing them in two parallel lines, back to back, in a position at a right angle to the one held a moment before. This quickly executed manoeuvre placed one half of my command squarely upon the right flank of one portion of the enemy's unbroken line, and the other half facing in exactly the opposite direction, squarely upon the left flank of the enemy's line."

Gordon's counterattack had saved the Confederate line in that spot, but the Confederate line to his right was also being attacked by Union brigades led by Roy Stone and James C. Rice. As those attacks were being repulsed, Warren tried to bring up artillery to help the advance, only to have the Confederates surge forward and initiate hand-to-hand fighting for control of the two guns in the field. In the melee, Saunders Field caught fire, consigning some of the unfortunate injured men lying on the field to literally watch flames creep up to them before burning them to death. One of the soldiers, Private Frank Wilkeson, later recalled, "I saw many wounded soldiers in the Wilderness who hung on to their rifles, and whose intention was clearly stamped on their pallid faces. I saw one man, both of whose legs were broken, lying on the ground with his cocked rifle by his side and his ramrod in his hand, and his eyes set on the front. I knew he meant to kill himself in case of fire—knew it is surely as though I could read his thoughts."

Warren's assault had failed to exploit any of its breakthroughs, but just as his V Corps was ending its fighting, Sedgwick's VI Corps came up on their right around 3:00 p.m. and started attacking Ewell's left. Sedgwick made the attack up the Spottswood Road, but Ewell's line forced him to try to align a battle line well into the Wilderness off the road as well. For the next hour, Sedgwick's corps tried to dislodge Ewell's line, but the inability to keep a line moving forward with any semblance of coordination doomed the attempts of Union and Confederates alike to attack and counterattack. After just an hour, Sedgwick's attack began to peter out.

About a mile to the southeast, A.P. Hill's corps was confronting Getty's division, which had come up on Warren's left to hold the crossroad where the east-west Orange Plank Road intersected the north-south Brock Road. It was essential for the Union to hold that intersection to make sure that Hancock could rejoin the other two corps by marching northwest up the Brock Road toward the now pitched battle. Getty was assisted in holding the spot with some a brigade of cavalry, keeping Hill's soldiers a few hundred yards to the west while Hancock's men began to trickle up.

Some of Hancock's men came up around 4:00 p.m., and with their arrival in mind, Getty's division was ordered to attack Hill. Lyman described the scene on the Union left that afternoon:

> At 3.15 I was sent with an order to General Getty to attack at once, and to explain to him that Hancock would join also. He is a cool man, is Getty, quite a wonder; as I saw then and after. 'Go to General Eustis and General Wheaton,' he said to his aides, 'and tell them to prepare to advance at once.' And so we were getting into it! And everybody had been ordered up, including Burnside, who had crossed that very morning at Germanna Ford. General Grant had his station with us (or we with him); there he took his seat on the grass, and smoked his briarwood pipe, looking sleepy and stern and indifferent. His face, however, may wear a most pleasing smile, and I believe he is a thoroughly amiable man. That he believes in his star and takes a bright view of things is evident. At 4.15 P. M. General Meade ordered me to take some orderlies, go to General Hancock (whose musketry we could now hear on the left) and send him back reports, staying there till dark. Delightful! At the crossing of the dotted cross-road with the plank sat Hancock, on his fine horse — the preux chevalier of this campaign — a glorious soldier, indeed! The musketry was crashing in the woods in our front, and stray balls — too many to be pleasant — were coming about. It's all very well for novels, but I don't like such places and go there only when ordered. 'Report to General Meade,' said Hancock, 'that it is very hard to bring up troops in this wood, and that only a part of my Corps is up, but I will do as well as I can.' Up rides an officer: 'Sir! General Getty is hard pressed and nearly out of ammunition!' 'Tell him to hold on and

General Gibbon will be up to help him.' Another officer: 'General Mott's division has broken, sir, and is coming back.' 'Tell him to stop them, sir!!' roared Hancock in a voice of a trumpet. As he spoke, a crowd of troops came from the woods and fell back into the Brock road. Hancock dashed among them. 'Halt here! halt here! Form behind this rifle-pit. Major Mitchell, go to Gibbon and tell him to come up on the double-quick!' It was a welcome sight to see Carroll's brigade coming along that Brock road, he riding at their head as calm as a May morning. 'Left face — prime — forward,' and the line disappeared in the woods to waken the musketry with double violence. Carroll was brought back wounded. Up came Hays's brigade, disappeared in the woods, and, in a few minutes, General Hays was carried past me, covered with blood, shot through the head.

As Lyman's account indicates, the fighting was back-and-forth, with both Hill's corps and Hancock's corps entangled in underbrush and forest near a small stream called the Ny River. Lee had made his headquarters at the Widow Tapp's house in a small clearing just behind Hill's defensive line, and at one point some Union soldiers came streaming out of the woods and into the clearing, coming into eyesight of Lee while he was discussing the fighting with Hill and JEB Stuart. Thankfully for the three Confederate officers, the Union soldiers were just as confused as they were, and when they realized there were Confederates in their front they turned right back around and reentered the forest.

When the fighting ended that night, both lines had maintained their respective positions, and the soldiers on both sides immediately started digging in and preparing strong defensive fortifications. There was still a gap separating the two armies from completely forming one line, something Grant would attempt to remedy the next day by bringing up Burnside's IX Corps and something that Lee could do nothing about other than to gamble that the confusing Wilderness would protect Hill's left flank and Ewell's right flank.

"After the close of the battle of the 5th of May my orders were given for the following morning. We knew Longstreet with 12,000 men was on his way to join Hill's right, near the Brock Road, and might arrive during the night. I was anxious that the rebels should not take the initiative in the morning, and therefore ordered Hancock to make an assault at 4.30 o'clock. Meade asked to have the hour changed to six. Deferring to his wishes as far as I was willing, the order was modified and five was fixed as the hour to move.

Hancock had now fully one-half of the Army of the Potomac. Wadsworth with his division, which had arrived the night before, lay in a line perpendicular to that held by Hill, and to the right of Hancock. He was directed to move at the same time, and to attack Hill's left.

Burnside, who was coming up with two divisions, was directed to get in between

Warren and Wadsworth, and attack as soon as he could get in position to do so. Sedgwick and Warren were to make attacks in their front, to detain as many of the enemy as they could and to take advantage of any attempt to reinforce Hill from that quarter. Burnside was ordered if he should succeed in breaking the enemy's centre, to swing around to the left and envelop the right of Lee's army. Hancock was informed of all the movements ordered."

Despite being outnumbered and not gaining any ground, Lee had kept Grant's army in the Wilderness, and he could count on Longstreet arriving at some point to fight tomorrow. Lee reported back to Richmond:

"The enemy crossed the Rapidan yesterday at Ely's and Germanna Fords. Two corps of this army moved to oppose him: Ewell's, by the old turnpike, and Hill's, by the plank road. They arrived this morning in close proximity to the enemy's line of march. A strong attack was made upon Ewell, who repulsed it, capturing many prisoners and four pieces of artillery. The enemy subsequently concentrated upon General Hill, who, with Heth's and Wilcox's divisions, successfully resisted repeated and desperate assaults. A large force of cavalry and artillery on our right flank was driven back by Rosser's brigade. By the blessing of God we maintained our position against every effort until night, when the contest closed."

Gordon summed up Confederate sentiments on the night of May 5:

"Both sides labored all night in the dark and dense woodland, throwing up such breastworks as were possible--a most timely preparation for the next day's conflicts. My own command was ordered during the night to the extreme left of Lee's lines, under the apprehension that Grant's right overlapped and endangered our left flank.

Thus ended the 5th of May, which had witnessed the first desperate encounter between Grant and Lee. The fighting had not involved the whole of either army, but it was fierce and bloody. It would be unjust to claim that either of the famous leaders had achieved a signal victory. Both sides had left their dead scattered through the bullet-riddled underbrush. The Confederates drew comfort from the fact that in the shifting fortunes of the day theirs was the last advance, that the battle had ended near where it had begun, and that the Union advance had been successfully repulsed."

Chapter 4: May 6

At the beginning of May 6, Grant was hoping that his advantage in manpower would make it possible for Burnside's IX Corps to interpose itself between Hill and Ewell, making it possible to cut Lee's army in half and destroy them. But he wasn't the only one intending to make an attack; the characteristically aggressive Lee had decided to keep Hill's outnumbered men in position and even use them to attack Hancock's corps, operating under the assumption that Longstreet's corps would be up in the morning and could sustain the momentum of the advance.

Naturally, things would not go according to plan for either Grant or Lee. Due to miscommunications, or due to the understanding that they would be used to attack the following morning, multiple divisions in Hill's corps decided not to dig in and build defensive fortifications on the night of May 5. While that may have been understandable and normal in 1862, experience had taught both sides by 1864 that the first thing to do once they had an established line was to start digging in and building earthworks that would protect them during an attack. By the end of the war, the Civil War had become a forerunner to the trench warfare of World War I, and if an army was given 24 hours to entrench, their position became practically unassailable. Grant described the process in his memoirs:

> "[I]n every change of position or halt for the night, whether confronting the enemy or not, the moment arms were stacked the men intrenched themselves. For this purpose they would build up piles of logs or rails if they could be found in their front, and dig a ditch, throwing the dirt forward on the timber. Thus the digging they did counted in making a depression to stand in, and increased the elevation in front of them. It was wonderful how quickly they could in this way construct defences of considerable strength. When a halt was made with the view of assaulting the enemy, or in his presence, these would be strengthened or their positions changed under the direction of engineer officers."

Moreover, Lee had expected that Longstreet's men would be up at dawn, allowing him to slide Hill's corps to the left and eventually link up with Ewell, which would have put Hill in the gap that Grant intended to push Burnside's IX Corps through. However, the nature of the night marching, the nature of the roads, and the nature of the terrain all delayed Longstreet's marching during the early morning hours of May 6. Longstreet expressed some of the causes of the inevitable delays:

> "About eleven o'clock in the night the guide reported from General Lee to conduct my command through the wood across to the Plank road, and at one o'clock the march was resumed. The road was overgrown by the bushes, except the side-tracks made by the draft animals and the ruts of wheels which marked occasional lines in its course. After a time the wood became less dense, and the unused road was more difficult to follow, and presently the guide found that there was no road under him; but no time was lost, as, by ordering the lines of the divisions doubled, they were ready when the trail was found, and the march continued in double line. At daylight we entered the Plank road, and filed down towards the field of strife of the afternoon of the 5th and daylight of the 6th."

Longstreet's men would be advancing down the Orange Plank Road toward Hill's corps and the Union line by the break of dawn, but by then Hancock's attack, which began at Grant's appointed time of 5:00 a.m., was already starting to steadily drive Hill's corps back. Even several decades later, Longstreet's frustration with Hill's corps was evident when explaining what happened in his memoirs:

> "R. H. Anderson's division of the Third Corps, marching on the Plank road, had rested at Verdierville during the night, and was called to the front in the morning. The divisions of Heth and Wilcox rested during the night of the 5th where the battle of that day ceased, but did not prepare ammunition nor strengthen their lines for defence, because informed that they were to be relieved from the front. Both the division commanders claim that they were to be relieved, and that they were ordered not to intrench or replenish supplies. So it seems that they were all night within hearing of the voices of Hancock's men, not even reorganizing their lines so as to offer a front of battle! General Heth has stated that he proposed to arrange for battle, but was ordered to give his men rest. While Hancock was sending men to his advanced line during the night and intrenching there and on his second line, the Confederates were all night idle."

Longstreet wouldn't be the only one frustrated. One of the reasons Meade had lobbied Grant to push back the time for Hancock's assault was concern that Burnside wouldn't be in position yet. While that convinced Grant to push back the attack to 5:00, that still wasn't enough time for Burnside's IX Corps to be in position, something that at least a few of his comrades anticipated. Lyman was ordered to ride over to Hancock and keep Meade and Grant informed of the attack's results, and he later recalled the morning attack:

> "It was after five when I mounted, and already the spattering fire showed that the skirmishers were pushing out; as I rode down the crossroad, two or three crashing volleys rang through the woods, and then the whole front was alive with musketry. I found General Hancock at the crossing of the plank: he was wreathed with smiles. 'We are driving them, sir; tell General Meade we are driving them most beautifully. Birney has gone in and he is just cleaning them out be-au-ti-fully!' This was quite apparent from the distance of the receding firing and the absence of those infernal minie balls. 'I

am ordered to tell you, sir, that only one division of General Burnside is up, but that he will go in as soon as he can be put in position.' Hancock's face changed. 'I knew it!' he said vehemently. 'Just what I expected. If he could attack now, we would smash A. P. Hill all to pieces!' And very true were his words. Meantime, some hundreds of prisoners were brought in; all from Hill's troops. Presently, however, the firing seemed to wake again with renewed fury; and in a little while a soldier came up to me and said: 'I was ordered to report that this prisoner here belongs to Longstreet's Corps.' 'Do you belong to Longstreet?' I hastened to ask. 'Ya-as, sir,' said grey-back, and was marched to the rear. It was too true!

Writing in his memoirs, Grant later expressed the belief that it was the Wilderness, not Longstreet, that would prove Hancock's undoing:

"I believed then, and see no reason to change that opinion now, that if the country had been such that Hancock and his command could have seen the confusion and panic in the lines of the enemy, it would have been taken advantage of so effectually that Lee would not have made another stand outside of his Richmond defences.

Gibbon commanded Hancock's left, and was ordered to attack, but was not able to accomplish much.

On the morning of the 6th Sheridan was sent to connect with Hancock's left and attack the enemy's cavalry who were trying to get on our left and rear. He met them at the intersection of the Furnace and Brock roads and at Todd's Tavern, and defeated them at both places. Later he was attacked, and again the enemy was repulsed.

Hancock heard the firing between Sheridan and Stuart, and thinking the enemy coming by that road, still further reinforced his position guarding the entrance to the Brock Road. Another incident happened during the day to further induce Hancock to weaken his attacking column. Word reached him that troops were seen moving towards him from the direction of Todd's Tavern, and Brooke's brigade was detached to meet this new enemy; but the troops approaching proved to be several hundred convalescents coming from Chancellorsville, by the road Hancock had advanced upon, to join their respective commands. At 6.50 o'clock A.M., Burnside, who had passed Wilderness Tavern at six o'clock, was ordered to send a division to the support of Hancock, but to continue with the remainder of his command in the execution of his previous order. The difficulty of making a way through the dense forests prevented Burnside from getting up in time to be of any service on the forenoon of the sixth."

Longstreet's counterattack

Longstreet's late arrival meant Lee could not slide Hill's corps to the left, but it meant that his corps was in just the right place to blunt Hancock's assault and launch a fierce counterattack itself. As Longstreet's column came marching up, Lee was so excited that he began riding at the head of the column, acting as though he intended to lead the counterattack himself. Writing about the episode decades later, Longstreet quipped that if Lee was going to lead the charge, he'd like to move farther behind the lines to safety:

> "Hancock advanced and struck the divisions before sunrise, just as my command reported to General Lee. My line was formed on the right and left of the Plank road, Kershaw on the right, Field on the left. As the line deployed, the divisions of Heth and Wilcox came back upon us in disorder, more and more confused as their steps hurried under Hancock's musketry. As my ranks formed the men broke files to give free

passage for their comrades to the rear. The advancing fire was getting brisk, but not a shot was fired in return by my troops until the divisions were ready. Three of Field's brigades, the Texas, Alabama, and Benning's Georgia, were formed in line on the left of the road, and three of Kershaw's on the right. General Lee, appalled at the condition of affairs, thought to lead the Texas brigade alone into desperate charge, before my lines were well formed. The ordeal was trying, but the steady troops, seeing him off his balance, refused to follow, begged him to retire, and presently Colonel Venable, of his staff, reported to me General Lee's efforts to lead the brigade, and suggested that I should try to call him from it. I asked that he would say, with my compliments, that his line would be recovered in an hour if he would permit me to handle the troops, but if my services were not needed, I would like to ride to some place of safety, as it was not quite comfortable where we were."

Of course, Lee would not end up leading the charge, and he wouldn't need to. Longstreet has often been criticized for being reluctant to move, and slow when he did, but once he put his corps into action, he was one of the best generals the Civil War had. As one Confederate soldier put it, "Like a fine lady at a party, Longstreet was often late in his arrival at the ball. But he always made a sensation and that of delight, when he got in, with the grand old First Corps sweeping behind him as his train."

Longstreet's counterattack also had the advantage of coming at a time when the Union charge had progressed a mile and inevitably resulted in soldiers getting intermingled with other commands and unit cohesion becoming relatively impossible. The Wilderness also hid Longstreet's impending attack until his men were within just a few hundred yards, but it also caused Longstreet some difficulty as well. Longstreet explained, "As full lines of battle could not be handled through the thick wood, I ordered the advance of the six brigades by heavy skirmish lines, to be followed by stronger supporting lines. Hancock's lines, thinned by their push through the wood, and somewhat by the fire of the disordered divisions, weaker than my line of fresh and more lively skirmishers, were checked by our first steady, rolling fire, and after a brisk fusillade were pushed back to their intrenched line, when the fight became steady and very firm, occasionally swinging parts of my line back and compelling the reserves to move forward and recover it."

While the counterattack blunted Hancock's momentum and also kept some of the men from Burnside's IX Corps occupied, Longstreet had heard about an unfinished railroad bed south of the Plank Road that his troops might be able to travel through and come up on Hancock's left flank by surprise. When the four brigades traveled through the railroad cut and hit Hancock's left flank at 11:00, it completely rolled up Hancock's battle line. Hancock would later claim that his line was rolled up "like a wet blanket", but Longstreet's men were still advancing as Hancock's men retreated. Longstreet wrote:

"As soon as the troops struck Hancock his line began to break, first slowly, then rapidly. Somehow, as they retreated, a fire was accidentally started in the dry leaves, and began to spread as the Confederates advanced. Mahone's brigade approached the burning leaves and part of it broke off a little to get around, but the Twelfth Virginia was not obstructed by the blaze and moved directly on. At the Plank road Colonel Sorrel rode back to join us. All of the enemy's battle on the right of the Plank road was broken up, and General Field was fighting severely with his three brigades on the left against Wadsworth and Stevenson, pushing them a little.

General Smith then came and reported a way across the Brock road that would turn Hancock's extreme left. He was asked to conduct the flanking brigades and handle them as the ranking officer. He was a splendid tactician as well as skilful engineer, and gallant withal. He started, and, not to lose time or distance, moved by inversion, Wofford's left leading, Wofford's favorite manoeuvre. As Wofford's left stepped out, the other troops moved down the Plank road, Jenkins's brigade by the road, Kershaw's division alongside. I rode at the head of the column, Jenkins, Kershaw, and the staff with me. After discussing the dispositions of their troops for reopening battle, Jenkins rode closer to offer congratulations, saying, 'I am happy; I have felt despair of the cause for some months, but am relieved, and feel assured that we will put the enemy back across the Rapidan before night." Little did he or I think these sanguine words were the last he would utter.'"

On May 2, 1863, almost a year to the day that the battle was raging in the Wilderness, Stonewall Jackson had been mortally wounded by his own men while leading a successful flank attack after being mistaken for advancing Union soldiers. On May 6, 1864, less than 5 miles to the west, Longstreet nearly suffered the same fate.

"As the Twelfth Regiment marched back to find its place on the other side of the Plank road, it was mistaken, in the wood, for an advance of the enemy, and fire was opened on it from the other regiments of the brigade. The men threw themselves to the ground to let the fire pass. Just then our party of officers was up and rode under the fire. General Jenkins had not finished the expressions of joyful congratulations which I have quoted when he fell mortally wounded.

Captain Doby and the orderly, Bowen, of Kershaw's staff, were killed. General Kershaw turned to quiet the troops, when Jenkins's brigade with levelled guns were in the act of returning the fire of the supposed enemy concealed in the wood, but as Kershaw's clear voice called out 'F-r-i-e-n-d-s!' the arms were recovered, without a shot in return, and the men threw themselves down upon their faces.

At the moment that Jenkins fell I received a severe shock from a minie ball passing through my throat and right shoulder. The blow lifted me from the saddle, and my right arm dropped to my side, but I settled back to my seat, and started to ride on, when in a minute the flow of blood admonished me that my work for the day was done. As I turned to ride back, members of the staff, seeing me about to fall, dismounted and lifted me to the ground."

Longstreet's day was done, and so was his involvement in the Overland Campaign as a whole. He would have to spend the next 5 months convalescing and wouldn't return to Lee's army until October, several months into the siege of Petersburg. To say his loss at this juncture would be an understatement, something acknowledged by both sides. Grant claimed, "His loss was a severe one to Lee, and compensated in a great measure for the mishap, or misapprehensions, which had fallen to our lot during the day." The leader of the artillery in Longstreet's corps, Porter Alexander, went even further, arguing, "I have always believed that, but for Longstreet's fall, the panic which was fairly underway in Hancock's Corps would have been extended and have resulted in Grant's being forced to retreat back across the Rapidan."

The delays and confusion brought about by Longstreet's injury hampered the effectiveness of his counterattack. Richard Anderson succeeded him, but he was unfamiliar with the entire corps' dispositions and needed to try to confer with the grievously wounded Longstreet to get the information after the corps commander had been shot through the throat. Lee would also be forced to take a more active role on his right, personally directing the line.

How much of a difference Longstreet's loss made continues to be debated, but there's no question that Hancock's defensive line ultimately held because of the defensive fortifications his men had constructed the night before. Although the Confederates were able to get into their rifle pits, the II Corps eventually repulsed them, forcing Lee to take time to reform his lines and prepare another attack for later in the afternoon.

Grant later wrote in his memoirs, "After Longstreet's removal from the field Lee took command of his right in person. He was not able, however, to rally his men to attack Hancock's position, and withdrew from our front for the purpose of reforming. Hancock sent a brigade to clear his front of all remnants that might be left of Longstreet's or Hill's commands. This brigade having been formed at right angles to the intrenchments held by Hancock's command, swept down the whole length of them from left to right. A brigade of the enemy was encountered in this move; but it broke and disappeared without a contest…Firing was continued after this, but with less fury. Burnside had not yet been able to get up to render any assistance. But it was now only about nine in the morning, and he was getting into position on Hancock's right."

When Burnside arrived, Anderson had to swing part of Longstreet's corps to face that new threat, until the corps had practically formed at a right angle. Burnside's arrival and Hancock's defensive fortifications ensured that the Army of the Potomac's left would remain secure throughout the day.

The afternoon of May 6

Grant's left flank had come close to disaster as a result of a surprise flank attack, and it turned out that his right would suffer nearly the same fate later in the day. While the fighting was going on south of them, John Gordon's scouts on the extreme left of the Confederate line reported the potential of turning Sedgwick's right flank. Gordon verified the situation for himself, and later wrote of his great surprise:

"THE night of the 5th of May was far spent when my command reached its destination on the extreme Confederate left. The men were directed to sleep on their arms during the remaining hours of darkness. Scouts were at once sent to the front to feel their way through the thickets and ascertain, if possible, where the extreme right of Grant's line rested. At early dawn these trusted men reported that they had found it: that it rested in the woods only a short distance in our front, that it was wholly unprotected, and that the Confederate lines stretched a considerable distance beyond the Union right, overlapping it. I was so impressed with the importance of this report and with the necessity of verifying its accuracy that I sent others to make the examination, with additional instructions to proceed to the rear of Grant's right and ascertain if the exposed flank were supported by troops held in reserve behind it. The former report was not only confirmed as to the exposed position of that flank, but the astounding information was brought that there was not a supporting force within several miles of it.

Much of this scouting had been done in the late hours of the night and before sunrise on the morning of the 6th. Meantime, as this information came my brain was throbbing with the tremendous possibilities to which such a situation invited us, provided the conditions were really as reported. Mounting my horse in the early morning and guided by some of these explorers, I rode into the unoccupied woodland to see for myself. It is enough to say that I found the reports correct in every particular. Riding back toward my line, I was guided by the scouts to the point near which they had located the right of the Union army. Dismounting and creeping slowly and cautiously through the dense woods, we were soon in ear-shot of an unsuppressed and merry clatter of voices. A few feet nearer, and through a narrow vista, I was shown the end of General Grant's temporary breastworks. There was no line guarding this flank. As far as my eye could reach, the Union soldiers were seated on the margin of the rifle-pits, taking their breakfast. Small fires were burning over which they were boiling their coffee, while their guns leaned against the works in their immediate front.

No more time was consumed in scouting. The revelations had amazed me and filled me with confident anticipations of unprecedented victory. It was evident that General Grant had decided to make his heaviest assaults upon the Confederate right, and for this purpose had ordered his reserves to that flank. By some inconceivable oversight on the part of his subordinates, his own right flank had been left in the extremely exposed condition in which my scouts had found it. Undoubtedly the officer who located that battle line for General Grant or for General Sedgwick was under the impression that there were no Confederates in front of that portion of it; and this was probably true at the time the location was made. That fact, however, did not justify the officer in leaving his flank (which is the most vulnerable part of an army) thus unguarded for a whole night after the battle...

During the night, while the over-confident Union officer and his men slept in fancied security, my men stole silently through the thickets and planted a hostile line not only in his immediate front, but overlapping it by more than the full length of my command. All intelligent military critics will certainly agree that such an opportunity as was here presented for the overthrow of a great army has rarely occurred in the conduct of a war."

Once he was certain of the Union line's situation, Gordon began forming the plan that he thought could destroy the entire Army of the Potomac:

"As later developments proved, one brigade on the flank was all that was needed for the inauguration of the plan and the demonstration of its possibilities. The details of the plan were as follows: While the unsuspecting Federals were drinking their coffee, my troops were to move quickly and quietly behind the screen of thick underbrush and form squarely on Sedgwick's strangely exposed flank, reaching a point far beyond that flank and lapping around his rear, so as to capture his routed men as they broke to the rear. While my command rushed from this ambush a simultaneous demonstration was to be made along his front. As each of Sedgwick's brigades gave way in confusion, the corresponding Confederate brigade, whose front was thus cleared on the general line, was to swing into the column of attack on the flank, thus swelling at each step of our advance the numbers, power, and momentum of the Confederate forces as they swept down the line of works and extended another brigade's length to the unprotected Union rear. As each of the Union brigades, divisions, and corps were struck by such an absolutely resistless charge upon the flank and rear, they must fly or be captured. The effective force of Grant's army would be thus constantly diminished, and in the same proportion the column of attack would be steadily augmented."

Despite the fact Gordon had determined the state of Sedgwick's flank in the early morning hours of May 6, the flank attack did not start until the late afternoon. As Gordon anticipated, the flank attack was decisive from the very beginning:

"The Georgia brigade (Gordon's) was directed to make the assault, and the North Carolina brigade (Johnson's) was ordered to move farther to the Union rear and to keep as nearly as possible in touch with the attacking force and to gather up Sedgwick's men as they broke to the rear. As the sun went down these troops were ordered forward. In less than ten minutes they struck the Union flank and with thrilling yells rushed upon it and along the Union works, shattering regiments and brigades, and throwing them into wildest confusion and panic. There was practically no resistance. There could be none. The Georgians, commanded by that intrepid leader, Clement A. Evans, were on the flank, and the North Carolinians, led by a brilliant young officer, Robert Johnson, were sweeping around to the rear, without a shot in their front. There was nothing for the

brave Federals to do but to fly. There was no time given them to file out from their
works and form a new line of resistance. This was attempted again and again; but in
every instance the swiftly moving Confederates were upon them, pouring a consuming
fire into their half-formed ranks and shivering one command after another in quick
succession. The gallant Union leaders, Generals Seymour and Shaler, rode among their
panic-stricken troops in the heroic endeavor to form them into a new line. Their brave
efforts were worse than unavailing, for both of these superb officers, with large
numbers of their brigades, were quickly gathered as prisoners of war in the Confederate
net; and nearly the whole of Sedgwick's corps was disorganized.

It will be seen that my troops were compelled to halt at last, not by the enemy's
resistance, but solely by the darkness and the cross-fire from Confederates. Had
daylight lasted one half-hour longer, there would not have been left an organized
company in Sedgwick's corps. Even as it was, all accounts agree that his whole
command was shaken. As I rode abreast of the Georgians, who were moving swiftly
and with slight resistance, the last scene which met my eye as the curtain of night shut
off the view was the crumbling of the Union lines as they bravely but vainly
endeavored to file out of their works and form a new line under the furious onset and
withering fire of the Confederates."

Gordon's flank attack on Sedgwick also led to one of Grant's most famous quotes of the war,
as remembered by Union general Horace Porter. Porter recalled the scene at headquarters when
Sedgwick's line began to unravel:

"It was now about sundown; the storm of battle which had raged with unabated fury
from early dawn had been succeeded by a calm . . . . . Just then the stillness was broken
by heavy volleys of musketry on our extreme right, which told that Sedgwick had been
assaulted and was actually engaged with the enemy. The attack against which the
general-in-chief during the day had ordered every precaution to be taken had now been
made . . . . . Generals Grant and Meade, accompanied by me and one or two other staff
officers, walked rapidly over to Meade's tent, and found that the reports still coming in
were bringing news of increasing disaster. It was soon reported that General Shaler and
part of his brigade had been captured; then that General Seymour and several hundred
of his men had fallen into the hands of the enemy; afterward that our right had been
turned, and Ferrero's division cut off and forced back upon the Rapidan . . . . . Aides
came galloping in from the right, laboring under intense excitement, talking wildly and
giving the most exaggerated reports of the engagement. Some declared that a large
force had broken and scattered Sedgwick's entire corps. Others insisted that the enemy
had turned our right completely and captured the wagon-train. . . . A general officer
came in from his command at this juncture and said to the general-in-chief, speaking
rapidly and laboring under considerable excitement:'General Grant, this is a crisis that

cannot be looked upon too seriously; I know Lee's methods well by past experience; he will throw his whole army between us and the Rapidan and cut us off completely from our communications.'

The general rose to his feet, took his cigar out of his mouth, turned to the officer, and replied, with a degree of animation which he seldom manifested: 'Oh, I am heartily tired of hearing about what Lee is going to do. Some of you always seem to think he is suddenly going to turn a double somersault, and land in our rear and on both of our flanks at the same time. Go back to your command, and try to think what we are going to do ourselves, instead of what Lee is going to do.' The officer retired rather crestfallen, and without saying a word in reply. This recalls a very pertinent criticism regarding his chief once made in my presence by General Sherman. He said: 'Grant always seemed pretty certain to win when he went into a fight with anything like equal numbers. I believe the chief reason why he was more successful than others was that while they were thinking so much about what the enemy was going to do, Grant was thinking all the time about what he was going to do himself.'"

Ultimately, Gordon's flank attack was conducted too late in the day to achieve the result he had hoped for. It would have been difficult enough in the Wilderness to conduct such an attack during the day, but with night falling and reinforcements brought up, Gordon's flank attack ultimately lost its momentum.

While Gordon obviously gave a rosy projection of what his flank attack could have achieved, the real historical question is why there was a delay of nearly 9 hours before the attack started. Gordon later blamed Ewell and his division commander, Jubal Early:

"When the plan for assault was fully matured, it was presented, with all its tremendous possibilities and with the full information which had been acquired by scouts and by my own personal and exhaustive examination. With all the earnestness that comes from deep conviction, the prompt adoption and vigorous execution of the plan were asked and urged. General Early at once opposed it. He said that Burnside's corps was immediately behind Sedgwick's right to protect it from any such flank attack; that if I should attempt such movement, Burnside would assail my flank and rout or capture all my men. He was so firmly fixed in his belief that Burnside's corps was where he declared it to be that he was not perceptibly affected by the repeated reports of scouts, nor my own statement that I myself had ridden for miles in rear of Sedgwick's right, and that neither Burnside's corps nor any other troops were there. General Ewell, whose province it was to decide the controversy, hesitated. He was naturally reluctant to take issue with my superior officer in a matter about which he could have no personal knowledge, because of the fact that his headquarters as corps-commander were located at considerable distance from this immediate locality. In view of General Early's protest, he was unwilling to order the attack or to grant me permission to make it, even upon my proposing to assume all responsibility of disaster, should any occur."

Early explained why he was hesitant to support making the flank attack in his own memoirs, and why the attack was made when it was:

"In the meantime General Gordon had sent out a scouting party on foot, which discovered what was supposed to be the enemy's right flank resting in the woods, in front of my division; and, during my absence while posting Johnston's brigade, he reported the fact to General Ewell, and suggested the propriety of attacking this flank of the enemy with his brigade, which was not engaged. On my return, the subject was mentioned to me by General Ewell, and I stated to him the danger and risk of making the attack under the circumstances, as a column was threatening our left flank and Burnside's corps was in rear of the enemy's flank, on which the attack was suggested. General Ewell concurred with me in this opinion, and the impolicy of the attempt at that time was obvious, as we had no reserves, and, if it failed, and the enemy showed any enterprise, a serious disaster would befall, not only our corps, but General Lee's whole army. In the afternoon, when the column threatening our left had been withdrawn, and it had been ascertained that Burnside had gone to Grant's left, on account of the heavy fighting on that flank, at my suggestion, General Ewell ordered the movement which Gordon had proposed…

Gordon succeeded in throwing the enemy's right flank into great confusion, capturing two brigadier generals (Seymour and Shaler), and several hundred prisoners, all of the 6th corps, under Sedgwick. The advance of Pegram's brigade, and the demonstration of Johnston's brigade in the rear, where it encountered a part of the enemy's force and captured some prisoners, contributed materially to the result. It was fortunate, however, that darkness came to close this affair, as the enemy, if he had been able to discover the disorder on our side, might have brought up fresh troops and availed himself of our condition. As it was, doubtless, the lateness of the hour caused him to be surprised, and the approaching darkness increased the confusion in his ranks, as he could not see the strength of the attacking force, and probably imagined it to be much more formidable than it really was. All of the brigades engaged in the attack were drawn back, and formed on a new line in front of the old one, and obliquely to it."

While Early may have been accurate in the belief that Burnside was behind Sedgwick early in the morning of May 6, it's also true that Burnside had been given orders to march further south and post himself on Sedgwick's left and Hancock's right. For his part, Grant pointed to the fact that he was sending reinforcements in his memoirs and also cited Early's memoirs, writing, "The defence, however, was vigorous; and night coming on, the enemy was thrown into as much confusion as our troops, engaged, were. Early says in his Memoirs that if we had discovered the confusion in his lines we might have brought fresh troops to his great discomfort. Many officers, who had not been attacked by Early, continued coming to my headquarters even after Sedgwick had rectified his lines a little farther to the rear, with news of the disaster, fully impressed with the idea that the enemy was pushing on and would soon be upon me."

Regardless, Gordon's attack brought an end to the fighting. On May 7, with the two armies in the same lines staring each other down, Grant issued marching orders to his army, beginning the process of delicately pulling out of his defensive lines in the face of Lee's army. The two days had produced nearly 30,000 casualties, with over 17,000 Union soldiers killed, wounded or captured and over 11,000 Confederates suffering the same fate.

Chapter 5: The Campaign Continues

The battle was over, but who had won it? Grant would later call the Battle of the Wilderness a Union victory, writing, "Our victory consisted in having successfully crossed a formidable stream, almost in the face of an enemy, and in getting the army together as a unit. We gained an advantage on the morning of the 6th, which, if it had been followed up, must have proven very decisive. In the evening the enemy gained an advantage; but was speedily repulsed. As we stood at the close, the two armies were relatively in about the same condition to meet each other as when the river divided them. But the fact of having safely crossed was a victory."

Naturally, Lee saw it from a different perspective, telling Richmond at the end of May 6, " Early this morning as the divisions of General Hill, engaged yesterday, were being relieved, the enemy advanced and created some confusion. The ground lost was recovered as soon as the fresh troops got into position and the enemy driven back to his original line. Afterward we turned the left of his front line and drove it from the field, leaving a large number of dead and wounded in our hands, among them General Wadsworth. A subsequent attack forced the enemy into his intrenched lines on the Brock road, extending from Wilderness Tavern, on the right, to Trigg's Mill. Every advance on his part, thanks to a merciful God, has been repulsed. Our loss in killed is not large, but we have many wounded; most of them slightly, artillery being little used on either side. I grieve to announce that Lieutenant-General Longstreet was severely wounded and General Jenkins killed. General Pegram was badly wounded yesterday. General Stafford, it is hoped, will recover."

Both sides claimed victory, but who was right? In a sense, they were both right and wrong. For the third straight year, Lee's army had successfully defended an advance toward Richmond by the Army of the Potomac and inflicted more casualties upon them. Moreover, it would be Grant who disengaged from the battle and left the field to Lee. But while these suggest the Confederates had won a tactical victory, the Battle of the Wilderness would not be a strategic victory because it would not end Grant's campaign.

Although Grant had suffered more casualties, he and Lee had both lost about 17% of their armies. This worked in Grant's favor not only because his army remained much larger than Lee's but also because he could replenish his manpower much more easily. While the casualties would astound and mortify the American public, it was all part of Grant's plan to grind down the Army of Northern Virginia until it could put up no resistance. This was evident to Lee, who became increasingly more desperate to score some kind of dramatic victory that would destroy the Army of the Potomac later in the Overland Campaign.

Ultimately, if there's any legacy to come out of the Battle of the Wilderness, or any way in which it was a turning point, it was enshrined in Grant's official orders on May 7.

"Make all preparations during the day for a night march to take position at Spottsylvania C. H. with one army corps, at Todd's Tavern with one, and another near the intersection of the Piney Branch and Spottsylvania road with the road from Alsop's to Old Court House. If this move is made the trains should be thrown forward early in the morning to the Ny River.

I think it would be advisable in making the change to leave Hancock where he is until Warren passes him. He could then follow and become the right of the new line. Burnside will move to Piney Branch Church. Sedgwick can move along the pike to Chancellorsville and on to his destination. Burnside will move on the plank road to the intersection of it with the Orange and Fredericksburg plank road, then follow Sedgwick to his place of destination.

All vehicles should be got out of hearing of the enemy before the troops move, and then move off quietly.

It is more than probable that the enemy concentrate for a heavy attack on Hancock this afternoon. In case they do we must be prepared to resist them, and follow up any success we may gain, with our whole force. Such a result would necessarily modify these instructions."

Unlike McClellan, Burnside and Hooker before him, Grant's orders directed the Army of the Potomac to continue heading south. The Battle of the Wilderness had only been a beginning, not an ending. As Grant would famously telegraph Washington, D.C. a few days later, "I propose to fight it out on this line, if it takes all summer."

If the Battle of the Wilderness had been a Confederate victory, that was an opinion lost on Grant's men when they learned the new marching orders. Grant himself would recount one such scene as he put his army into motion on May 7:

"Soon after dark Warren withdrew from the front of the enemy, and was soon followed by Sedgwick. Warren's march carried him immediately behind the works where Hancock's command lay on the Brock Road. With my staff and a small escort of cavalry I preceded the troops. Meade with his staff accompanied me. The greatest enthusiasm was manifested by Hancock's men as we passed by. No doubt it was inspired by the fact that the movement was south. It indicated to them that they had passed through the 'beginning of the end' in the battle just fought. The cheering was so lusty that the enemy must have taken it for a night attack. At all events it drew from him a furious fusillade of artillery and musketry, plainly heard but not felt by us."

With that, Grant began marching his army toward Spotsylvania Court House, the area he had hoped to reach before fighting Lee in a pitched battle. Things hadn't gone according to plan in the Wilderness, but Grant and Lee would have their battle at Spotsylvania soon enough.

Bibliography

Alexander, Edward P. Military Memoirs of a Confederate: A Critical Narrative. New York: Da Capo Press, 1993.

Bonekemper, Edward H., III. A Victor, Not a Butcher: Ulysses S. Grant's Overlooked Military Genius. Washington, DC: Regnery, 2004.

Grant, Ulysses S. Personal Memoirs of U. S. Grant. 2 vols. Charles L. Webster & Company, 1885–86.

Grimsley, Mark. And Keep Moving On: The Virginia Campaign, May–June 1864. Lincoln: University of Nebraska Press, 2002.

Jaynes, Gregory, and the Editors of Time-Life Books. The Killing Ground: Wilderness to Cold Harbor. Alexandria, VA: Time-Life Books, 1986.

Longstreet, James. From Manassas to Appomattox: Memoirs of the Civil War in America. New York: Da Capo Press, 1992. First published in 1896 by J. B. Lippincott and Co.

Lyman, Theodore. With Grant and Meade: From the Wilderness to Appomattox. Edited by George R. Agassiz. Lincoln: University of Nebraska Press, 1994.

Rhea, Gordon C. The Battle of the Wilderness May 5–6, 1864. Baton Rouge: Louisiana State University Press, 1994.

Rhea, Gordon C. The Battles of Wilderness & Spotsylvania. National Park Service Civil War series. Fort Washington, PA: U.S. National Park Service and Eastern National, 1995.

Rhea, Gordon C. In the Footsteps of Grant and Lee: The Wilderness Through Cold Harbor. Baton Rouge: Louisiana State University Press, 2007.

Trudeau, Noah Andre. Bloody Roads South: The Wilderness to Cold Harbor, May–June 1864. Boston: Little, Brown & Co., 1989.

U.S. War Department, The War of the Rebellion: a Compilation of the Official Records of the Union and Confederate Armies. Washington, DC: U.S. Government Printing Office, 1880–1901.

The Battle of Spotsylvania Court House

Chapter 1: Racing to Spotsylvania

When Grant ordered Meade on the night of May 7 to have the Army of the Potomac march to Spotsylvania Court House, he did so for several reasons. In addition to disengaging from Lee at the Wilderness and bring him out into the open, Grant hoped that swift marching might get his army inbetween Lee and Richmond, which would make the Confederates even more desperate. But there was also another reason, as Grant noted in his memoirs:

"On the afternoon of the 7th I received news from Washington announcing that Sherman had probably attacked Johnston that day, and that Butler had reached City Point safely and taken it by surprise on the 5th. I had given orders for a movement by the left flank, fearing that Lee might move rapidly to Richmond to crush Butler before I could get there.

My object in moving to Spottsylvania was two-fold: first, I did not want Lee to get back to Richmond in time to attempt to crush Butler before I could get there; second, I wanted to get between his army and Richmond if possible; and, if not, to draw him into the open field. But Lee, by accident, beat us to Spottsylvania. Our wagon trains had been ordered easterly of the roads the troops were to march upon before the movement commenced. Lee interpreted this as a semi-retreat of the Army of the Potomac to Fredericksburg, and so informed his government. Accordingly he ordered Longstreet's corps—now commanded by Anderson—to move in the morning (the 8th) to Spottsylvania. But the woods being still on fire, Anderson could not go into bivouac, and marched directly on to his destination that night. By this accident Lee got possession of Spottsylvania. It is impossible to say now what would have been the result if Lee's orders had been obeyed as given; but it is certain that we would have been in Spottsylvania, and between him and his capital. My belief is that there would have been a race between the two armies to see which could reach Richmond first, and the Army of the Potomac would have had the shorter line. Thus, twice since crossing the Rapidan we came near closing the campaign, so far as battles were concerned, from the Rapidan to the James River or Richmond. The first failure was caused by our not following up the success gained over Hill's corps on the morning of the 6th, as before described: the second, when fires caused by that battle drove Anderson to make a march during the night of the 7th-8th which he was ordered to commence on the morning of the 8th. But accident often decides the fate of battle."

Grant's route to Spotsylvania Court House had been opened by Phil Sheridan's cavalry in the days before, due to the fact that Grant had initially intended to march there before engaging in battle. Sheridan's cavalry had been holding important spots, including crossings of the Ny and Po Rivers, in anticipation of that movement, but when Hancock's left was turned by Longstreet's corps on May 6, the cavalry had been hurried back north. As a result, when Grant issued the orders to march toward Spotsylvania on May 7, it was once again incumbent on the Union cavalry to ride to those spots and hold them for the infantry advance. Sheridan explained in his memoirs:

> "On the 7th of May, under directions from headquarters, Army of the Potomac, the trains were put in motion to go into park at Piney Branch Church, in anticipation of the movement that was about to be made for the possession of Spottsylvania Court House. I felt confident that the order to move the trains there had been given without a full understanding of the situation, for Piney Branch Church was now held by the enemy, a condition which had resulted from the order withdrawing the cavalry on account of the supposed disaster to Hancock's left the day before; but I thought the best way to remedy matters was to hold the trains in the vicinity of Aldrich's till the ground on which it was intended to park them should be regained.
>
> This led to the battle of Todd's Tavern, a spirited fight for the possession of the crossroads at that point, participated in by the enemy's cavalry and Gregg's division, and two brigades of Torbert's division, the latter commanded by Merritt, as Torbert became very ill on the 6th, and had to be sent to the rear. To gain the objective point — the crossroads — I directed Gregg to assail the enemy on the Catharpen road with Irvin

Gregg's brigade and drive him over Corbin's bridge, while Merritt attacked him with the Reserve brigade on the Spottsylvania road in conJunction with Davies's brigade of Gregg's division, which was to be put in on the Piney Branch Church road, and unite with Merritt's left. Davies's and Irvin Gregg's brigades on my right and left flanks met with some resistance, yet not enough to deter them from executing their orders. In front of Merritt the enemy held on more stubbornly, however, and there ensued an exceedingly severe and, at times, fluctuating fight. Finally the Confederates gave way, and we pursued them almost to Spottsylvania Court House; but deeming it prudent to recall the pursuers about dark, I encamped Gregg's and Merritt's divisions in the open fields to the east of Todd's Tavern."

As previously noted by Grant in his memoirs, the Confederates were not idle on May 7. The movements of the Union Army's logistics train had suggested to him that Grant was either moving east toward Fredericksburg or south toward Spotsylvania. Either way, Lee needed to hold the crossroads at Spotsylvania, so he gave orders to Richard Anderson's corps to occupy Spotsylvania Court House on May 8. Luckily for the Confederates, however, the desperate fighting of the 6th by that corps had sparked fires in the area of the fighting, and the putrid smells of the burning and death compelled Anderson and his soldiers to go ahead and march to Spotsylvania that night, rather than try to bivouac near the burning and dying. By 10:00 p.m., Anderson's corps was on the march toward Spotsylvania.

The same fires that had compelled the Confederates to march that night were also causing logistical problems for the Army of the Potomac's movement. In addition to the inevitable traffic jams on the roads, the Union's unfamiliarity with the area caused fits and starts, as Grant mentioned in his memoirs:

"Meade and I rode in advance. We had passed but a little way beyond our left when the road forked. We looked to see, if we could, which road Sheridan had taken with his cavalry during the day. It seemed to be the right-hand one, and accordingly we took it. We had not gone far, however, when Colonel C. B. Comstock, of my staff, with the instinct of the engineer, suspecting that we were on a road that would lead us into the lines of the enemy, if he, too, should be moving, dashed by at a rapid gallop and all alone. In a few minutes he returned and reported that Lee was moving, and that the road we were on would bring us into his lines in a short distance. We returned to the forks of the road, left a man to indicate the right road to the head of Warren's column when it should come up, and continued our journey to Todd's Tavern, where we arrived after midnight."

While the infantry struggled to get underway in the right direction, the poor relationship between Meade and Sheridan played an important role on the night of the 7th. After Sheridan's cavalry had taken up their posts to hold the necessary ground for the infantry, Meade lost his temper when he and Grant arrived near Todd's Tavern and found Sheridan's cavalry troopers sleeping near their posts. At that point, Meade ordered part of Sheridan's cavalry to help clear the road for the infantry's march, which incensed Sheridan. Sheridan later claimed that this decision prevented his cavalry from blocking the Confederates at Spotsylvania, writing:

> "Had Gregg and Merritt been permitted to proceed as they were originally instructed, it is doubtful whether the battles fought at Spottsylvania would have occurred, for these two divisions would have encountered the enemy at the Po River, and so delayed his march as to enable our infantry to reach Spottsylvania first, and thus force Lee to take up a line behind the Po. I had directed Wilson to move from the left by 'the Gate' through Spottsylvania to Snell's bridge, while Gregg and Merritt were to advance to the same point by Shady Grove and the Block House. There was nothing to prevent at least a partial success of these operations; that is to say, the concentration of the three divisions in front of Snell's bridge, even if we could not actually have gained it. But both that important point and the bridge on the Block House road were utterly ignored, and Lee's approach to Spottsylvania left entirely unobstructed, while three divisions of cavalry remained practically ineffective by reason of disjointed and irregular instructions.
>
> On the morning of the 8th, when I found that such orders had been given, I made some strong remonstrances against the course that had been pursued, but it was then too late to carry out the combinations I had projected the night before, so I proceeded to join Merritt on the Spottsylvania road. On reaching Merritt I found General Warren making complaint that the cavalry were obstructing his column, so I drew Merritt off the road, and the leading division of the Fifth Corps pushed up to the front. It got into line about 11 o'clock, and advanced to take the village, but it did not go very far before it struck Anderson's corps, and was hurled back with heavy loss. This ended all endeavor to take Spottsylvania that day."

As Sheridan's account indicates, Anderson's corps eventually forced the advanced elements of his cavalry to fall back up the road. At the same time, it's unclear whether Sheridan's two divisions of cavalry could have held off an entire Confederate corps of infantry long enough for Warren's V Corps to beat Anderson's corps to the spot. For his part, Grant later insisted it would have been likely, writing, "Wilson, who was ordered to seize the town, did so, with his division of cavalry; but he could not hold it against the Confederate corps which had not been detained at the crossing of the Po, as it would have been but for the unfortunate change in Merritt's orders. Had he been permitted to execute the orders Sheridan gave him, he would have been guarding with two brigades of cavalry the bridge over the Po River which Anderson had to cross, and must have detained him long enough to enable Warren to reinforce Wilson and hold the town."

If Grant was going to occupy Spotsylvania, he now needed to dislodge Anderson's corps or destroy it on May 8 before the rest of the Confederate army joined him.

Chapter 2: May 8

As soon as the sun came up on May 8, the Union cavalry busied itself trying to break through the Confederate defenses on Brock Road just north of Spotsylvania. If Sheridan's cavalry could dislodge the Confederates there, it would prevent the rest of the Confederate army from being able to march northeast toward Spotsylvania along the Old Court House Road, which would have required Lee's army to fall back several miles south to the next natural defensive line along the Po River. While Wesley Merritt's division skirmished with Fitzhugh Lee's Confederate cavalry on the Brock Road, Anderson's corps and Warren's corps marched toward the action, both intending to hold Brock Road for their respective armies.

While Fitzhugh Lee's cavalry fought a delaying action around the Alsop farm, two brigades from Anderson's corps marched north to arrive at Laurel Hill, just south of the farm. As those men pulled into position on the ridge of Laurel Hill, they spotted men from Warren's V Corps just 100 yards away.

Warren was operating under the assumption that the men he saw on Laurel Hill were just Confederate cavalry, unaware that an entire corps of Confederate infantry was in the vicinity.

While Warren's men prepared for that assault, Joseph Kershaw's division of Anderson's corps was clearing away a brigade of Union cavalry south of Laurel Hill, ensuring that the rear was safe and then allowing the rest of Anderson's corps to march up to the impromptu line at Laurel Hill. Perhaps due to his incorrect belief that he was only dealing with a small number of Confederate cavalry, Warren's initial attacks consisted of piecemeal maneuvers by separate divisions. Grant discussed the morning fighting in his memoirs, as well as a candid appraisal of Warren, whose strengths as an engineer led to frequent criticism that he was too slow and cautious as an infantry corps commander:

"Anderson soon intrenched himself—if indeed the intrenchments were not already made—immediately across Warren's front. Warren was not aware of his presence, but probably supposed it was the cavalry which Merritt had engaged earlier in the day. He assaulted at once, but was repulsed. He soon organized his men, as they were not pursued by the enemy, and made a second attack, this time with his whole corps. This time he succeeded in gaining a position immediately in the enemy's front, where he intrenched. His right and left divisions—the former Crawford's, the latter Wadsworth's, now commanded by Cutler—drove the enemy back some distance.

At this time my headquarters had been advanced to Piney Branch Church. I was anxious to crush Anderson before Lee could get a force to his support. To this end Sedgwick who was at Piney Branch Church, was ordered to Warren's support. Hancock, who was at Todd's Tavern, was notified of Warren's engagement, and was directed to be in readiness to come up. Burnside, who was with the wagon trains at Aldrich's on our extreme left, received the same instructions. Sedgwick was slow in getting up for some reason—probably unavoidable, because he was never at fault when serious work was to be done—so that it was near night before the combined forces were ready to attack. Even then all of Sedgwick's command did not get into the engagement. Warren led the last assault, one division at a time, and of course it failed.

Warren's difficulty was twofold: when he received an order to do anything, it would at once occur to his mind how all the balance of the army should be engaged so as properly to co-operate with him. His ideas were generally good, but he would forget that the person giving him orders had thought of others at the time he had of him. In like manner, when he did get ready to execute an order, after giving most intelligent instructions to division commanders, he would go in with one division, holding the others in reserve until he could superintend their movements in person also, forgetting that division commanders could execute an order without his presence. His difficulty was constitutional and beyond his control. He was an officer of superior ability, quick perceptions, and personal courage to accomplish anything that could be done with a small command."

Gouverneur Warren

While Warren was miscalculating the force in his front, the confusion of the marches and the armies' relative dispositions led to an encounter further north at the intersection of Brock Road and Catharpin Road, where a division of Jubal Early's corps encountered Winfield Scott Hancock's II Corps protecting the rear of the Union army. The aggressive Early tested Barlow's division of Hancock's corps but ultimately chose not to test the rearguard. Grant took this as evidence that Lee was unaware of Grant's intentions and movements, and that Anderson's arrival at Spotsylvania had thus been by chance, not due to Lee's skill: "Lee had ordered Hill's corps—now commanded by Early—to move by the very road we had marched upon. This shows that even early in the morning of the 8th Lee had not yet become acquainted with my move, but still thought that the Army of the Potomac had gone to Fredericksburg. Indeed, he informed the authorities at Richmond he had possession of Spottsylvania and was on my flank. Anderson was in possession of Spottsylvania, through no foresight of Lee, however. Early only found that he had been following us when he ran against Hancock at Todd's Tavern. His coming detained Hancock from the battle-field of Spottsylvania for that day; but he, in like manner, kept Early back and forced him to move by another route."

As a result of Warren's inability to push Anderson's men at Laurel Hill, men from Ewell's corps were able to slide into the line to the right of Anderson before John Sedgwick's VI Corps was in position on Warren's left. The two Union corps attempted a coordinated assault on the night of May 8, with Warren finally willing to put in all his men, but by then they were surprised to find Ewell's men in position and the assault was quickly and sharply repulsed.

May 8 had not been a good day for the Union. Delays in their marches and countermanded cavalry orders had let Anderson occupy the crossroads at Spotsylvania in force, Warren's inability to initially beat back two brigades on Laurel Hill allowed those defenders to allow two whole corps to take up positions there, and Sedgwick's inability to get up quickly enough prevented the Union from launching a decisive assault that night. Grant wrote about what he may have been able to do differently that day in his memoirs, both noting that he was still not familiar enough with the army's corps commanders and weighing the risks and rewards:

> "Had I ordered the movement for the night of the 7th by my left flank, it would have put Hancock in the lead. It would also have given us an hour or earlier start. It took all that time for Warren to get the head of his column to the left of Hancock after he had got his troops out of their line confronting the enemy. This hour, and Hancock's capacity to use his whole force when necessary, would, no doubt, have enabled him to crush Anderson before he could be reinforced. But the movement made was tactical. It kept the troops in mass against a possible assault by the enemy. Our left occupied its intrenchments while the two corps to the right passed. If an attack had been made by the enemy he would have found the 2d corps in position, fortified, and, practically, the 5th and 6th corps in position as reserves, until his entire front was passed. By a left flank movement the army would have been scattered while still passing the front of the enemy, and before the extreme right had got by it would have been very much exposed. Then, too, I had not yet learned the special qualifications of the different corps commanders. At that time my judgment was that Warren was the man I would suggest to succeed Meade should anything happen to that gallant soldier to take him from the field. As I have before said, Warren was a gallant soldier, an able man; and he was beside thoroughly imbued with the solemnity and importance of the duty he had to perform."

Meanwhile, Meade was in his notorious "snapping turtle" mode, with his short temper long gone by the end of the day. He was irate at Warren's caution, Sedgwick's slowness, and Sheridan's command of the cavalry, over which they had serious philosophical differences of opinion. Meade preferred having his cavalry perform traditional duties like screening army movements and reconnaissance, but Sheridan was a soldier who had previously commanded infantry and spoiled for a fight. Sheridan explained the roots of the friction between the two of them in his memoirs:

> "Before and at the review I took in this situation, and determined to remedy it if possible; so in due time I sought an interview with General Meade and informed him

that, as the effectiveness of my command rested mainly on the strength of its horses, I thought the duty it was then performing was both burdensome and wasteful. I also gave him my idea as to what the cavalry should do, the main purport of which was that it ought to be kept concentrated to fight the enemy's cavalry. Heretofore, the commander of the Cavalry Corps had been, virtually, but an adjunct at army headquarters — a sort of chief of cavalry-and my proposition seemed to stagger General Meade not a little. I knew that it would be difficult to overcome the recognized custom of using the cavalry for the protection of trains and the establishment of cordons around the infantry corps, and so far subordinating its operations to the movements of the main army that in name only was it a corps at all, but still I thought it my duty to try.

At first General Meade would hardly listen to my proposition, for he was filled with the prejudices that, from the beginning of the war, had pervaded the army regarding the importance and usefulness of cavalry, General Scott then predicting that the contest would be settled by artillery, and thereafter refusing the services of regiment after regiment of mounted troops. General Meade deemed cavalry fit for little more than guard and picket duty, and wanted to know what would protect the transportation trains and artillery reserve, cover the front of moving infantry columns, and secure his flanks from intrusion, if my policy were pursued. I told him that if he would let me use the cavalry as I contemplated, he need have little solicitude in these respects, for, with a mass of ten thousand mounted men, it was my belief that I could make [194] it so lively for the enemy's cavalry that, so far as attacks from it were concerned, the flanks and rear of the Army of the Potomac would require little or no defense, and claimed, further, that moving columns of infantry should take care of their own fronts. I also told him that it was my object to defeat the enemy's cavalry in a general combat, if possible, and by such a result establish a feeling of confidence in my own troops that would enable us after a while to march where we pleased, for the purpose of breaking General Lee's communications and destroying the resources from which his army was supplied.

The idea as here outlined was contrary to Meade's convictions, for though at different times since he commanded the Army of the Potomac considerable bodies of the cavalry had been massed for some special occasion, yet he had never agreed to the plan as a permanency, and could not be bent to it now. He gave little encouragement, therefore, to what I proposed, yet the conversation was immediately beneficial in one way, for when I laid before him the true condition of the cavalry, he promptly relieved it from much of the arduous and harassing picket service it was performing, thus giving me about two weeks in which to nurse the horses before the campaign opened.

The interview also disclosed the fact that the cavalry commander should be, according to General Meade's views, at his headquarters practically as one of his staff, through whom he would give detailed directions as, in his judgment, occasion required.

Meade's ideas and mine being so widely divergent, disagreements arose between us later during the battles of the Wilderness, which lack of concord ended in some concessions on his part after the movement toward Spottsylvania Court House began, and although I doubt that his convictions were ever wholly changed, yet from that date on, in the organization of the Army of the Potomac, the cavalry corps became more of a compact body, with the same privileges and responsibilities that attached to the other corps-conditions that never actually existed before."

On the night of May 8, Meade and Sheridan continued arguing over the use of cavalry, when Sheridan suggested that his cavalry be massed and allowed to find and engage JEB Stuart's cavalry in mass. While Meade was against it, Grant held his former Western subordinate in higher regard and acceded to Sheridan's request, stating, "Well, he generally knows what he is talking about. Let him start right out and do it." As a result, Sheridan's entire force of 10,000 cavalry left the Army of the Potomac and would end up missing the most important fighting of the battle on May 12. Although they fought Stuart's cavalry at the Battle of Yellow Tavern on May 11 and mortally wounded the iconic Confederate cavalry chieftain in the process, most modern historians have since sided with Meade's side of the argument, with Overland Campaign historian Gordon Rhea going so far as to write, "In the larger picture, Sheridan's raid proved to be a costly mistake. Chasing Stuart was another side show for the campaign, which would be decided by what the armies did at Spotsylvania. By abandoning the main theater of conflict to pursue his whimsical raid south, Sheridan deprived Grant of an important resource. His victory at Yellow Tavern offered scant solace to the blue-clad soldiers hunkering in trenches above the courthouse town. Sheridan's absence hurt Grant at Spotsylvania in much the same way that Stuart's absence from Gettysburg had handicapped Lee."

Chapter 3: Digging In

The armies' positions on May 9

By the end of the war, the Civil War had become a forerunner to the trench warfare of World War I, and if an army was given 24 hours to entrench, their position became practically unassailable. Grant described the process in his memoirs:

> "[I]n every change of position or halt for the night, whether confronting the enemy or not, the moment arms were stacked the men intrenched themselves. For this purpose they would build up piles of logs or rails if they could be found in their front, and dig a ditch, throwing the dirt forward on the timber. Thus the digging they did counted in making a depression to stand in, and increased the elevation in front of them. It was wonderful how quickly they could in this way construct defences of considerable strength. When a halt was made with the view of assaulting the enemy, or in his presence, these would be strengthened or their positions changed under the direction of engineer officers."

Thus, the Army of the Potomac's inability to clear Brock Road on May 8 allowed the Confederates to begin the process of digging in, a crucial advantage. By the end of the Civil War, some generals who fought in it had come to believe that a well-entrenched defensive line could only be taken if there were 4 times as many attackers as defenders. John Gordon, who led a brigade in Early's corps, discussed the nature of the line as the Confederates dug in on the night of May 8:

> "As the heads of the columns collided, the armies quickly spread into zigzag formation as each brigade, division, or corps struck its counterpart in the opposing lines. These haphazard collisions, however, rapidly developed a more orderly alignment and systematic battle, which culminated in that unparalleled struggle for the possession of a short line of Lee's breastworks. I say unparalleled, because the character of the fighting, its duration, and the individual heroism exhibited have no precedent, so far as my knowledge extends, in our Civil War, or in any other war.
>
> During these preliminary and somewhat random engagements, General Lee, in order to secure the most advantageous locality offered by the peculiar topography of the country, had placed his battle line so that it should conform in large measure to the undulations of the field. Along the brow of these slopes earthworks were speedily constructed. On one portion of the line, which embraced what was afterward known as the 'Bloody Angle,' there was a long stretch of breastworks forming almost a complete semicircle. Its most advanced or outer salient was the point against which Hancock made his famous charge.
>
> My command had been withdrawn from position in the regular line, and a role was assigned me which no officer could covet if he had the least conception of the responsibilities involved. I was ordered to take position in rear of that salient, and as nearly equidistant as practicable from every point of the wide and threatened semicircle, to watch every part of it, to move quickly, without waiting for orders, to the support of any point that might be assaulted, and to restore, if possible, any breach that might be made. We were reserves to no one command, but to all commands occupying that entire stretch of works. It will be seen that, with no possibility of knowing when or where General Grant would make his next effort to penetrate our lines, the task to be performed by my troops was not an easy one, and that the tension upon the brain and nerves of one upon whom rested the responsibility was not light nor conducive to sleep."

As the Confederates dug in, they were well aware that a salient was being created in the line at the Mule Shoe, which jutted out nearly a mile in front of the rest of their defensive line. Civil War armies always tried to avoid creating a salient in the line because it allowed the salient to be attacked in multiple directions. In this case, despite the fact the Mule Shoe was a salient, the Confederates dug in there to hold onto the nearest high ground in the area, hoping to prevent Union soldiers from occupying it and disrupting the rest of their line.

At the same time, the Army of the Potomac began digging in and erecting earthworks along their own lines, just as aware of their importance. With that, the two armies hunkered down into the kind of trench warfare that would've seemed foreign to the soldiers and generals in 1861. With sharpshooters among the lines, which were about half a mile away from each other, soldiers were afraid to even show their heads above their trenches for fear of being sniped.

While this process was going on during the morning of May 9, Union VI Corps commander John Sedgwick was placing his artillery and directing the men in his line when scattered shots from snipers started coming in from several hundred yards away. The soldiers in his corps had been harassed by the sharpshooters all morning, and one bullet had already knocked one of Sedgwick's brigadier-generals off his horse. Nevertheless, Sedgwick projected calm as he went about his business, even acting amused when some of his staff joined the soldiers in taking cover. Sedgwick mocked them, "What? Men dodging this way for single bullets? What will you do when they open fire along the whole line? I am ashamed of you. They couldn't hit an elephant at this distance." After one bullet whizzed by, one of his soldiers told Sedgwick that he had already nearly had his own head taken off by an artillery shell, to which Sedgwick reassured him and told him to stay in his position. His men would note that Sedgwick kept repeating, "I'm ashamed of you, dodging that way. They couldn't hit an elephant at this distance."

Sedgwick

Just then, another shot whizzed through the air, the unmistakable sound of a bullet fired by a .451 caliber Whitworth rifle. But this one found a mark, as noted by one of the soldiers in the vicinity, Lieutenant Colonel Martin McMahon, who wrote, "For the third time the same shrill whistle, closing with a dull, heavy stroke." Far from being unable to hit an elephant, a Confederate sharpshooter had just hit Sedgwick right in the face, killing him almost instantly. McMahon would later note that as he tried to catch Sedgwick from falling, blood spurted out just below his left eye, and that Sedgwick died so quickly that he still had a smile on his face.

Sedgwick was the highest ranking Union officer to die during the war (though James McPherson died while commanding an army during Sherman's Atlanta campaign that same year). When news reached Grant's headquarters, Grant was so shocked that he repeatedly asked, "Is he really dead?" Grant later wrote, "His loss was a severe one to the Army of the Potomac and to the Nation. General H. G. Wright succeeded him in the command of his corps." According to Grant's aide, Horace Porter, the grief-stricken Grant was telling those around him, "His loss to this army is greater than the loss of a whole division of troops."

Meanwhile, Burnside's IX Corps, which had been late to show up at the Battle of the Wilderness, marched southwest along the Fredericksburg Road and came up on the far left of the Union line, leaving a gap between his men and Wright's VI Corps. When Burnside's corps were confronted by cavalry led by Fitzhugh Lee, the cautious Burnside stopped moving forward and began digging in. That skirmish induced Grant into thinking that Lee might be trying to turn his left flank, when Lee had no such plan. As a result, Grant prepared Hancock's II Corps to make an attack on the Confederates' left flank, figuring that would be the weaker part of their line, while Lee was actually shifting some of Early's corps along his left in the hopes of attacking Hancock's flank.

Grant had no idea that Burnside's corps was poised to strike Lee's right flank and had only been opposed by cavalry, and he would not realize it until after the war, much to his consternation.

Chapter 4: May 10

The action on May 10

On several occasions throughout the Overland Campaign, Grant ordered general attacks out of a sense that he could break Lee's army, and he had conceived of such an attack for May 10:

> "Accordingly in the morning, orders were issued for an attack in the afternoon on the centre by Warren's and Wright's corps, Hancock to command all the attacking force. Two of his divisions were brought to the north side of the Po. Gibbon was placed to the right of Warren, and Birney in his rear as a reserve. Barlow's division was left south of the stream, and Mott of the same corps was still to the left of Wright's corps. Burnside was ordered to reconnoitre his front in force, and, if an opportunity presented, to attack with vigor."

Grant's plan actually started to go haywire on the evening of May 9, when the Confederates noticed some of Hancock's II Corps shifting their position that night. This allowed Lee to counter the perceived threat by trying to outflank Hancock's corps with Early's corps, which led the Union high command to mistakenly assume that Early's men were being shifted to the Confederates' right flank. By the morning of May 10, Grant realized his mistake, but when he pulled back most of Hancock's corps behind the Po River, he left Francis Barlow's division on the other side to keep manning the earthworks there, which all but invited a Confederate attack.

Sure enough, that attack came at 2:00 p.m., with Henry Heth's division of Early's corps and William Mahone's division in support on the right. Early noted in his memoirs:

"Our line was then north of the Po, with its left, Fields' division of Longstreet's corps, resting on that stream, just above the crossing of the Shady Grove road. The whole of the enemy's force was also north of the Po, prior to this movement of his. Mahone's division was sent to occupy the banks of the Po on Fields' left, while with Heth's division and a battalion of artillery I moved to the rear, crossing the Po on the Louisa Court-House road, and then following that road until we reached one coming in from Waite's Shop on the Shady Grove road. After moving about a mile on this road, we met Hampton gradually falling back before the enemy, who had pushed out a column of infantry considerably to the rear of our line. This column was in turn forced back to the posi tion on Shady Grove road which was occupied by what was reported to be Hancock's corps. Following up and crossing a small stream just below a mill pond, we succeeded in reaching Waite's Shop, from whence an attack was made on the enemy, and the entire force, which had crossed the Po, was driven back with a loss of one piece of artillery, which fell into our hands, and a considerable number in killed and wounded. This relieved us from a very threatening danger, as the position the enemy had attained would have enabled him to completely enfilade Fields' position and get possession of the line of our communications to the rear, within a very short distance of which he was, when met by the force which drove him back. In this affair Heth's division behaved very handsomely, all of the brigades (Cook's, Davis', Kirkland's and Walker's) being engaged in the attack. General H. H. Walker had the misfortune to receive a severe wound in the foot, which rendered amputation necessary, but otherwise our loss was slight. As soon as the road was cleared, Mahone's division crossed the Po, but it was not practicable to pursue the affair further, as the north bank of the stream at this point was covered by a heavily entrenched line, with a number of batteries, and night was approaching."

While Hancock was trying to extricate Barlow's division, it left Warren in command of the general attack that Grant intended to make on the center. Warren was eager to make the assault, still smarting from perceived criticism over his timidity the previous two days, but in so doing he ended up ordering an attack that was uncoordinated with Hancock's men on the right or Wright's men on the left. Despite having tried to reconnoiter in force twice and being pushed back both times, Warren recommended making an assault on the Confederate center, and his uncoordinated attack was quickly repulsed at 4:00 p.m.

As Warren began reforming his lines, this time to make a coordinated attack, one of the divisions in Wright's VI Corps did not realize that the general attack at 5:00 p.m. had been delayed. Gershom Mott, whose division had performed poorly at the Wilderness, had even less luck when it made an uncoordinated attack at that hour.

When Early's two divisions had shifted to the left to attack Hancock, it left Cadmus Wilcox's division on the right flank, where it opposed Burnside's entire corps. Luckily for the Confederates, Grant had thought that the Confederates had been shifting more soldiers to their right instead of their left, leaving the Union high command with no idea that Burnside so heavily outnumbered the enemy in his front. Since Burnside was only ordered to reconnoiter in force, he stopped advancing down the road almost as soon as he came into contact with Wilcox's division, and at that point Grant started to worry about the gap between Wright's corps and Burnside's corps. Had Grant kept Sheridan's cavalry with him, such a reconnaissance might have already been done by the cavalry, and he would have had a better idea of what was in Burnside's front. But since he had allowed Sheridan to leave the army with no cavalry, later that night he pulled Burnside back to close the gap with Wright's corps, losing a chance to overwhelm Lee's right flank. It was something he greatly regretted after the war, writing, "Burnside on the left had got up to within a few hundred yards of Spottsylvania Court House, completely turning Lee's right. He was not aware of the importance of the advantage he had gained, and I, being with the troops where the heavy fighting was, did not know of it at the time. He had gained his position with but little fighting, and almost without loss. Burnside's position now separated him widely from Wright's corps, the corps nearest to him. At night he was ordered to join on to this. This brought him back about a mile, and lost to us an important advantage. I attach no blame to Burnside for this, but I do to myself for not having had a staff officer with him to report to me his position."

There had been fighting by all of the Union corps along each sector of the lines, but the most famous assault on the 10th was made by 12 regiments under the command of 24 year old Colonel Emory Upton, consisting of mixed elements of Wright's corps. This "storming party" was sent out at 6:00 p.m. with the intention of quickly rushing into the Confederate trenches and creating at least a minor breakthrough in the Confederate lines that could then be further breached by reinforcements. By using an unusual battle formation and not pausing to stop and fire, Upton's small attack force gained a surprising success, at least at first. Grant explained:

> "Wright also reconnoitred his front and gained a considerably advanced position from the one he started from. He then organized a storming party, consisting of twelve regiments, and assigned Colonel Emory Upton, of the 121st New York Volunteers, to the command of it. About four o'clock in the afternoon the assault was ordered, Warren's and Wright's corps, with Mott's division of Hancock's corps, to move simultaneously. The movement was prompt, and in a few minutes the fiercest of struggles began. The battle-field was so densely covered with forest that but little could be seen, by any one person, as to the progress made. Meade and I occupied the best

position we could get, in rear of Warren.

Warren was repulsed with heavy loss, General J. C. Rice being among the killed. He was not followed, however, by the enemy, and was thereby enabled to reorganize his command as soon as covered from the guns of the enemy. To the left our success was decided, but the advantage was lost by the feeble action of Mott. Upton with his assaulting party pushed forward and crossed the enemy's intrenchments. Turning to the right and left he captured several guns and some hundreds of prisoners. Mott was ordered to his assistance but failed utterly. So much time was lost in trying to get up the troops which were in the right position to reinforce, that I ordered Upton to withdraw; but the officers and men of his command were so averse to giving up the advantage they had gained that I withdrew the order. To relieve them, I ordered a renewal of the assault. By this time Hancock, who had gone with Birney's division to relieve Barlow, had returned, bringing the division with him. His corps was now joined with Warren's and Wright's in this last assault. It was gallantly made, many men getting up to, and over, the works of the enemy; but they were not able to hold them. At night they were withdrawn. Upton brought his prisoners with him, but the guns he had captured he was obliged to abandon. Upton had gained an important advantage, but a lack in others of the spirit and dash possessed by him lost it to us. Before leaving Washington I had been authorized to promote officers on the field for special acts of gallantry. By this authority I conferred the rank of brigadier-general upon Upton on the spot, and this act was confirmed by the President. Upton had been badly wounded in this fight."

Upton

Had Upton's successful assault been made in a coordinated fashion along with Mott's previous attack at 5:00 p.m. or Warren's attack at 4:00 p.m., it's possible that there would have been a much bigger breakthrough that wouldn't have allowed Lee to flush Upton's attack party out with reinforcements. But as it was, Upton's success in reaching the western side of the Mule Shoe salient had established both the model for attacking the line and the point at which the Confederate line should be attacked.

Chapter 5: May 11

Every attack made by the Army of the Potomac on May 10 had been repulsed, and the lines had barely moved since the end of fighting on May 8, but Grant had reason for optimism. On May 11, he began plans to conduct another attack in the innovative style Upton had used, but with Hancock's entire II Corps instead of just 5,000 men. He also continued to believe that Lee's army was on the verge of being broken, partly the result of overestimating how many casualties he had inflicted on the Army of Northern Virginia and underestimating the Confederates. That day, he telegraphed Washington:

"We have now ended the 6th day of very hard fighting. The result up to this time is much in our favor. But our losses have been heavy as well as those of the enemy. We have lost to this time eleven general officers killed, wounded and missing, and probably twenty thousand men. I think the loss of the enemy must be greater—we having taken over four thousand prisoners in battle, whilst he has taken from us but few except a few stragglers. I am now sending back to Belle Plain all my wagons for a fresh supply of provisions and ammunition, and propose to fight it out on this line if it takes all summer.

The arrival of reinforcements here will be very encouraging to the men, and I hope they will be sent as fast as possible, and in as great numbers. My object in having them sent to Belle Plain was to use them as an escort to our supply trains. If it is more convenient to send them out by train to march from the railroad to Belle Plain or Fredericksburg, send them so.

I am satisfied the enemy are very shaky, and are only kept up to the mark by the greatest exertions on the part of their officers, and by keeping them intrenched in every position they take.

Up to this time there is no indication of any portion of Lee's army being detached for the defence of Richmond.

U. S. GRANT,

Lieut.-General."

After a couple of days in which Grant's incorrect assumptions had cost him chances for success, Lee made a terrible mistake on May 11 while reacting to movements by the Union army. Grant's plan for Hancock's assault required pulling his men out of the line and assembling them about a mile north of the Mule Shoe. By having Hancock attack the north face of the Mule Shoe while Wright advanced on the west face and Burnside advanced on the east face, the salient in the Confederate line would be as exposed as possible. Hancock's men would be advancing over open ground, while the part in the line they pulled out of was woody, which would keep Lee from fully understanding the movements and prevent the Confederates from launching a potentially devastating attack in the gap while Warren shifted to the left to replace Hancock's men.

Even worse, the movements of Hancock's corps and intelligence reports that Lee received convinced him that Grant was actually starting to retreat. Thinking this was the case, Lee intended to try to attack Grant's army while it was most vulnerable on the move, and since that would require improving the Army of Northern Virginia's mobility, he started withdrawing his artillery from around the salient for the purpose of having it prepared to advance more quickly. His nephew Fitzhugh Lee explained, "On the 11th he thought Grant was preparing for another move, and that night ordered most of the cannon out of the salient so as to be ready for a counter move, all of which a deserter from [Allegheny] Johnson's line reported, and which may account for the assault which, though favored by a climatic condition, was courageously executed."

Though Fitzhugh Lee credited that Confederate deserter for the assault, it was apparent that Grant already had it in mind. As Hancock's men began moving to their staging ground at the Brown farm, thunderstorms provided a torrential downpour, making it that much harder to truly understand the purpose of the movement. That was of little comfort to Allegheny Johnson and his division, who were defending the salient in the line and watching Hancock's men marching north in their front even while their artillery was being withdrawn. Johnson pleaded with corps commander Richard Ewell to bring the guns back to his line, but by the time Ewell accepted the request and the orders reached the artillery units, it was 3:30 a.m. on the morning of May 12. Hancock's assault was scheduled to come crashing right into Allegheny Johnson's division just half an hour later.

Allegheny Johnson

Chapter 6: The Bloody Angle

"I fancy this war has furnished no parallel to the desperation shown here by both parties. It must be called, I suppose, the taking of the Salient." – Theodore Lyman, George Meade's aide-de-camp

The ugly weather conditions had slowed Hancock's men to the extent that they reached the Brown farm around midnight, and then had to spend most of the next 4 hours forming their battle lines. The attack was delayed half an hour, back to 4:30 a.m., and Grant ordered Burnside to attack the east face of the Mule Shoe at the same time in force.

As if Grant's attack hadn't already been aided by Lee pulling the artillery away from the salient, there was a dense fog over the battlefield when Hancock's men stepped off to begin their assault. Hancock's men would not have come into view until they were within 300 yards of the Confederate lines, and now they would be obscured by mist.

At 4:30 a.m. that morning, nobody could have believed what the salient would look like 24 hours later. Gettysburg hero Rufus Dawes, Colonel of the 6th Wisconsin in the Iron brigade, described the final approach to the salient and the nature of the entrenchments:

"We stood perhaps one hundred feet from the enemy's line, and so long as we maintained a continual fire they remained hidden in their entrenchments. But if an attempt to advance was made, an order would be given and they would all rise up together and fire a volley upon us. They had constructed their works by digging an entrenchment about four feet deep, in which at intervals there were traverses to protect the flanks. This had the effect of making a row of cellars without drainage, and in them was several inches of mud and water. To protect their heads, they had placed in front logs which were laid upon blocks, and it was intended to put their muskets through the chinks under the head logs, but in the darkness this became impracticable and the head log proved a serious obstruction to their firing."

Battle of Spotsylvania Court House
Actions May 12, 1864

Hancock's corps, nearly 15,000 strong, quickly overwhelmed the salient and almost immediately destroyed the initial defenders comprised of William Witcher's brigade. As Hancock's men entered the Confederate trenches, Barlow's division fanned out to their left and flanked George Steuart's brigade facing Burnside's men on the eastern face of the Mule Shoe, capturing both Steuart and Allegheny Johnson. Meanwhile, David Birney's division advanced along the western part of the Mule Shoe until confronting the old Stonewall Brigade, once commanded by the legendary Stonewall Jackson but now commanded by James Walker.

Within half an hour, Hancock's corps had breached the Confederates' main line, capturing nearly 4,000 men and 20 guns, including their horses and ammunition. As the men kept advancing, Hancock had the captured Confederate guns turned around and began firing them down the Confederate lines, providing a devastating enfilade. Around this time, news of the initial success was making its way back to Grant's headquarters, and Theodore Lyman described the scene:

"At a little after five o'clock, General Williams approached from the telegraph tent; a smile was on his face: Hancock had carried the first line! Thirty minutes after, another despatch: he had taken the main line with guns, prisoners and two generals! Great rejoicings now burst forth. Some of Grant's Staff were absurdly confident and were sure Lee was entirely beaten. My own experiences taught me a little more scepticism. Hancock presently sent to ask for a vigorous attack on his right, to cover and support his right flank. General Wright was accordingly ordered to attack with a part of the 6th Corps. As I stood there waiting, I heard someone say, 'Sir, this is General Johnson.' I turned round and there was the captured Major-General, walking slowly up. He was a strongly built man of a stern and rather bad face, and was dressed in a double-breasted blue-grey coat, high riding boots and a very bad felt hat. He was most horribly mortified at being taken, and kept coughing to hide his emotion. Generals Meade and Grant shook hands with him, and good General Williams bore him off to breakfast. His demeanor was dignified and proper. Not so a little creature, General Steuart, who insulted everybody who came near him, and was rewarded by being sent on foot to Fredericksburg, where there was plenty of mud and one stream up to his waist."

Horace Porter also recounted a rather tense exchange between Steuart and Hancock: "General George H. Steuart was also captured, but was not sent in to general headquarters on account of a scene which had been brought about by an unseemly exhibition of temper on his part. Hancock had known him in the old army, and in his usual frank way went up to him, greeted him kindly, and offered his hand. Steuart drew back, rejected the offer, and said rather haughtily, 'Under the present circumstances, I must decline to take your hand.' Hancock, who was somewhat nettled by this remark, replied, 'Under any other circumstances, general, I should not have offered it.'"

Burnside's men had attacked in concert with Hancock's and had greatly assisted in destroying the Confederate line on the eastern face of the Mule Shoe, but in the process his men had lost contact with the faster advancing II Corps. When Burnside informed Grant that his men had lost contact with Hancock's men, Grant responded, "Push the enemy with all your might; that's the way to connect."

Now, with a breach in the Confederate line nearly half a mile wide, both sides began quickly reacting by ordering more men to the fighting. For Grant, this meant that Wright's corps would support Hancock on the right, but because Grant had only planned for Wright to remain in a defensive posture during the initial assault, it required time for Wright's men to prepare for a similar kind of advance.

Meanwhile, Lee was so desperate that as he was ordering up reinforcements from John Gordon's division, he rode to the front of their marching column as though he was going to lead the charge himself. Fitzhugh Lee recalled the scene, writing, "On this occasion the general rode to the head of the column forming for the charge, took off his hat, and pointed to the captured line; but General John B. Gordon proposed to lead his own men, and no one in the army could do it better, for he was in dash and daring inferior to none. 'These are Virginians and Georgians who have never failed,' said Gordon. 'Go to the rear, General Lee.' And appealing to his men, he cried: 'Is it necessary for General Lee to lead this charge?' 'No, no,' they exclaimed; 'we will drive them back if General Lee will go to the rear.'

Gordon was unquestionably one of the toughest soldiers in the South. He had led a desperate flank attack at the Battle of the Wilderness on May 6, and he had been wounded several times at Antietam. But not even Gordon was ready for his division's initial contact with Hancock's corps:

> "So rapidly and silently had the enemy moved inside of our works-- indeed, so much longer time had he been on the inside than the reports indicated--that before we had moved one half the distance to the salient the head of my column butted squarely against Hancock's line of battle. The men who had been placed in our front to give warning were against that battle line before they knew it. They were shot down or made prisoners. The sudden and unexpected blaze from Hancock's rifles made the dark woodland strangely lurid. General Johnson, who rode immediately at my side, was shot from his horse, severely but not, as I supposed, fatally wounded in the head. His brigade was thrown inevitably into great confusion, but did not break to the rear. As quickly as possible, I had the next ranking officer in that brigade notified of General Johnson's fall and directed him at once to assume command. He proved equal to the emergency. With great coolness and courage he promptly executed my orders. The Federals were still advancing, and every movement of the North Carolina brigade had to be made under heavy fire. The officer in charge was directed to hastily withdraw his brigade a short distance, to change front so as to face Hancock's lines, and to deploy his whole force in close order as skirmishers, so as to stretch, if possible, across the entire front of Hancock. This done, he was ordered to charge with his line of skirmishers the solid battle lines before him. His looks indicated some amazement at the purpose to make an attack which appeared so utterly hopeless, and which would have been the very essence of rashness but for the extremity of the situation. He was, however, full of the fire of battle and too good a soldier not to yield prompt and cheerful obedience. That order was given in the hope and belief that in the fog and mists which concealed our numbers the sheer audacity of the movement would confuse and check the Union advance long enough for me to change front and form line of battle with the other

brigades. The result was not disappointing except in the fact that Johnson's brigade, even when so deployed, was still too short to reach across Hancock's entire front. This fact was soon developed: not by sight, but by the direction from which the Union bullets began to come."

As Gordon's account indicated, the fog and damp conditions made musket volleys and firing far more ineffective than they otherwise would have usually been. Moreover, the nature of the Confederate lines, which were composed of trenches that were upwards of 4 feet deep in some positions, made it all but impossible for Hancock's corps to reform their battle lines once they had stormed the Confederates' positions. With men getting mixed up in the chaos, it became impossible for officers to control their commands, and the fighting around the breached salient began to devolve into hand-to-hand fighting.

As Hancock was proudly boasting, "I have used up Johnson and am going into Early", Gordon's division came countercharging into the breach and checked Hancock's progress with a series of desperate attacks. As they began to push back Hancock's now-exhausted attackers on the eastern portion of the Mule Shoe, division commander Robert Rodes was reestablishing the Confederate line on the western part of the Mule Shoe.

The Confederates had just desperately stopped Hancock's momentum, but the worst was yet to come. By the time the Confederates had fought off Hancock, Wright's entire corps was ready to press forward around 6:30 a.m., and Grant had also ordered Warren's corps to attack the Confederates on their left and pin them down. By now, the steady rain that was still coming down had combined with the mud and the blood of the fighting soldiers to produce a nauseating stream in the trenches near the salient that one soldier recalled being half-way up to his knees. It was only about to get worse.

Around 6:30 a.m., Wright's corps had been assembled in a similar manner to Upton's assault, and they rushed forward into the salient even while some of Hancock's men were streaming to the rear. G. Norton Galloway, a member of the 95th Pennsylvania in Wright's corps, described the scene:

"Under cover of the smoke-laden rain the enemy was pushing large bodies of troops forward, determined at all hazards to regain the lost ground. Could we hold on until the remainder of our brigade should come to our assistance? Regardless of the heavy volleys of the enemy that were thinning our ranks, we stuck to the position and returned the fire until the 5th Maine and the 121st New York of our brigade came to our support, while the 96th Pennsylvania went in on our right ; thus reenforced, we redoubled our exertions. The smoke, which was dense at first, was intensified by each discharge of artillery to such an extent that the accuracy of our aim became very uncertain, but nevertheless we kept up the fire in the supposed direction of the enemy. Meanwhile they were crawling forward under cover of the smoke, until, reaching a certain point, and raising their usual yell, they charged gallantly up to the very muzzles of our pieces and reoccupied the Angle.

Upon reaching the breastwork, the Confederates for a few moments had the advantage of us, and made good use of their rifles. Our men went down by the score; all the artillery horses were down ; the gallant Upton was the only mounted officer in sight. Hat in hand, he bravely cheered his men, and begged them to 'hold this point.' All of his staff had been either killed, wounded, or dismounted.

At this moment, and while the open ground in rear of the Confederate works was choked with troops, a section of Battery C, 5th United States Artillery, under Lieutenant Richard Metcalf, was brought into action and increased the carnage by opening at short range with double charges of canister. This staggered the apparently exultant enemy. In the maze of the moment these guns were run up by hand close to the famous Angle, and fired again and again, and they were only abandoned when all the drivers and cannoneers had fallen. The battle was now at white heat.

The rain continued to fall, and clouds of smoke hung over the scene. Like leeches we stuck to the work, determined by our fire to keep the enemy from rising up. Captain John D. Fish, of Upton's staff, who had until this time performed valuable service in conveying ammunition to the gunners, fell, pierced by a bullet. This brave officer seemed to court death as he rode back and forth between the caissons and cannoneers with stands of canister under his 'gum' coat. 'Give it to them , boys! I'll bring you the canister,' said he; and as he turned to cheer the gunners, he fell from his horse, mortally wounded. In a few moments the two brass pieces of the 5th Artillery, cut and hacked by the bullets of both antagonists, lay unworked with their muzzles projecting over the enemy's works, and their wheels half sunk in the mud. Between the lines and near at hand lay the horses of these guns, completely riddled. The dead and wounded were torn to pieces by the canister as it swept the ground where they had fallen."

Earthworks near the Bloody Angle

With Wright's VI Corps crashing into the line, the Confederates were forced to quickly bring in more reinforcements, beginning with William Mahone's division. Mahone had been near the extreme left the previous day while Heth's division was attacking the Union's right flank, and now he was forced to quickly countermarch two of his brigades from the extreme left to the Mule Shoe. By 9:30 a.m., all of the VI Corps had been committed and were desperately fighting to hold on as more Confederates streamed to the breach.

Grant had hoped to avoid allowing massive reinforcements by having Warren's corps pin down the Confederate left. Given that Mahone was able to march his entire division from that sector to the Mule Shoe, it was apparent that Warren's assault was a failure. Warren's men had been ordered to attack near Laurel Hill multiple times the past few days, and the failures of the previous days had demoralized them. Despite the fact that Warren's entire corps was opposed by just one division of Anderson's corps, their attack completely stalled in under an hour. When Warren had to tell Meade that he could not advance, the short-tempered Meade exploded and ordered him to attack "at once at all hazards with your whole force, if necessary." Once again, Warren's men made a half-hearted advance that was quickly bogged down, and by now Grant was so frustrated that he authorized Meade to relieve Warren of command. Although Warren technically avoided being relieved, one of his divisions was placed under Wright's command and another was placed under Hancock's, leaving him with only one division. For the one division still nominally under Warren's command, Meade had his chief of staff, General Humphreys, attached to Warren's division and the authority to give it orders in his name. Grant would ruefully note in his memoirs, "If the 5th corps, or rather if Warren, had been as prompt as Wright was with the 6th corps, better results might have been obtained."

As Lee kept pulling men from his left to reinforce the Mule Shoe, a stalemate developed in which neither side could fully dislodge the other. For Lee, this meant that Union artillery positions made his current defensive line precarious, while Grant was still holding out hope of achieving a decisive breakthrough that would cut Lee's army in two, separating Ewell and Early from Anderson. As a result, both commanders kept ordering more and more men forward into the salient.

By the mid-afternoon, the Union and Confederate soldiers had been fighting at the salient for over 10 hours. Galloway discussed the nature of the fighting at the Bloody Angle during this time:

"The great difficulty was in the narrow limits of the Angle, around which we were fighting, which precluded the possibility of getting more than a limited number into action at once. At one time our ranks were crowded in some parts four deep by reenforcements. Major Henry P. Truefitt, commanding the 119th Pennsylvania, was killed, and Captain Charles P. Warner, who succeeded him, was shot dead. Later in the day Major William Ellis, of the 49th New York, who had excited our admiration, was shot through the arm and body with a ramrod during one of the several attempts to get the men to cross the works and drive off the enemy. Our losses were frightful. What remained of many different regiments that had come to our support had concentrated at this point and planted their tattered colors upon a slight rise of ground close to the Angle, where they staid during the latter part of the day.

To keep up the supply of ammunition pack mules were brought into use, each animal carrying three thousand rounds. The boxes were dropped close behind the troops engaged, where they were quickly opened by the officers or file-closers, who served the ammunition to the men. The writer fired four hundred rounds of ammunition, and many others as many or more. In this manner a continuous and rapid fire was maintained, to which for a while the enemy replied with vigor.

Finding that we were not to be driven back, the Confederates began to use more discretion, exposing themselves but little, using the loop-holes in their works to fire through, and at times placing the muzzles of their rifles on the top logs, seizing the trigger and small of the stock, and elevating the breech with one hand sufficiently to reach us."

However, while more and more men packed into the tight lines, Lee was busy creating a new defensive line south of the Mule Shoe that would prevent him from having to defend a salient. All throughout the afternoon Confederate engineers began shuffling men south of the fighting and digging in, so that there would be a new set of entrenchments for the Confederates to use once the new line was established.

By the time the Confederates were ready to dislodge Wright's corps, the men from Hancock's corps had been reformed and ordered back to the salient, keeping the fight going throughout the night. It was not until 4:00 a.m. on the 13th, nearly 24 hours after Hancock's assault began, that the Confederates at the salient began to pull back to the newly formed trenches a few hundred yards south. Nearly 9,000 Union soldiers had been killed or wounded, while 5,000 Confederates had been killed or wounded and 3,000-4,000 had been captured.

When dawn broke on the 13th, the Bloody Angle produced a sight unlike anything the battle hardened soldiers had seen before. Theodore Lyman recounted injured men being pulled out from under multiple corpses, and seeing one corpse that looked like it had been shot 80 times. Dawes, who had fought at Antietam and Gettysburg, was so horrified by the Bloody Angle that he ordered his men to pull out so they wouldn't have to sleep near the spot, writing, "In the morning the rebel works presented an awful spectacle. The cellars were crowded with dead and wounded, lying in some cases upon each other and in several inches of mud and water. I saw the body of a rebel soldier sitting in the corner of one of these cellars in a position of apparent ease, with the head entirely gone, and the flesh burned from the bones of the neck and shoulders. This was doubtless caused by the explosion of a shell from some small Cohorn mortars within our lines."

Grants aide, Horace Porter, was astounded by what he saw: "The appalling sight presented was harrowing in the extreme. Our own killed were scattered over a large space near the "angle," while in front of the captured breastworks the enemy's dead, vastly more numerous than our own, were piled upon each other in some places four layers deep, exhibiting every ghastly phase of mutilation. Below the mass of fast-decaying corpses, the convulsive twitching of limbs and the writhing of bodies showed that there were wounded men still alive and struggling to extricate themselves from the horrid entombment. Every relief possible was afforded, but in too many cases it came too late. The place was well named the 'Bloody Angle.'"

Galloway noted one morbid way that the Union soldiers still holding the salient went about burying the dead: "Hundreds of Confederates, dead or dying, lay piled over one another in those pits. The fallen lay three or four feet deep in some places, and, with but few exceptions, they were shot in and about the head. Arms, accouterments, ammunition, cannon, shot and shell, and broken foliage were strewn about. With much labor a detail of Union soldiers buried the dead by simply turning the captured breastworks upon them. Thus had these unfortunate victims unwittingly dug their own graves. The trenches were nearly full of muddy water. It was the most horrible sight I had ever witnessed."

Grant was more circumspect, writing, "Lee massed heavily from his left flank on the broken point of his line. Five times during the day he assaulted furiously, but without dislodging our troops from their new position. His losses must have been fearful. Sometimes the belligerents would be separated by but a few feet. In one place a tree, eighteen inches in diameter, was cut entirely down by musket balls. All the trees between the lines were very much cut to pieces by artillery and musketry. It was three o'clock next morning before the fighting ceased. Some of our troops had then been twenty hours under fire. In this engagement we did not lose a single organization, not even a company. The enemy lost one division with its commander, one brigade and one regiment, with heavy losses elsewhere. Our losses were heavy, but, as stated, no whole company was captured. At night Lee took a position in rear of his former one, and by the following morning he was strongly intrenched in it."

Chapter 7: Lee Lives to Fight Another Day

"The enemy are obstinate, and seem to have found the last ditch." – Ulysses S. Grant, May 12 telegraph to Washington.

Movements on May 13-14

Lee's army had barely escaped disaster on the 12th, leaving Grant anxious to continue offensive operations, but he was also well aware that an attack against the newly entrenched line would be suicidal. Thus, he began the delicate process of marching the men on his right flank to come up on the left flank of the army, requiring them to countermarch and then head south and southeast. From May 13-14, he accomplished this by having the VI Corps and the remaining men of the V Corps move behind Hancock's men and march to the left of Burnside's IX Corps. The steady rains, which had now continued for nearly 4 days, slowed the progress and bogged them down. In response to these movements, Lee shifted Anderson's corps from his left to his right to counter them.

On May 16, Grant telegraphed Washington to explain that the rain had all but halted his campaign: "We have had five days almost constant rain without any prospect yet of it clearing up. The roads have now become so impassable that ambulances with wounded men can no longer run between here and Fredericksburg. All offensive operations necessarily cease until we can have twenty-four hours of dry weather. The army is in the best of spirits, and feel the greatest confidence of ultimate success."

The attack on May 18

The following day, Grant devised plans for another assault, hoping to catch the Confederates by surprise. Since Grant had been marching men from his right to his left, he hoped and guessed that Lee was countering that by building up that flank to meet the new threat, so he decided to try to attack Lee's left flank with Hancock's men and Burnside's men, near the Mule Shoe. The problem with the plan was that Lee was still fearful that an assault might come at any time, so the Confederates were alert. Moreover, Ewell's men had been in the same defensive lines for several days, which had allowed them to dig in so effectively that their line was all but impregnable. When Hancock's corps led this attack, the felled trees (abates) bogged them down and made them sitting ducks for Confederate artillery, which had not been withdrawn this time. The Union attack was repulsed without Ewell's infantry having to fire a single musket.

With that, Grant had finally been convinced of the hopelessness of striking a decisive blow at Spotsylvania Court House, noting in his memoirs, "I immediately gave orders for a movement by the left flank, on towards Richmond, to commence on the night of the 19th. I also asked Halleck to secure the cooperation of the navy in changing our base of supplies from Fredericksburg to Port Royal, on the Rappahannock."

On May 19, as Grant was getting ready to march south by pulling his right flank out of the lines, Lee ordered Ewell's corps to conduct a reconnaissance in force that would probe the Union's right flank. This was the kind of reconnaissance that would have been assigned to JEB Stuart's cavalry in previous years, but Stuart's badly outnumbered cavalry had their hands full with Sheridan, and the famous cavalier had been mortally wounded in a skirmish at the Battle of Yellow Tavern on May 11. As a result, two of Ewell's divisions pushed forward until they came across some of Hancock's corps at Harris Farm, a skirmish that lasted most of the 19th. By the time Lee withdrew Ewell's men, they had suffered 900 casualties. Meanwhile, Grant was disappointed by Warren yet again, writing, "Warren had been ordered to get on Ewell's flank and in his rear, to cut him off from his intrenchments. But his efforts were so feeble that under the cover of night Ewell got back with only the loss of a few hundred prisoners, besides his killed and wounded. The army being engaged until after dark, I rescinded the order for the march by our left flank that night."

After Harris Farm, the last major fighting of the Battle of Spotsylvania Court House was finished. From May 8-21, the two armies had inflicted nearly 32,000 casualties on each other. Grant had lost over 18,000 killed, captured or wounded, meaning he had lost over 35,000 since entering the Wilderness less than three weeks earlier. Meanwhile, Lee had lost another 13,000 soldiers, over 20% of his entire army. It was the deadliest battle of the Overland Campaign and one of the 5 bloodiest battles of the entire Civil War.

At Spotsylvania, just like at the Battle of the Wilderness, Lee's army had skillfully defended against Grant's attacks and had inflicted more casualties than they suffered. But once again, the

Confederates had suffered a larger % of casualties within their army and failed to stop Grant's campaign. The Army of the Potomac and Army of Northern Virginia would continue to move south, destined to meet again along the North Anna River.

Bibliography

Alexander, Edward P. Military Memoirs of a Confederate: A Critical Narrative. New York: Da Capo Press, 1993.

Bonekemper, Edward H., III. A Victor, Not a Butcher: Ulysses S. Grant's Overlooked Military Genius. Washington, DC: Regnery, 2004.

Grant, Ulysses S. Personal Memoirs of U. S. Grant. 2 vols. Charles L. Webster & Company, 1885–86.

Grimsley, Mark. And Keep Moving On: The Virginia Campaign, May–June 1864. Lincoln: University of Nebraska Press, 2002.

Jaynes, Gregory, and the Editors of Time-Life Books. The Killing Ground: Wilderness to Cold Harbor. Alexandria, VA: Time-Life Books, 1986.

Longstreet, James. From Manassas to Appomattox: Memoirs of the Civil War in America. New York: Da Capo Press, 1992. First published in 1896 by J. B. Lippincott and Co.

Lyman, Theodore. With Grant and Meade: From the Wilderness to Appomattox. Edited by George R. Agassiz. Lincoln: University of Nebraska Press, 1994.

Rhea, Gordon C. The Battle of the Wilderness May 5–6, 1864. Baton Rouge: Louisiana State University Press, 1994.

Rhea, Gordon C. The Battles of Wilderness & Spotsylvania. National Park Service Civil War series. Fort Washington, PA: U.S. National Park Service and Eastern National, 1995.

Rhea, Gordon C. In the Footsteps of Grant and Lee: The Wilderness Through Cold Harbor. Baton Rouge: Louisiana State University Press, 2007.

Trudeau, Noah Andre. Bloody Roads South: The Wilderness to Cold Harbor, May–June 1864. Boston: Little, Brown & Co., 1989.

U.S. War Department, The War of the Rebellion: a Compilation of the Official Records of the Union and Confederate Armies. Washington, DC: U.S. Government Printing Office, 1880–1901.

Printed in Great Britain
by Amazon.co.uk, Ltd.,
Marston Gate.